PENGUIN BOOKS

THE RAJA, THE REBEL AND THE MONK

J N. Sinha was born in Majhawalia (Siwan), north Bihar, and ducated at Patna University. He earned his PhD in the history of cience from the University of Delhi, and did a stint at its Cluster nnovation Centre, teaching history in innovative formats. He as researched at the foremost centres in Europe, North America nd Asia and is associated with many professional bodies nternationally. He has published and presented globally. For he popular audience in India, he writes in the leading national press, on aspects of history, culture and environment, and about hings ordinary and mundane. He has appeared on the BBC (London), Asianet TV (New York) and Sputnik (Moscow), and on several media platforms in India. He loves nature, heritage and travelling, and has visited noted heritage locations across the globe. In India, he endeavours to conserve and preserve these sites.

The Raja, The Rebel and The Monk

Fateh Sahi's War Against the East India Company

J. N. Sinha

PENGUIN BOOKS
An imprint of Penguin Random House

PENGUIN BOOKS

Penguin Books is an imprint of the Penguin Random House group of companies whose addresses can be found at global.penguinrandomhouse.com

Published by Penguin Random House India Pvt. Ltd
4th Floor, Capital Tower 1, MG Road,
Gurugram 122 002, Haryana, India

First published in Penguin Books by Penguin Random House India 2025

10 9 8 7 6 5 4 3 2

ISBN 9780143468370

Typeset in Requiem Text by Manipal Technologies Limited, Manipal
Printed at Replika Press Pvt. Ltd, India

www.penguin.co.in

To,
All those who ever made me happy

Contents

Word Usage

The proper names of many places and individuals occurring in the story of Fateh Bahadur Sahi have been spelt variously in different sources. I use the ones most popular and widely used until now. In cases where identification is difficult to synchronize with currently existing names, the spellings used in the original sources have been accepted. Honorifics and decorations have generally been dropped, except in quotations or wherever they are likely to illustrate an issue or context. Words of Indian origin or those typically used are generally italicized unless they are accepted in English as well.

At present, Huseypur is situated in the Gopalganj district of north-west Bihar, but the erstwhile Huseypur Raj included a major part of the old Sarkar Saran, which consisted of the present-day districts of Gopalganj, Siwan and Saran and Champaran in the time of Fateh Sahi. It extended into the territories of Gorakhpur in Awadh and probably into Nepal, too. The territorial and administrative boundaries in the olden days were not as well-defined as they are today. They were fluid and often shifted with the victory or defeat of territorial contenders, and after natural disasters. In some cases, they were undefined due to difficult accessibility, when boundaries were more a notion than a reality.

With the passage of time, the territorial nomenclatures of the areas around Huseypur and Saran changed. The earliest territorial units had emerged as the ancient republics like Vaishali, Kosal and Mall, which changed over centuries in shape and nature under the successive ruling regimes. The territorial expanse of the Kalyanpur-Huseypur Rajas gradually became part of Sarkar Saran under Subah Bihar in the Mughal Empire. This further changed during the British rule to Bengal, Bihar, the United Provinces of Agra and Oudh, shortened to the United Provinces in 1935, and finally, to Uttar Pradesh in independent India. Coincidentally, the last two names bear the same acronym—UP, which I have used frequently in this account, hoping that the readers would visualize it in its chronological context.

Along with standard citations, in some cases, the original sentences or words have been rearranged or altered to reduce quotation marks and footnotes to facilitate readability. This is in no way intended to deny the contribution of their original authors, who are also footnoted at intervals. Since the citation of popular sources, such as folklore, is cumbersome, they are used in such a manner that the readers can recognize them easily.

Glossary

Akhara: A traditional monastery of the Hindu monks and ascetics (grouped as Dasnamis, including the Nagas), organized in the eighth century by Adi Shankaracharya to protect and preserve Sanatan Dharma, now located at places like Allahabad and Varanasi.

Amil: An officer responsible for maintaining peace and realizing revenue in late Medieval India; like the modern Collector.

Arzee: A petition; an address; a memorial.

Ayachak: The Brahmin who does not beg and depends on farming and other professions for a living.

Bag: Garden.

Bagh: Tiger.

Bahadur: Brave; an honorific generally suffixed after the name of a raja or notable.

Bali: Sacrifice of a living animal as offering to a deity.

Banjara: Nomad traders.

Basta: A bundle of papers wrapped in cloth.

Bazaar: Marketplace.

Begum: A Muslim noblewoman.

Bhavani: An incarnation of Goddess Kali in Hinduism.

Bhutt/Bhat: A branch of Brahmins, hence their surname.

Brahmin: Hindu priestly class, at the top of the Indian caste pyramid.

Brahmottar: A rent-free land allotted to someone with religious purpose.

Brit: A maintenance grant given by a raja or notable to someone for religious and charitable purposes, usually rent free; its holder called *Britdar*.

Bungy bardar: Porter.

Chhattri: A decorative domed kiosk supported on pillars.

Chauth: An annual tax or tribute (one-fourth of revenue or produce, hence the name) imposed by the Maratha Empire on lands under nominal Mughal rule in India from the early eighteenth century; a type of protection money charged to provide armed security for a state by the Marathas.

Chobdar: A person carrying a staff or baton of office, who accompanied an officer, often responsible for maintaining order in the royal court or official gatherings.

Cutcherry/Kucheri: A Hindustani word initially used for revenue collector's office in the colonial administration, still in use in India; also an

	office, a court, a place where public business is conducted.
Dam:	A coin; money of account; in Akbar's time, 40 dams equalled Re 1.
Danka:	Big drum.
Darbar:	Royal court.
Darbari:	Courtier; members of the nobility at the royal court.
Dargah:	Sufi shrine, usually built over the grave of a saint.
Darh:	A folk sport of pig hunting, collectively by villagers and their domestic animals, a primitive game vanishing now.
Dawk/Dak:	Post, postal system.
Dharma:	Duty, also used for religion.
Diara:	The tract of an island-like land formation created by rivers along with their stream.
Diwan:	Prime minister; *wazir* in charge of administrative finance.
Diwan-e-Khana:	Court, a tribunal, hall of audience, public room (detached from residence).
Durbar:	Court; the one who attended such royal courts was called *durbari*.
Fakir:	Sufi holy man, wandering Muslim ascetic; literally, poor.
Farman/Firman:	A formal order issued by a king.
Faujdar:	Fort keeper or garrison commander.
Gadi Ledo:	A tenure-title granted to someone to manage some kind of local affairs under a regional ruler, prevalent in early modern Bihar.
Gadi/Gaddi:	Throne, ruler's seat; a high ruling position.

Garh: Mud-walled fort.

Ghat: A broad flight of steps leading down to a river; also used as *shamshanghat* (burial ground).

Ghatwal: A holder of feudal tenure/*jagir* (called *ghatwali*) for quasi-military services in south Bihar before Independence. Their chiefs were also known as *gaddi*, responsible for maintaining law and order in their estates. They were originally created in the eighteenth century to defend against the invasion of the Marathas and others. A few of them became rulers of their respective estates after 1793. This also refers to a person in charge of permits for passage on the riverbank or in the mountains; increasingly associated with a local chief in the period of this study.

Gomastah: Agent looking after land revenue at the village level under the East India Company government.

Jagir: A landed estate, granted by the ruler in return for service, whose revenue would go to the holder—*jagirdar*.

Jama/Jumma: Assessed revenue from agricultural land.

Khillat: A ceremonial robe or other gifts given to someone by a superior as a mark of honour.

Kiladar/Qiladar: In charge of a fort.

Kotwal: Police chief, chief magistrate or city administrator in the Mughal period.

Mahal: In the time of Akbar, a revenue subdivision, usually corresponding to *pargana*.

Mahanth: Chief of a Hindu monastery; the head of the Dasnami sanyasis.

Malguzar: A landholder or proprietor in the context of the Indian land revenue system; one who paid rent or revenue.

Malguzari: System and amount of revenue.

Mansabdar: A high-ranking servant of a king assigned with salary and jagir in return for his services whenever required by the king. His rank was determined by the material benefits and obligation of maintaining a particular size of militia.

Marzaban: Used in Persian sources for big *zamindars*, called raja in indigenous parlance, referred to fully or semi-autonomous chiefs, ruling over their respective territories for a long time.

Mauza: Village. The lowest level of the Mughal administration; its head was called *Mustajir*, *Pradhan* or *Mulrayat*.

Mulrayat: A kind of ghatwal, with quasi-military powers and responsibilities.

Musnad: Low arrangement of cushions and bolsters that formed the throne of the Indian rulers in the late Mughal period.

Nabob: A corruption of Hindustani *nawab*, literally 'deputy', the title of the regional governors of the Mughal Empire (hence the adjective—*nawabi*).

Nagara: Indian ceremonial kettledrum.

Naib Nazim: A deputy subahdar who assisted the Nawab in administering outlying areas, introduced in the eighteenth century to tackle rebellions, invasions and the growing political and commercial ambitions of the European powers.

Naib: A deputy, appointed to assist the provincial Governor whenever the latter was busy with some other duty.

Nautanki: Folk theatre, consisting of music, dance and drama, with dialogue in a typical style—generally popular in the Bhojpuri-speaking north India and in some of the British colonies with a Bhojpuri diaspora.

Nazim: The Governor or *subahdar* of a province.

Nishan: A formal order issued by the prince or Governor of a province during the Mughal period.

Nizamat: The office of the administrator and its system of working.

Panchayat: A village or community council of elders.

Pargana: A smaller unit of the revenue administration containing a few villages; named after its biggest village.

Parwana: An order issued by a higher authority or a legal grant that conferred enforceable privileges; a letter of conferment of a piece of land, generally a revenue-free grant given to the destitute and the needy, by the wazir, under supervision of the emperor.

Peshkash: The money given to the high officials or the king in advance to get something done. It was in vogue also when zamindars or rulers submitted to the Mughals and accepted their suzerainty.

Pindari: Member of a criminal group looting strangers, an occupation prevalent in the eighteenth-nineteenth century in central India.

Pir: Sufi holy man.

Poojari: Worshipper, especially associated with a temple.

Rais: A nobleman.

Raja: King, also used for big zamindar in India.

Rani: Queen.

Ryot or *Ryott*: Peasant or tenant farmer.

Sanad: The document containing all types of imperial orders, as a document of witness and testimony—issued by the emperor or the Governor; charter or warrant.

Sanyas: Renunciation; the fourth and final stage of life when one renounced all the worldly ties and meditated about the ultimate truth; its practitioner is called *sanyasi* (Hindu ascetic).

Sarai: A wayside inn in medieval India where travellers would rest after a day's travel; something like a modern-day hotel.

Sarkar: District, an administrative unit generally containing sixty to seventy villages.

Sati: A woman who immolated herself, voluntarily or under duress, on the funeral pyre of her husband.

Sepoy: An Indian soldier in the British army.

Shroff: Trader, merchant, banker or moneylender.

Sicca rupee: Metallic coin with changing values, prevalent in the eighteenth century.

Sipahi/Sepoy: Infantry soldiers of Indian origin, during the colonial rule in India.

Suba: Province; a unit comprising not less than two sarkars and not more than twenty. It was a province of the Mughal Empire.

Subadhar: Governor in Mughal times.

Sudder: A high court of civil and revenue jurisdiction; main, chief, upper.

Tahsildar: In-charge of revenue collection of a mauza or a pargana; he also assisted the *faujdar* and the amil.

Taluka: An estate comprising several villages; controlled by a *talukdar*.

Tantrik: A practitioner of Tantra, well-versed in spiritual rituals and esoteric practices.

Tappa/Tuppeh: The collection of a few mauzas, forming a large group of villages under a local controller.

Thana: Police station or military post.

Thuggee: Robbery and murder formerly practised in India by members of a group or organization known as the Thugs.

Vakil: Representative, lawyer.

Wazir: During the Mughal period, the wazir was the revenue and finance minister, sometimes called diwan.

Yachak: The Brahmin who begs for a living.

Zamindar: A land holder; a big zamindar was called Raja.

Chronology

The Life and Times of Fateh Bahadur Sahi

BCE **Sixth** – BCE **Fifth Century**: Approximate date of origins of the Huseypur family lineage, calculated on the basis of its genealogy, currently running in its 114th generation.

BCE **Fourth** – BCE **Second Century**: According to living traditions of the Huseypur families, Beer Sen established their dynasty around 150 BCE, at Bharhe Choura in the Deoria district of modern Uttar Pradesh. When the Greco-Bactrian king Menander (ruled from Sagala in Punjab c. 165–130 BCE), advanced up to Saket in Koshal (Ayodhya), he encountered the Mauryan commander, supported by Jagat Sinha, descendant of Beer Sen. On repulsing Menander, Jagat Sinha was rewarded with the recovered territory, which strengthened his roots at Bharhe Choura.

The sources are lacking on the ensuing gap up to CE seventh century, which may be seen as a time of transition from their priestly occupation to farming under the influence of Buddhism.

CE **Seventh Century:** Sudden emergence of Mayyur Bhutt, along with Vanabhatta, as court poets of Harshvardhan (CE 606–47). Their writings indicate they were relatives; Vana claimed to belong to a Bhojak family of Saran.

Eighth – Fifteenth Century: Family history not clear; but noted Indologist Rahul Sankrityayan believed they ruled through the thirteenth to eighteenth centuries (Turko-Afghan-Mughal period) from the north-western corner of Saran.

Sixteenth Century: Raja Jai Mull, eighty-third Raja in line, helped Humayun after his defeat by Sher Shah at Chausa (1539). After his victory, Sher Shah tried to punish Jai Mull, who fled into the jungles and engaged in rebellion. Once back in power, Humayun rewarded Jai Mull's grandson Raja Jubraj with four parganas, inaugurating a tradition of friendly relations with the Mughals. Akbar collaborated with Kalyan Mull (eighty-sixth Raja) to contain the local rebels; on suppression of the Afghan chief of Barharia, he rewarded Kalyan with the territory recovered from the rebel, together with the title of *Raja* and, later, of *Maharaja.* Jahangir reconfirmed it with higher honorifics as *Raja Bahadur*, and finally *Maharaja Bahadur* and *Sahi*.

Kalyan Mull established his capital at a place named after him as Kalyanpur (present Gopalganj district). He established his paramountcy over the area, and the family started ruling as autonomous rajas under the nominal suzerainty of the Mughals. Later, the capital shifted from Kalyanpur to Huseypur, nearby; an imposing fort and other facilities were created there. Fateh Bahadur was born here as son to the ninety-eighth Raja Sardar Sahi.

1628: Peter Mundy visited India during 1628–34; met the Raja of Kalyanpur in Patna, who presented unique gifts to the local Governor and was welcomed; but arrested soon after, suggesting fragile relations between the two.

1733: Bihar was attached to Subah Bengal, when Emperor Muhammad Shah granted Subah Bihar to the Subadar of Bengal, Shuja-ud-Din Muhammad Khan.

1750: Fateh Bahadur Sahi was crowned the ninety-ninth Raja of Huseypur. Warren Hastings joined the East India Company as a clerk at Calcutta.

1756: The Seven Years' War (1756–63) between Britain and France commenced for global supremacy; their relations were deeply embittered in India, too.

1757: The Battle of Plassey (23 June): Bengal Nawab defeated by the Company forces and replaced by its favourite, allowing it to interfere in local affairs. Robert Clive (1725–74) appointed Governor of Bengal (1757–60), laying the foundations of Company rule in Bengal; his tenure was known for rampant corruption. A hazy indication of cooperation between Mir Kasim and Fateh Sahi.

1760: Marathas invaded eastern India; used Naga sanyasis as mercenaries for the first time. Subsequently, sanyasis were used by Fateh Sahi and by local chiefs to resolve their domestic disputes. End of the first term of Clive as the Governor of Bengal.

1761: The Third Battle of Panipat (14 January): Between Maratha Confederacy and the invading army of the Durrani Empire. After losing the battle to Durrani, some groups of Chitpawan Brahmins of the Maratha Army emigrated eastward, settled near Patna, emerged as local chiefs and, later, developed social relations with the local nobility, including Huseypur families.

1763: After William Ellis failed to seize Patna (25 June), the Company forces tried to flee to the neutral territory towards Awadh, but were encountered near Chapra by the local faujdar (identified with Fateh Sahi by popular sources), with the support of Walter Reinhardt Sombre (1725–78), nicknamed Sumru, an Alsatian German mercenary assisting the anti-British clique in India, who imprisoned the escapees and executed hundreds of them on orders from Mir Kasim (Patna Massacre, 6 October). Nagas also fought for Mir Kasim during the siege.

1764: The Battle of Buxar (22–23 October) between East India Company forces under Major Hector Munro, and the combined armies of the Mughal emperor, nawabs of Bengal and Awadh, and Raja Balwant Singh of Benares. Indian allies were defeated. Concluded by the Treaty of Allahabad laying the foundation of British rule in India. Fateh Sahi and some of his clansmen fought against the Company, as also the Naga sanyasis and Walter Reinhardt Sombre, on behalf of the Allies.

1765: Right of *Diwani* for the fiscal administration of Bengal, Bihar and Orissa granted to the East India Company by the Treaty of Allahabad (16 August) signed by Mughal Emperor

Shah Alam II and Robert Clive, representing the East India Company. A turning point in Indian history, it allowed the Company to encroach upon the country's political and economic matters, accelerating the drain of wealth from India. Clive reappointed Governor of Bengal (1765–67).

1766: Mutiny of European soldiers in Monghyr, and of the sepoys at Manjhi near Chapra in Saran. Clive convened at Chapra a conference with General Carnac, Nawab Vizier of Awadh, envoy of the Mughal emperor, Raja Balwant Singh of Benares, a Jat Raja and Rohilla chiefs, laying the foundation of their treaty for mutual defence against a Maratha invasion.

1767: Robert Clive left for England with huge wealth acquired during his corrupt tenure as Governor of Bengal. Captain Kinlock's expedition to Nepal to explore possibilities of trade with Betia and Nepal failed.

Fateh Sahi approached by Company officials demanding land revenue under their Diwani rights. But he asserted his status of a hereditary raja of his territory, who would not recognize any higher authority over him. Company forces acted to enforce obedience. Sahi retaliated with military action but could not stand against them and retreated to the neighbouring jungle of Gorakhpur to fight them another day.

1769–71: Famine in Bengal and Bihar. Failure of crops, pestilence, hunger-deaths, cannibalism, crime. Spread of social and political discontent. Unusual movements of hordes of sanyasis and *fakirs* around Huseypur reported. Revenue collection fell sharply; the Calcutta Council appointed revenue councils at Patna and Murshidabad to improve the collection.

1770: Bengal Famine at its peak: unprecedented conditions prevailed. Chait Singh crowned as Raja of Benares (r. 1770–81), succeeding his father Raja Balwant Singh.

Around this time, the British visited Fateh Sahi's camp on a peace mission to settle their mutual disputes, probably with the mediation of Basant Sahi, a cousin of Fateh Sahi. But once face-to-face, the British party became violent and a skirmish followed, resulting in the death of a few camp members. Some people believe it involved the rebel's son, too.

1771: In May, Company forces besieged the fort of the Afghan chief at Burharia, near Huseypur, and compelled its owners to surrender; although old adversaries of Fateh's family, their surrender facilitated the Company's presence close to Huseypur.

1772: Warren Hastings (1732–1818) appointed Governor of Bengal and the de facto first Governor-General of India in April, starting a period of internal reforms and consolidation of the Company's power, impinging upon the privileges of old local zamindars. Fateh Sahi marched into Huseypur; killed the Company's revenue farmer Govind Ram; incessant incursions followed. Fateh Sahi persuaded to meet the Governor: was offered a monthly stipend of Rs 300, with a promise of cessation of military action against him and full autonomy within his territory.

1773: Narrowney Rajput zamindars too rebelled like Fateh Sahi, when Company agents sought to recover revenue arrears from them. They killed a *gomastah* and his servants, and fled into the Awadh territory.

1774: Warren Hastings was appointed first Governor-General of Bengal. Philip Francis, an Irish politician, reached Calcutta in October as a member of the supreme council of the Governor-General, and his conflict with Hastings started almost immediately; Francis engineered his impeachment later.

1775: Fateh Sahi raided the Company agent's camp, and killed Mir Jamal, the revenue farmer, and Basant Sahi, his own cousin and a Company sympathizer, who was also present there. Fateh Sahi's attacks on Company agents and revenue offices continued; he enlarged his army and forged an anti-Company group with the neighbouring zamindars. In June, Warren Hastings requested the Nawab of Awadh to help in arresting Fateh Sahi.

1776: The minor heir of deceased Basant Sahi relocated to Patna. The American War of Independence commenced, which, together with the French Revolution (1789), showed many common features with the rebellion of Fateh Sahi.

1777: Fateh Sahi attacked the Company's Baragaon military station: tore down the Company office and officers' quarters, and placed his own men in charge of the buildings. He also undertook to rebuild his Huseypur fort, and reasserted his right of rent collection.

Catherine Noël Worlée (1761–1834) married George François Grand at Chandarnagar on 10 July; they emerged as elusive actors in this story, whose shadows loomed for long.

1778: Hastings asked Chait Singh for an additional Rs 5 lakh as a war-levy—as a prelude to confiscating all his possessions.

A vicious scandal caught a member of the supreme council (Philip Francis) trespassing into the residence of Catherine Grand (wife of a Company employee) in a nightly assignation. Francis was tried for adultery and punished. This left serious consequences for all concerned and exposed the ugliness of the top Company bureaucracy. Curiously, the issue seems to have incited a gunfight between Francis and Warren Hastings, the Governor-General himself. Francis was injured seriously; utterly humiliated, he returned to England, rebuilt his political clout and engineered the impeachment of Warren Hastings for his misdeeds in India. Catherine's marriage floundered; she moved to Europe and lived with noted French diplomat Talleyrand in Paris.

Walter Reinhardt Sombre died; his wife Begum Sumru inherited his principality of Sardana yielding about £90,000 annually, and a huge mercenary army. Begum Sumru rose to become a rare powerbroker of her time. Sombre fought for the anti-British camp through the Plassey and Buxar Wars and was likely in touch with Fateh Sahi. The couple are elusive characters in the Fateh story.

1779: Saran created as a separate district; with Charles Grome as its Collector.

1780: Ahilya Bai Holkar (1725–95), a contemporary of Fateh Sahi (and of Maratha general and statesman Mahadaji Shinde), initiated the restoration of Kashi Vishvanath Temple and renovation of several others in north India, generally patronized by Fateh Sahi's clansmen and relations.

1781: Beginning October 1781 through 1782, Fateh Sahi met with successive defeats and setbacks as at Ramnagar and in the eighteen-day war with the Dhujju Singh–Company coalition. Warren Hastings asked Chait Singh for extra levy in violation of the earlier treaty, inciting a military retaliation in which Fateh Sahi participated.

1782: On reports of Fateh Sahi's presence at Ramnagar, British troops deployed to capture him; the attempt failed. The Governor-General directed Samuel Charters of Patna Council to probe the rebellion of Fateh Sahi; Samuel submitted his comprehensive report on 25 June 1782, discussing the rebellion's causes, nature and the reasons why the rebel was able to sustain it until then, besides such matters as his supporters and those who sided with the Company government.

1784: Golghar, a huge granary, was constructed by the East India Company during 1784–86, as a part of a long-term plan to prevent famine in the provinces.

1785: Warren Hastings resigned: was accused of misconduct, mismanagement and personal corruption during his service in India; leading to his impeachment.

1786: Charles Cornwallis appointed Governor-General and commander-in-chief of India (February), with instructions to avoid conflict with the Company's neighbours. He inaugurated a period of comparative peace and reconciliation for all stakeholders in India. The decrease in Fateh Sahi's aggression now may be seen in its light.

1787: Impeachment of Warren Hastings (1787–95) commenced: for his alleged crimes in India, notably embezzlement, extortion and coercion, and killing of Maharaja Nandkumar; its prosecution led by Edmund Burke, managed by Philip Francis; it failed ultimately.

1790: Fateh Sahi maintained his sway over the north-western part of the Huseypur estate, contiguous with Bhagjogni Jungle of Gorakhpur; entered secretly into some kind of settlement on the land under his possession but falling under the Awadh territory, and developed his campsite there into his capital to be known as Tamkuhi. Finally, he relinquished his *gaddi* to his son, and gradually withdrew from public life.

1791: Mahesh Dutt's estate was bestowed on his infant son Chhattardhari Sahi by Lord Cornwallis, which passed under the Court of Wards.

1793: Permanent settlement was introduced, but it was not applied to the erstwhile Huseypur zamindari the way it was settled with others, in view of its record of rebellion.

1794: By now, Catherine Grand had reached Paris where she attracted the attention of the noted French diplomat Charles Maurice de Talleyrand, French foreign minister and, later, the first prime minister of Napoleon Bonaparte; on Napoleon's insistence, Talleyrand married her (1802), but they gradually drifted apart; eventually, Talleyrand divorced her, with enough money for her to live luxuriously in London.

1795: Fateh Sahi is believed to have raided Champaran; also seen holding periodic panchayats (social platform of mediators) in its riverine areas to resolve local disputes. Some believe he was killed by British agents in one such panchayat.

Hastings finally acquitted (24 April) of all charges listed in the impeachment prosecution.

1795–96: The Treaty of Tamkuhi was concluded between the Raja of Tamkuhi and the Company, recognizing Tamkuhi as a separate zamindari, claim a few sources, although there is no documentary evidence to prove it.

1797: The fourth Nawab of Awadh, Vazir Ali Khan, ascended the throne with the support of the British in September; within months, they replaced him with his uncle Saadat Ali Khan II. Vazir Ali was granted a pension of Rs 3 lakh and shifted to Benares.

1798: Richard Wellesley appointed fifth Governor-General of Bengal (1798–1805); his regime known for the Subsidiary Alliance.

1799: Jagat Singh, related by kinship with Chait Singh, conspired with Awadh Nawab Vazir Ali, then exiled in Benares, to oust the Company from there, but the plan leaked. Jagat Singh was arrested, tried and sentenced to death—later converted into deportation to St Helena, but, allegedly, he committed suicide in the last hours and passed away.

1801: Saadat Ali Khan II of Awadh acted as a puppet and ceded half of his territory to the British by the treaty of 1801; also disbanded his troops in favour of a hugely expensive army under their control. Consequently, a portion of Awadh became a vassal of the Company, though Mughal suzerainty over it continued nominally until 1819. All this happened in the neighbourhood of Fateh Sahi.

1802: Fateh Sahi's family did not give up its claim over the original estate. His wife continued to press for their title and rights.

1807: During 1807–14, Francis Buchanan made a comprehensive survey of the districts of Bhagalpur, Patna, Shahabad, Palamu in Bihar, Gorakhpur in UP and Nepal, which he reported in a series of accounts.

1808: Fateh Sahi was last seen; believed to have gone thereafter, on a pilgrimage, via Gwalior, to Nasik. In 1808, he had 100 villages under his control; the Tamkuhi family continued efforts to regain their authority over the original Huseypur Raj, but the British refused, and recognized Hathwa as its legal heir.

1811: Chait Singh died in exile in Gwalior on 28 March, leaving behind three sons whose descendants are settled there.

1817: A court document claims Fateh Sahi lived up to 1817.

1829: In June, the great-grandson of Fateh Sahi brought a regular suit for the recovery of the Huseypur Raj, but it was dismissed as barred by limitation.

1834: In her last years, Madam Grand returned from London to Paris and died there on 10 December 1834; buried in Montparnasse Cemetery.

1836: Some sources indicate Fateh Sahi died in 1836.

1837: The British formally recognized Hathwa as the natural heir of the Huseypur Raj, understandably when the original claimant Fateh Sahi was not heard of any more and he was assumed to be dead. A source says he died in 1835/36. As such, on 27 February, the Government of Auckland conferred on the Hathwa Raja the title of Maharaja Bahadur with the usual khillat.

1844: On 21 June, Bujhawan Misir, a Brahmin of Bhore, rose in revolt, claiming the whole territory on the other side of the Jharahi River as his brit (Brahmottar) donated by the Huseypur Raja. At their height, such risings involved twenty ringleaders supported by six thousand armed men. At last, with the help of the Company government, he was confronted, captured and imprisoned for ten years. The areas controlled by him were reclaimed and order restored.

1848: A legal suit by Tamkuhi family for the recovery of the Huseypur Raj was brought, but it was dismissed again as barred by limitation.

1857: During the Revolt of 1857, this Bhojpuri region remained a hotbed of anti-British activities. Beginning with the rebellion of Fateh Sahi, Chait Singh, Jagat Singh, and the Nawabs and Begams of Awadh, they resurged in the Revolt of 1857, led by Mangal Pandey (Balia), Kunwar Singh (Shahabad) and others, to later climax at the Chauri Chaura massacre and the extraordinary feat of defiance by Chitu Pandey of Balia in the Quit India Movement (1942).

1858: Chattardhari Sahi of Hathwa died on 16 March. An able administrator, he left behind about Rs 40 lakh in his treasury.

1871: Rajendra Pratap Sahi of Hathwa died in 1871, leaving behind a minor son of fifteen, Krishna Pratap Sahi; therefore, the Court of Wards took over the administration of Hathwa, again.

1872: Bhubaneshwar Dutt was appointed superintendent of the Court of Wards (1872) and diwan and manager of Hathwa (1874). His nephew, Devendra Nath Dutt, was first appointed private secretary to Hathwa Maharaja (1885), and diwan and joint manager in 1891; he was succeeded by his son Brajendra Nath Dutt as diwan in 1915.

1873: On 15 December, Bankim Chandra Chattopadhyay was manhandled by a British army officer at Berhampur (Bengal), causing his antagonism against the British; the zamindars of Lalgola sided with him, who are believed to have told him the story of Fateh Sahi that finally served as the background story of his *Anandamath*.

1877: Delhi Imperial Durbar: Hathwa invited during celebrations. The local Sonepur Durbar listed twenty-seven invitees in order of precedence. Members of the Hathwa family occupied the highest positions in the protocol. Of the twelve families represented by twenty-seven *durbaris* of 1877, four—Hathwa, Chainpur, Chirand and Manjha—were among the nine leading zamindars.

1878: Bihar Landlords' Association formed. The participants included the Maharaja of Hathwa, Ram Saran Sinha, Achabar

Prasad Narain Sinha (Parsa), Parsid Narain Sinha (Chainpur) and Raghubans Sahai of Chapra.

1880s: Kharag Bahadur Sahi was recognized by the British government as the 'Raja' of Tamkuhi.

1902: In recognition of her generous charity and kindly gestures, the Kaiser-i-Hind Gold Medal was conferred on the Hathwa Rani by the Queen Empress of Great Britain, invested by the Lieutenant-Governor of Bengal, at a durbar at Hathwa in January 1902. The deaths of Raja Rajendra Pratap Sahi and Krishna Pratap Sahi of Hathwa were marked by two famines in Bihar, in which the Hathwa Raj spent more than Rs 10 lakh to relieve the distress of its people, besides several other contributions for similar causes for the rest of India that brought this recognition.

1903: Delhi Durbar: Hathwa participated.

1905: First history of Hathwa Raj by Girindra Nath Dutt, *History of the Hutwa Raj*, published (1905), followed by the publication of Devendra Nath Dutt's *A Brief History of the Hathwa Raj* (1909).

1911: Delhi Durbar: Both Hathwa and Tamkuhi attended. Like Hathwa, the British now started placating the Tamkuhi rajas with protocol privileges, official decorations and the like, and they were trapped with successive colonial projects and programmes.

1914: Indrajit Pratap Sahi of Tamkuhi reached majority, and assumed actual charge of the estate, comprising 362 villages—232 in the district of Gorakhpur and 130 in Bihar. For public welfare measures within his territory, he was awarded a Silver Medal, and for his war services, presented with a *sanad* by the War Board, and a Sword of Honour by the Lieutenant-Governor of UP.

1930s: After losing the legal battles to regain authority over the original Huseypur Raj continually, the Tamkuhi family endeavoured to restore and consolidate themselves as rulers of an independent estate. In the course of their legal wrangle, they had engaged Motilal Nehru as their lawyer much earlier. During 1937–49, they became close to Jawaharlal Nehru and other nationalist leaders, and the masses, and entered the civic bodies, with corresponding favour from the colonial authorities.

1947: India became independent.

1949: Merger of Indian native states into the Indian Republic.

1950: India declared a republic. In the following years, the zamindari system under Permanent Settlement in eastern India was abolished, technically doing away with the last vestiges of the rajaship in Tamkuhi and Hathwa as elsewhere in the country.

Preface

Over a decade ago, I came across a few references about Fateh Sahi, an enigmatic character in India's history, lost in the vortex of myth and reality—not because he did not exist, but because his different avatars in the public domain masked his real identity. Historically, he was the Raja of Huseypur in the erstwhile Saran district of Bihar. He revolted against the British in 1767, soon after the Battle of Buxar, and continued his guerrilla war for nearly three decades. As such, for the British, he was an outlaw and a public nuisance. Even until recently, he was depicted as a *dakoo* (dacoit) on a Government of Bihar web portal! A generous or ingenious observer may characterize him as Robin Hood. Curiously, though, mainstream historians have not taken him seriously.

Somehow, the references to Sahi struck a chord with me. They referred to some thrilling episodes, a few heard about in my childhood, which prompted me to dig deeper into his history. *The Limited Raj* by Anand A. Yang (Oxford, 1989) led me to his hideout in the jungles of Gorakhpur in the latter half of the eighteenth century. I would think of those episodes whenever I passed through the terrain of his operations on the border between Uttar Pradesh and Bihar. The typical traits and nuances of the Bhojpuri culture and geography, with its semi-wild topography of forests, lakes and riverine locations, and the way of life of the local people laid out the historical landscape for my story.

Meanwhile, I came to know of some locals trying to resurrect Fateh Sahi as a folk hero. I read the writings of Akshayvar Dikshit and others in Hindi and Bhojpuri, and reviewed them in *Social Science Probings* (2007), a serious academic journal. The response was encouraging. However, as these writers were basically litterateurs and not historians, their work lacked in professionalism. Yet, I appreciated their endeavour to reinstate this historic figure with whatever information they could gather from oral traditions and popular memory. They tried to present their protagonist as a great warrior and a patriot who dared to challenge the mighty East India Company, single-handedly.

After all, city-based historians had never cared to look closely at this hero.

Looking into the historicity of the legend, I published a long article in *The Hindu* (2011), and was stunned at the volume of applause and queries it brought in about this little-known Raja, from countless readers from India and abroad. For most people, the find was a surprise, and they paid glowing tributes to the patriot. A Tamil NRI scientist based in Paris, for example, took details of the raja's location so that he could visit his abode and pay tributes. The story also attracted some movie-makers. Since I hail from the same region, I have been interested in the history and culture of the Gangetic heartland, and, off and on, write on them in the popular press. All this is the inspiration behind this book, which, above all, is a tribute to the bravery of the forgotten hero.

I am deeply obliged to a host of scholars, intellectuals, and to my audience at large who appreciated my perspective in my earlier presentations on the subject, and offered valuable comments. First of all, I am particularly grateful to noted writer, historian and public intellectual Ramachandra Guha for encouraging me to write about the lesser-known characters of history. I am indebted to Anand A. Yang, from whose work I have drawn liberally. I have no words to thank Vaidurya Pratap Sahi, a 114th-generation scion of Fateh Sahi's dynasty, a scientist and a heritage enthusiast interested in the history of his family. He has helped me in so many ways, with information, source material and discussion. I am beholden also to other members of his family, A.P. Sahi, R.P. Sahi, Shruti Sahi and others, for their cordiality and support. My thanks are due also to Maheshwar Pratap Sahi and Veena Sahi (daughter of Khagendra Pratap Sahi) from another sibling branch of the Tamkuhi family, for their help.

I am equally grateful to Mrigendra Pratap Bahadur Sahi, Poonam Sahi, Kaustuvmani Pratap Sahi and other members of the Hathwa Raj family, for their help and generosity. They have provided me with some rare sources; and, in course of our interactions, valuable information and insights into their relations with Fateh Sahi's Tamkuhi family (their cousin line), with the British and the freedom movement. I am beholden to both the families and their relatives for cooperation and help. The documents apart, I came to know through them, how the hostility between the Tamkuhi and Hathwa families were more due to contemporary circumstances and mischief of the Company authorities and their agents than due to the personal volition or animosity of the two families. I wish and hope, after reading this book, the two sibling families would realize the price their ancestors paid for the cause of freedom, and look back with pride at their shared contribution to the nation.

During my research, I reached out to many across north India, who could provide some information about the life and times of Fateh Sahi. Shubhrendu Singh of Chainpur-Salemgarh estate, Krisna Nandan Singh of Sheohar and Smita Parashar of the Revteeth families, Kashinath Singh and Aditya Narayan Singh of Parsa Garh, Amite Swarendra Shahi of Manjha, and Shefali Roy (Patna University, connected with the Singhabad-Tilasan family), provided me information and helped me reach out to descendants of some forgotten players of this saga. In Bengal, I am beholden in particular to the descendants of the Lalgola (Murshidabad) and Mahishadal (East Midnapore) *zamindar* families, especially to Rakesh Roy of Singhabad-Tilasan (Malda), who provided me many details, reinforcing the historical links between the western provinces (UP and Bihar) and Bengal, and the link of his own family with the *Anandamath* story. Kishan Chand Bhakat, an *Anandamath* aficionado from Lalgola, reinforced my information on eighteenth-century Bengal in the throes of the famines and the Sanyasi Rebellion. All of them informed me on the migrations from the United Provinces and Bihar to Bengal over the past centuries, strengthening my surmise regarding Fateh's connection with *Anandamath*, Lalgola and the Bengal nawabs. I am thankful also to Dileep Singh and his son, Anurag Singh Kashiwale, the descendants of Chait Singh settled in Gwalior, for providing me information about their exit from Benares.

I am grateful to many scholars whose work I have used or have gained insights from, countless popular writers, commentators, poets and folk artists. I am thankful in particular to Anand A. Yang (Washington State University, USA), Manager Pandey (JNU, New Delhi), Awadhesh Pradhan (BHU, Varanasi), and late Akshayvar Dixit (Siwan) and his literary associates, for having used their writings. I deeply appreciate the help and support of Deepak Kumar (JNU, New Delhi), Santosh Rai (DU, Delhi), Prasun Chatterjee (Primus Books) and Priyadarshini Sharma (*The Hindu*). They have gone through parts of my drafts and made valuable suggestions. Sanjeev Kumar (BAS) helped me research in Patna, and Rai Murari (Patna University), Nripendra Kumar Rai, Rai Brijmohan Sharma and Rai Chandrabhushan Sharma (all from Belaspur), and Binod Verma (Shikarpur), facilitated my visits to the interiors of Champaran. The Bihar Police helped me access some of the most difficult terrains of the region. P.K. Shukla (ICHR) encouraged me to work on the theme despite its obscurity, and Nalin Sharma (publishing consultant), Gautam Chandra, Pushpa Kumari and Neel Rekha (BRA Bihar University) helped me at different stages. I have gained encouragement from the discussions at the Creative History Group on the web, and am beholden to Devendra Chaube, Rashmi Chaudhury (JNU) and others for their initiative. While concluding this project, I fondly remember my long-time friends P.K. Dubey (IRS), A.R. Sinha, Kishore Kunal, Sunil Kumar (all three IPS), Manoj Singh (IRTS), Pramod Kumar and P.S. Chaudhury (Delhi University), P.N. Tiwary (Patna University) and Prabhakar Singh (Bihar University) who have always been there to extend a helping hand. And there are many more, not mentioned here, to whom I am beholden.

With regard to institutions, I owe a lot in particular to the State Archives of West Bengal (Kolkata), Bihar State Archives

(Patna) and the National Archives of India (New Delhi). For Kolkata consultations, I deeply appreciate the help received from Bidisha Chakraborty (archivist) and Sarmistha De (archivist) at Bengal State Archive, and the help received from Saumitra Basu (independent scholar), Malika Basu (Burdwan University) and Nilanjana Patra (independent scholar). At the India Office Library, and the British Library, London, I am beholden especially to Margaret Makepeace and Karen Stapley, curators, East India Company Records. I accessed the libraries of Chicago University and the University of California (USA) and many others through their portals, as also onsite resource providers, including Wikipedia Commons and the Internet Archive. My thanks are due also to the NMML and ICHR Library (New Delhi). Tahir M. Ansari (AMU, Aligarh), Shashi Sheikh (Bankura University), Riteshwar Nath Tiwary (JP University), and my former students, Saurav Kumar Rai (NMML) and Vivek Ranjan (NAI, New Delhi) were also of great help.

Since there has been no significant work on Fateh Sahi until now and written sources are extremely scarce, I have also depended on folklore enshrined in popular memory, and on cultural heritage and material remains. I am thankful in particular to Sanjeev Tyagi (poet, Ghazipur) in this regard. In my account, I might have erred on certain issues and could be oblivious of others despite my best efforts. I hope my work will inspire others to delve deeper and present a fuller account of the life and times of Fateh Bahadur Sahi.

While completing this project, I thankfully remember some media platforms, both print and audiovisual, who have appreciated my approach to history and have presented my write-ups and interviews on the lesser-known aspects of history, most notably *The Hindu*, *Frontline*, *Pioneer* and *Telegraph*, and the BBC (London), Asianet TV (New York), Sputnik (Moscow), and News24 and All India Radio (New Delhi).

For helping me shape this work, I am thankful to Narayani Basu, and to my literary agent Kanishka Gupta of the Writer's Side for facilitating its early publication. To my Penguin editors Karthik Venkatesh and Ralph Rebello, I remain grateful for their diligent editing and encouraging cooperation. Finally, I am beholden to all at Penguin—administrative authorities and technical staff for helping me reach out to my readers.

Like all of my other works, this volume owes much to my family—Kiran, Supriya, Rajat, Shailesh and Udayan for their contributions in so many ways. They share the credit for all that is good in this book; I alone am responsible for any slips or shortcomings.

New Delhi J.N. Sinha
4 July 2024

Introduction

A Rebel's Tryst with History

The hero of this story—Fateh Bahadur Sahi—is an unknown and extremely obscure character in modern Indian history. In popular perception, he is more of a mythological figure. In the folklore of the middle Gangetic plain, he features as a gallant warrior, rather than a real historical character. Indeed, he is still remembered as the ruler of the obscure principality of Huseypur in northwest Bihar, where he is said to have challenged the authority of the mighty East India Company, soon after the Battle of Buxar in 1764. Displaced from his capital, he retreated to the jungles of the Himalayan foothills, from where he continued his guerrilla wars against the East India Company for nearly thirty years. He did not spare even their supporters and often looted their property. It is not surprising, then, that he is remembered as a brigand as well—a dakoo in local parlance.

How did he manage all this, who supported him, and who constituted his army? How did he lead his life in the jungles?

And, finally, what happened of him and his family afterwards? His story remains a mystery. This book is an effort to unlock it.

The little information that has trickled down to us places him in the latter half of the eighteenth century. When he became old, he relinquished his gaddi to his son in 1790, took *sanyas,* and finally left home for a pilgrimage to Nasik. He was last seen in 1808. Nothing is clearly known thereafter. This book is an attempt to understand his life and times in transition, on the borders of Awadh and Bengal in the Ganga valley.

Through contemporary relics and the history of events connected with him, we have a faint glimpse of his life at Huseypur, Line Bazar and other places in the old Saran district of Bihar. Popular memory and folklore apart, the structural remains of his time at and around Tamkuhi and Hathwa, his family heirlooms and the collections of his descendants are other important sources of information. A direct scion of Fateh Bahadur Sahi, now in the 114th generation of their founding dynasty, Vaidurya Pratap Sahi of the Tamkuhi Raj family, a scientist and heritage buff, is deeply interested in his family history. He is forever on the lookout for more information about his illustrious ancestors and is in touch with a number of archives, libraries and collectors throughout the world. His cousin line, the Hathwa Raj family, now in its 106th generation, also possesses sources in print, manuscripts and artefacts which may help to chronicle Fateh Sahi's story.

The key to many unknown facts about his life is likely to lie in moth-eaten official records stored at the administrative headquarters in Chapra, Patna, Lucknow, Allahabad, Calcutta (now Kolkata) and in London, as also in private collections elsewhere. Yet another source for a curious biographer may be found in the memoirs left by European officials, soldiers, missionaries and adventurers, such as Peter Mundy, Major J. Browne and Francis Buchanan.

Among professional historians, Anand A. Yang, a professor of history at Washington State University in the United States, has unearthed volumes of documents from obscure locations, which shed light on Fateh Sahi and happenings of the time in his native region. However, much more seems to be waiting to be discovered. Until then, we could also rely on popular legends, folklore and the ballads of local bards.

Why historians have missed telling the story of Fateh Sahi may be attributed, to begin with, to the lack of sources, as he was the most dreaded enemy of the Company in his day, and so they blocked all information about him, lest it spread across the region and encourage others to revolt. Logistically speaking, the geographical remoteness of Huseypur from the administrative headquarters in Patna (across the then unbridged Ganga) and far-off Calcutta, and the wild and marshy topography of the region further hindered the easy spread of the news of Sahi's exploits.

Given this background, official Company records are bound to be prejudicial. Any conspiracy against the State was always kept secret; most communications were transmitted verbally in utter privacy; and to avoid disclosure and reprisal, sources relating to a plot were destroyed by their authors or handlers at the earliest. That aside, if a historian or biographer were to search for evidence of the same in an archive, they would find that many records concerning local issues—social or political, including military movements and operations of the Huseypur Raja, were filed under the headings of Revenue or Crime.

Seventy-five years of Independence later, the bulk of these documents are still scattered, disorganized or simply untraceable in the respective state archives. During the storming of the Huseypur fort by Company forces in 1767, most of its records are said to have been destroyed; parts of the remaining are believed to have been seized by the English or taken away by Fateh Sahi himself. Some of the more sensitive documents were probably weeded out or destroyed outright. As for private holdings, the concerned families have not maintained their papers properly. Most of the family collections—literary sources, artefacts, etc.—were taken away by the managers under the Court of Ward regimes, claims Maheshwar Pratap Sahi of the Tamkuhi family.

Geography has played its own role in hindering explorations into the life of Fateh Sahi. For instance, the remote location of his establishment at Huseypur and later, at Tamkuhi in the Jogini jungle, or of his cousins' at Hathwa further obstructed prospective researchers from using their documents at their natural sites. Thus, the history of the region has generally gone unattended by city-based professional historians.

Intriguingly, *Anandamath*, the novel by Bankim Chandra Chattopadhyay, written nearly 300 miles away in Bengal, is believed to be based on the life and adventures of Fateh Sahi.[1] It was written against the background of the Famine of 1770 and the Sanyasi Rebellion, both of which took place in the time of Sahi; its protagonists, their life in the jungle and the wars they fought are almost identical with those connected with the Huseypur Raja.[2] Popular sources suggest that the story of Fateh Sahi was narrated to Bankim Chandra by the zamindars of Lalgola of Murshidabad district in West Bengal, where Bankim stayed for some time in 1873–74.[3] Lalgola's Roys (originally Rai, migrants from Ghazipur, UP) were Bhumihar Brahmins like Sahi, who later entered into matrimonial relations with his relatives, too.[4] In fact, the stories of *Anandamath* and Fateh Sahi are so similar that it is difficult to disbelieve the claim. A local historian, Kishan Chand Bhakat, has tried to prove Lalgola's links with *Anandamath* and the anti-British Sanyasi rebellion of the time. Not long ago, noted film director Satyajit Ray based his award-winning film *Jalsaghar* at the Nimtita Rajbari, a neighbouring zamindari estate within the Lalgola fraternity, to portray the decline of the zamindars under the British in Bengal.[5] Lalgola awaits its explorer.

A formal historical account referring to Fateh Sahi appeared in 1905, when G.N. Dutt chronicled the *History of the Hathwa Raj*,[6] followed soon by the publication of *A Brief History of the Hutwa Raj* by D.N. Dutt in 1909.[7] These works provide valuable information on the Hathwa Raj and also discuss Fateh Sahi, up until the moment when he was dislodged from Huseypur; but they do not dwell much on his life in exile. Since both writers were British appointees responsible for assisting the Hathwa Raja of the cadet line in administering his estate, they treated Fateh Sahi as a fugitive revenue defaulter of the East India Company, rather than as a patriot fighting against foreign intruders.

The *District Gazetteer of Saran* of 1930 referred to the Huseypur affair in some detail, but not as a revolt for autonomy or independence.[8] Fateh Sahi received fairer treatment after Independence in the *Saran District Gazetteer* of 1960, wherein he is portrayed as the leader of the 'First Freedom Struggle in Saran'.[9] *The Comprehensive History of Bihar* (1976) also accorded him a better place in the history of modern Bihar, but still only indirectly and not as a harbinger of the freedom struggle in India.[10] However, as these publications could not reach a wide audience, Fateh Sahi largely remained invisible to academia. More studies have followed, but all of them refer to him in the context of some other events, such as the rebellion of Chait Singh[11] or the revenue administration of the British Raj.

Happily, despite these limitations, Anand A. Yang has produced a masterly volume, *The Limited Raj*, on agrarian relations in Saran district between 1793 and 1920.[12] It is focused primarily on the Hathwa Raj land revenue operations, wherein he also refers to Fateh Sahi in considerable detail. Still, this book is not exclusively devoted to Sahi either. However, Yang takes a broad view of his subject, with a keen eye on the varieties of sources that can help future researchers in studying the two families descending from the Huseypur Raj—Hathwa and Tamkuhi. Yang's *Bazaar India* offers more information, sources and perspectives,[13] but, again, it is not a study devoted to Fateh Sahi. Despite many broader studies on eighteenth century India that also cover this region, such as those by B.S. Cohn, S. Nurul Hasan, Richard Barnet and B.P. Ambashthya,[14] and many publications on neighbouring Benares,[15] none have accorded Fateh Sahi the attention he deserves in India's history.

While writing this book, I puzzled over why even subaltern historians have missed out on studying this rebel, who revolted at the first threat of colonialism and fought from the grassroots with the support of the subalterns. Historians like Georges Lefebvre and George Rudé have talked of agrarian disturbances in the French Revolution and of the role of the 'crowd' in it.[16] In some ways, a similar situation prevailed in Huseypur, where a local chief rebelled against an exploitative foreign regime, with support from the rural masses, and his army comprised a whole lot of people from outside mainstream society—religious warriors, vagabonds, destitute and brigands.

Working on Benares, C.A. Bayly diligently focused on the rise and role of the Bhumihar Brahmins, the caste Fateh

Sahi belonged to, but, again, he missed Sahi.[17] More recently, Shashi Tharoor and William Dalrymple have come out with magnificent histories of the time and have closely followed many of the happenings around Huseypur, which are also concerned with Fateh Sahi, but the Raja is nowhere in sight.[18] As a rebel against the state, it seems as though he was destined to remain invisible and elusive. Therefore, until more sources are discovered and information retrieved, the gaps in his story may be filled with circumstantial evidences, popular memories and with the informed imagination of the historian.

Compared with the slip by professional historians who wrote in English, the works of some vernacular writers in Hindi and Bhojpuri are noteworthy. Decades ago, Rahul Sankrityayan had written about Fateh Sahi and praised him for his rebellion against foreign rule.[19] In 1987, a Delhi University history book, *Adhunik Bharat ka Itihas* (in Hindi) edited by Ramlakhan Shukla, briefly discussed Sahi's uprising as a people's revolt during 1757–1857 in British India.[20] After the initial writings of Sankrityayan on Fateh Sahi, a few short interventions from contemporary scholars of the Hindi language like Manager Pandey (JNU) and Awadhesh Pradhan (BHU) have added to the literature on the subject.[21] But this was not enough to satisfy local intelligentsia. So, around 2010, some literary writers from Sahi's region, led by Akshaywar Dixit, took it upon themselves to mine the past and resurrect the warrior from the shadows of history. However, they were not trained historians; as such, they relied mainly on popular literature and folktales, lore, legends and the heritage of the time.[22]

Their writings show how historical figures and events are perceived by the common people, how they view their own past and how they visualize it as having happened. Is the growing need for a story like that of Fateh Sahi the manifestation of the disappointment of people with their present leaders, or their unspoken disillusionment with an elitist perspective of history? Why can't we see such alternative histories as a collective concern of the masses in democracy to appropriate their share in history? Fateh Sahi appears to be their ideal, as the common masses and the marginalized supported him, and together, they fought against foreign aggression and oppression.

As a career historian, I realized over a decade ago how my fraternity had failed to look at this warrior patriot and his feats. I did some preliminary research and published an article on Fateh Sahi in *The Hindu* in 2011.[23] I was surprised by the overwhelming response I received from readers from everywhere, and the ensuing spurt of interest in this forgotten hero. These events have inspired me to write this book.

The subsequent pages present the saga of Sahi's extraordinary deeds and adventures of his guerrilla wars against the Company in the latter half of the turbulent eighteenth century in India. I will try to trace his rise to power, the flashpoint for his revolt, his decades-long raids from his jungle hideout and eventually, his farewell to arms, his royal retreat and his voyage to the ultimate freedom—unknown and unexplained.

And, lastly, a question for us: Was his rebellion India's First War of Independence?

I

A Hero Forgotten

This is a semi-wild terrain on the borders of Uttar Pradesh and Bihar. Bounded by the Himalayan foothills in the north, the Ganga in the south, and by its two tributaries, the Ghagra and the Gandak in the west and the east, respectively, it is remote, but endowed with variegated flora and an abundance of waterbodies. It is a region rich in history as well. Kushinagar, where the Buddha breathed his last, is situated to its west, and Balmiki Nagar, the abode of the revered saint-poet and author of the epic Ramayana, Valmiki, to the east. You may also hear of Bhartharihari, the yogi king of yore, and of the cult of Gorakhnath. Kabir, the saint poet, Ghagh, the wise man of the rural masses, and many others are enshrined in its popular culture. In this conclave of the greats, folklore also admires an obscure hero—Fateh Bahadur Sahi, a lone warrior always in the saddle, waging bloody wars against the East India Company day and night and unleashing a reign of terror in the region. Yet, he does not have any great memorial nor do history books talk much of him.

A dilapidated fort at Huseypur, a war cemetery at Company Bagh and an infamous orchard (Mudkatwa Bagh) where bloody clashes are said to have taken place, remind us of his existence. Nearby, there is a string of memorial mounds where thirteen women—whose husbands were killed during Fateh Sahi's raids—are believed to have committed *sati* in the footsteps of the wife of the deceased prince. This is a popular memory, albeit vague and incoherent. If you talk to the local residents of the area, they may often utter a phrase or an anecdote that catches your attention: they address a stubborn child by the name of this elusive warrior; and the elderly recall how, in their childhood, their mothers used to evoke his name to lull the children to sleep. But, in intimate moments of triumph and loss, happiness or despair, the vanishing recounters in the surrounding hamlets still remember him and sing of his love for the land, his ordeals, and of his valour and sacrifice.

The Enigma of Fateh Sahi

Maharaja Fateh Bahadur Sahi was the independent ruler of Huseypur in the erstwhile Saran district of Bihar. In 1767, he was probably the first Indian king of ancient origins to challenge the British soon after they came to power, in the aftermath of the Battle of Buxar of 1764. This happened at Huseypur. The English retaliated with full force and compelled Fateh Sahi to retreat into the neighbouring Bhagjogni (Jogini) jungles of Gorakhpur, but he did not surrender. From within those dense forests, he waged a guerrilla war against the British for over a quarter of a century. Indeed, he became such a vexing problem for the East India Company that eventually, they established an army garrison nearby at Baragaon to contain him. Yet he continued to push back, attacking the establishments of the Company and its agents from his refuge. He killed his cousin in one of these raids, because he had a soft attitude towards the English. This was probably a tactical error, as this murder would allow the British the opportunity to win over to their side the aggrieved family to act as their supporters in the future.[1]

Fateh Sahi continued his raids in the following years and remained in contact with his *ryots* who paid him taxes even in exile. He organized his supporters and received help from many feudatories of subah Bihar (then loosely allied to Bengal) and Awadh (present eastern Uttar Pradesh) of the Mughal Empire, especially the rajas of Benares, Majhauli and Padrauna and the Awadh nawabs. Many zamindars of his clan also helped him, and support came from the Rajput and Muslim chiefs, too. Above all, he was supported by his subjects.

Fateh Sahi was crowned as the Raja of Huseypur around 1750, seven years before the Battle of Plassey and fourteen years before Buxar. It was a turbulent time. The aftermath of Plassey and Buxar would consolidate the foundation of the British Empire on the Indian subcontinent, leading to widespread oppression, corruption, crime and utter chaos. Locally, the inaccessible geographical location of Saran, its wild and marshy terrain and multiple administrative controls added to the chaos. It became a free zone for the powerful, the ingenious and the enterprising.

The East India Company acquired Saran after the Battle of Buxar, but its hold was tenuous. The region remained defiant, with its chiefs acting according to their own will. It had always been this way in Saran. Even in the heyday of the Mughals, the region was defiant and its local chiefs acted independently. The Mughal rulers attempted to appease them by granting *jagirs* and honours, or overlooked their autonomy. So, the British thought it wiser to ally with them, in order to consolidate their own position, and extract revenue and resources from the area. They would soon realize that there was no other way for them. The exploitation that followed only deepened poverty and confusion.

The Bengal famine of 1770 made the situation worse. Official correspondence and contemporary tracts tell horrifying stories of the failure of crops and pestilence, of hunger, death and lawlessness in the towns and countryside of Bihar. As a result, the tax returns of the Company, which had initially increased manifold after the introduction of the Diwani rights, now suddenly dwindled. When the higher authorities pressed for the augmentation of the tax collection, their agents resorted to harsh measures that hurt the taxpayers. The old zamindars, who had been enjoying privileges since Mughal times, reacted strongly and connived at paying any new taxes imposed by the Company. The situation was so nasty that it pricked the conscience of even some Company officers.[2]

The native chiefs and notables reacted adversely, as their hereditary, traditional privileges and status were challenged by the new regime, and the common masses harboured a general hatred towards the Company, because they were oppressed by its agents. Traditionally, local masters had always protected them in hard times, allowing exemptions from many feudatory obligations. Additionally, they launched public welfare schemes, like the construction of ponds, public wells, roads and dams to provide employment and earnings to the sufferers. Small cottage-industries had always stood them in good stead, but the commercial activities and policy of the Company ruined them, and gravely dented the traditional self-sufficient village economy. The Company was concerned only with economic gains, overlooking the welfare of the people completely.[3] In such a desperate situation, the popular psyche looked for a liberator with a magic wand in hand to change their destiny overnight.

Fateh Bahadur fitted well in that mould. His long heredity of kingship and power, and the topography of the region shaped the future course of his life. The local geography dictated the means and methods of his actions to some extent. The Huseypur Raj was part of the alluvial middle Gangetic plain, crisscrossed by rivers and smaller water channels, and dotted with marshy depressions called *chaur*. The maps and survey reports prepared in the last quarter of the eighteenth century by Major James Rennell (1742–1830), the first surveyor general of the East India Company, give us an understanding of the geography of the region then.[4] The sources, folk traditions in particular, recount frequent group clashes and internecine fights among local chiefs over issues arising out of floods, famines and scarcities. There are also instances of significant demographic displacement and growing rivalry among stakeholders for exploiting the local resources.[5]

Lest We Forget

Not much has changed since then. Perpetual changes in the flow of the Ghagra and the Gandak rivers often result in floods in the area and the creation of lagoons and *diaras* (tiny islands). New tracts emerge after floods whose nature depends on the quality of the silt. The good quality alluvial deposit creates fertile *diaras* in a certain part, while an adjoining tract is rendered infertile on account of an accumulation of sand there. Their location keeps changing with the direction of flow and load of water according to the topography.[6] As a result, locals scramble for fertile tracts after the rains, in the hope of getting rich crops. However, their frequently changing sites complicate the issue of property ownership, leading to recurrent community violence, often involving multiple stakeholders, including the State. This has long been a historical phenomenon.

Such conditions rendered life unsettled and insecure in the past, encouraging the frequent use of muscle power and violence in day-to-day life. In Saran, which also included Champaran then, pre-monsoon summer cyclones, heavy rains and floods have been a cause of people's woes for ages. Even Babar was the victim of such a cyclone. He has given graphic details of how, in the dead of night in the month of May, a violent tempest blew down his camp at Chapra (then a village). The papers he was writing on in candlelight were blown away along with his books; his pavilion collapsed and everything was drenched in rain water, and he could not sleep throughout the night. [7] However, at the same time, abundant rivers, marshes and wild tracts offered the natives useful resources to survive—food, navigation, even sports and entertainment. This is well reflected in local folktales and certain traditional social practices, such as foraging, hunting and the practice of *Darh*.[8] Though many of them may appear primitive and weird to us and are rarely practised now, such activities entertained the natives, and helped them hone their hunting skills and survive in a subsistence economy. This must have also whetted their abilities for group action against their adversaries, especially in difficult terrains.

But these conditions on the other hand, also acted to keep them socially backward and cut off from the rest of the society and progress at large. This encouraged clever and articulate outsiders to bring them under their sway—with lure and persuasion, and, if needed, by force. In this way, external fortune-seekers entered the region and acquired land and enough power to act freely in scattered pockets. We will see later how it became difficult for any central authority, including the Mughals and the British, to exert control over the territorial chiefs of the region like the Huseypur rajas.

The origins of some of these new regional chiefs may be traced to the seventh century, right after the Gupta period. Among them, the Brahmin, Rajput (Kshatriya) and Muslim chiefs gained a stronger footing. They tended to defy the imperial authority, which was already on the wane. Since no associations of chiefs and group interests had emerged by then, like the ones that formed centuries later, caste alignments and religion served as a means of unity for the protection of mutual or group interests whenever needed. This is why the caste or religion of the main players in the present story are crucial and hence, occasionally identified while assessing their implications for the events concerned.

The latter half of the eighteenth century was a period of fast transition in India. The Mughal control declined rapidly as its governors increasingly became independent. Politically, the most important change that affected the whole of eastern India, from Allahabad to Bengal, was the consolidation of the Hindu states under the two dominant Hindu agrarian castes—the Rajputs and the Bhumihar Brahmins.[9] In view of the fact that Mughal rule in eastern India had always been rather superficial, these two castes, especially of the dynasty of Gautam Bhumihar Brahmins in the Benares region, were consequential.[10]

These developments would considerably influence Fateh Sahi's struggle against the British in the years to come. The geo-ethnic legacy he had inherited encouraged him to assert his autonomy and defy the diktats of the new masters of Hindustan. Not all chiefs of his time were so daring though—and that makes him stand out. Indeed, it is noteworthy that Fateh Sahi undertook his actions three decades before Tipu Sultan challenged the East India Company in the closing years of the eighteenth century.

The Folk Hero

In the background of these developments around him, Fateh Sahi lived a life of relentless wars, occasional diplomacy and, above all, one of extreme courage, violence and endurance, fired by a deep yearning for freedom. This showed in the pursuit of his targets. He was in league with the nawabs of Awadh, the Raja of Benares and many chiefs of the region, such as those of Majhauli and Padrauna, some of whom also claimed hereditary connections with him. Chait Singh of Benares was his relative; the Rajput chiefs rallied behind him because they had common interests; and, for similar reasons, many Muslim feudatories and other zamindars of the region supported him covertly. This was enough to frighten the fledgling regime of the East India Company, which was compelled to fight him tooth and nail. They engaged in several battles with Fateh Sahi. Skirmishes occurred sporadically, but the guerrilla bounced back each time.

Desperately worried, the British resorted to diplomacy, pardoned his atrocities and offered to live amicably. Sahi used the opportunity to bide his time for a short spell. Soon, he resumed his attacks, and met with his supporters in the forest and the riverine areas, and continued his operations from the wild.

As Fateh Sahi aged, he handed over the reins of power to his eldest son in 1790. A new capital was established at his forest retreat at Tamkuhi, in today's Kushinagar District of Uttar Pradesh. It is still home to his descendants. In this way, out of the Huseypur Raj, two separate principalities emerged—one, the Hathwa Raj (representing the original Huseypur Raj under the descendants of Basant Sahi, the deceased prince who was Fateh Sahi's cousin), and the other, Tamkuhi Raj (direct descendants of Fateh Sahi). The British succeeded in their much-known policy of divide and rule. Yet, they could not subdue Fateh Sahi, who never gave up his claim on Huseypur, nor did he ever surrender.

2

Prelude to Power

The Ancestry

Fateh Sahi's earliest known ancestor—Mayyur Bhutt—is believed to have travelled from Gujarat to Benares for studies. He excelled in Sanskrit and astrology. So impressed was the ruler of Shravasti by Mayyur's scholarship that he got his daughter Suryaprabha married to him, so goes the legend. Shravasti, in modern Uttar Pradesh, was a major city in the time of the Buddha. Situated near the West Rapti River in the north-eastern part of Uttar Pradesh, close to the Nepalese border, it was the capital of the ancient kingdom of Kosala from the sixth century BCE to sixth century CE. It was one of the most revered sites in Buddhism, believed to be the place where the Buddha stayed many times during *Chaturmas* (the four months of the monsoon when Buddhist monks stayed home in order to avoid killing insects), and delivered his famous sermons and performed miracles—as portrayed in numerous reliefs, sculptures and Buddhist literature. Shravasti was at the junction of major trading routes in ancient India, and remained prosperous until the twelfth century CE.[1]

After his marriage, Mayyur settled initially in the district of Azamgarh, where he acquired *pargana* Sikandarpur in the modern-day Ballia District, probably received as a land gift from his father-in-law, which elevated his status. Later, he shifted to Karkotpur (Kikora) before moving to Kundin Gram (Kudwa) near Kushinara in today's Kushinagar. From there, the family finally relocated to Saran District in Bihar, where they prospered as a principality.[2] In Saran, they settled first in a village close to modern Gopalganj in north-west Bihar called Kalyanpur, named after the reigning king Kalyan Mull. Later, they shifted to the neighbouring village of Huseypur. It was here that Fateh Sahi would succeed as the Raja of his principality.

While scanty and scattered sources reveal this trajectory, we still don't know much about the period of the origins and the ancestry of the family.[3]

There are two main possibilities: first, the family emerged in the fifth–sixth century BCE, during the time of Gautam Buddha who hailed from the Malla Republic;[4] the second possibility places them during the reign of Harshvardhan in the first half of the seventh century CE. According to the noted scholar Rahul Sankrityayan, the word *Bagauchhia*, the sub-clan (*mool* denoting root) of the Huseypur rulers, was derived from the Byagrapad *gotra* of the Mallas who lived in the region. Sankrityayan holds that although the region was under Islamic control from the thirteenth to the eighteenth century, its north-western corner was ruled by a Bagauchhia Bhumihar family with its capital at Kalyanpur,[5] implying that they ruled even through the Turko-Afghan-Mughal period. The Mallas had nine branches. The Kolis, who claimed to be a branch of Kshatriyas, into which the Buddha was married, were one of them.[6] The fact that several predecessors of Huseypur rajas used the title of Mull after their names, up to Kalyan Mull, supports this idea of their relationship with the Mallas. The association of the Buddha both with the Kolis and Shravasti, and Mayyur's connection with Shravasti may well provide not only a linkage with the Kalyanpur rajas, but could also help explain their historicity.

The marriage of Mayyur with the princess of Shravasti in the time of the Buddha also seems to reinforce his identity with the Bhumihar Brahmins, to which caste his present descendants claim to belong. It is believed that a section of Brahmins who did not favour ritualism turned to Buddhism; gradually, they took to agriculture and eventually became landlords, gradually known as Bhumihar Brahmin.[7] Indeed, from the Turko-Afghan period onwards, several Brahmin families seem to have migrated from western India to the eastern provinces—to what is now Uttar Pradesh, Bihar and Bengal. Since many of them engaged in agriculture, they aspired to have their own identity and called themselves Bhumihar Brahmin, Bhumihar, or Babhan. The term 'Babhan' for the Brahmins occurs in the *Jatakas*, indicating a Buddhist connection, which is further reinforced by the fact that a section of Bhumihars is also called Gautami Brahmans. This may help retain Mayyur's Gujarat-Brahmin connection, his location in the Buddha's time as also his caste identity. Taking this a step further, another strong possibility is that the evolution of Mayyur's progeny passed through this process as well. Their patronymic of Pachhima Babhan clearly shows their migration from the west (*pachhim*) and their identity as a branch of the Brahmins. We will soon come across their sub-castes, like the Eksaria and the Gautam, who prospered in the vicinity of Huseypur and collaborated with Fateh Sahi in the course of time.

At present, the Baghochia families trace their roots to Baghoch and Bharhichowra (in pargana Salempur in the modern Gorakhpur in Uttar Pradesh), as the ancient seats of the Huseypur rulers. The name Baghauch may have been associated with their clan from its totemic stages, considering that the word refers to *bagh* (tiger), which was the clan's totem. The name of the family's first capital was also Baghauch. They claim to be a sub-group of the Vats gotra Bhumihar Brahmins. According to both genealogy and family legend, the founder of the dynasty was Raja Beer Sen, who played an important role during the invasion of the Sakyas by the Kosala Maharaj Vidudabha, son of Pasenadi, who was a contemporary as well as a patron of the Buddha.

Later traditions say that the Sakyas were defeated during the Buddha's time. As a result, Beer Sen gained part of the vanquished country, which he added to his territory. It is possible, therefore, that he received the title of Raja from Vidudabha for his services. The fact that the ancient seat of the earliest Huseypur rajas was Bharhichowra in the same region further endorses this inference. This suggests their presence in the time of the Buddha; in the successive centuries, too, there are references to the rajas and events that can be related to their ancestors.[8]

The change in the surname of Beer Sen (or Sein) to Sinha with the sixteenth Raja seems to have some anchorage in history. A genealogical table submitted in the great Hathwa case of 1861 and subsequently published as a pamphlet in 1870 claims that the patronymic of the earlier rajas was 'Sein', which changed to 'Sinha' with the sixteenth descendant, who received the title of Raja from the emperor of Delhi.[9] However, it is not clear which emperor; thus, it hints at least at the presence of the family in the medieval period. Going by genealogy, Jagat Sinha might have lived around 150 BCE, which brings him close to a historical event: Menander I Soter (reigned c. 165/155–130 BCE), the Indo-Greek king of Sagala in the Punjab, had advanced as far as the city of Saketa in Kosala (Ayodhya) in 141 BCE, but he was forced to retreat by Pushyamitra, the general of the last Mauryan king, Brihdratha. It appears Jagat Sinha assisted the king in driving out the invader, for which he was honoured with the title of 'Sinha', meaning lion—an emblem of the Mauryas, set up on the Ashokan pillars found in the area.[10] There are no further clues thereafter, until we meet Mayyur Bhutt in the time of Harsh of the Vardhan dynasty in the seventh century CE.

At the height of his power, Harshvardhan (CE 606–647) ruled over most of north India, with his capital at Kannauj. The peace and prosperity of his reign made for a cosmopolitan court, attracting scholars, artists and religious men from far-off places. The Chinese traveller Xuanzang was one of them. Banabhatta, the well-known seventh-century Sanskrit scholar, was his court poet who chronicled the happenings of his time in Harsha's biography *Harsha Charita*. Eclectic in his religious views, the king patronized scholars of all faiths.[11] Mayyur Bhutt is also believed to have lived at his court. But, except for these assumptions and a few testimonies from later scholars, there is not much tangible evidence to prove such a long antiquity. However, Fateh Sahi's descendants from Tamkuhi, and their cousin line of Hathwa, assert that they are currently in their 114th and 106th generations, respectively. By conventional estimation, this claim puts their origin somewhere in the time of the Buddha, though this genealogical count has a tricky side. The standard practice of granting about thirty years for a generation may be deceptive, especially in the case of rulers who were crowned later in life, those who ruled only briefly or who died or abdicated prematurely. In case of these probabilities, the timing may be substantially contracted towards the end of the Gupta period.

Mayyur's surname—Bhutt—provides a clue in our search. It is the surname of a branch of Brahmins variously called Bhutt, Bhat or Bhaat, found in some parts of India. They are known to have been scholars, writers, bards, astrologers and traditional physicians. Professionally, some of them are known to have orally maintained the genealogy of reigning kings and nobles. Probably, Banabhatta belonged to this branch. In his *Harsha Charita*, India's first historical text, and his novel *Kadambari*, he mentions that he was born in a village in a Bhojaka family of the Vātsyāyana gotra at a place believed to have been in the erstwhile Saran District of Bihar.[12] Like Banabhatta, Mayyur Bhutt was also a great scholar. His *Suryasatak* and *Mayurashtak* are highly praised for their linguistic maturity and artistry, and poetic beauty. Deriving from certain episodes, it appears that Mayyur was either Banabhatta's father-in-law or his sister's husband. Both of them are said to have lived in Saran.

But, again, except for legend, there is not much to relate Mayyur or his family to any happenings in the following centuries, until one reaches the medieval period. This shrinks the chronological gap between the Kalyanpur rajas and their ancestor Mayyur, who probably lived in the time of the Buddha or Harsha. Still, a long gap of well over a thousand years remains. The legend that the Bhumihars engaged in farming, under the influence of Buddhism, resolves the problem to an extent, if we presume the Kalyanpur-Huseypur lineage passed through this process in the intervening period.

Moreover, the changes in the surname of the Kalyanpur-Huseypur rajas, from Bhutt to Sen to Mull, Sinha and Sahi are a little intriguing. Leaving Mayyur Bhutt aside, the patronymic of the earlier rajas was Sen (with Beer Sen); it was changed to Sinha with the sixteenth Raja in descent Jagat Sinha, to Mull (also spelt as Malla) with the eighty-third Raja Jai Mul, and to Sahi with the eighty-seventh, Raja Khem Karan Sahi in the line. The title of 'Maharaja' was conferred by Emperor Akbar on the eighty-sixth Raja Kalyan Mull and that of 'Maharaj Bahadur' on the eighty-seventh Raja Khem Karan Sahi.[13] The traditions of the Majhauli estate, a Rajput family, also attribute their origins to Mayyur Bhutt, who is variously associated with multiple castes. Mayyur is said to have had three wives, one each from the Brahmin, Bhumihar and Rajput castes. From each of them, his sons founded major estates.[14]

We have already referred to Mayyur's marriage with Suryaprabha. She gave birth to Vishwasen, with whom started the line of Surajbans Rajputs, who founded the Majhauli estate. At the time of his marriage with Suryaprabha, the royal priest of Shravasti also got his daughter married to Mayyur, who became the mother of Nagsen, the founder of the line of the Mishra group of the Sarupari Brahmanas. Mayyur's Bhumihar Brahmin wife, probably named Chhavi Kumari, gave birth to Beer Sen, who did penance at Baghoch Ghat wearing a tiger skin; hence, he became known as Baghambar. He was the progenitor of the Bagauchhia Bhumihars, the Vats gotra *Ayachak* Brahmins, the founders of the future Kalyanpur Raj in the region.[15]

The genesis of the Mull surname may be traced to the Malla-Koli-Kshatriya connection and the Kshatriya progeny of Mayyur Bhutt. Sen appears to have been a generic title for rulers, and Sinha (also spelt Singh, meaning 'lion'), an honorific decoration or a title generally assumed to show power and a high/ruling-class status. The last title of Sahi (originally Shahi, meaning 'royal'), which the family still retains, was bestowed upon them as an honorific by the Mughal Emperor Jahangir. The cadet branches of the Bagauchias also held several zamindaris, *ghatwali* and *mulraiyati* estates in Bihar, Jharkhand and eastern Uttar Pradesh, where they assumed surnames like Singh and Rai.[16]

The tradition of marriages across castes, creeds or territories among ruling families was common in the past; as such, the social status, and not the caste, was the prime prerequisite for social interaction among them, leading to changes in surnames.[17] Such changes took place also because of religious conversions, both in medieval and colonial periods, as we shall soon see in the case of the Kharagpur rajas in Bihar.[18]

But what about the title of Raja? Was it bestowed upon someone by a higher authority or was it self-assumed by the ruler of a territory or a clan chief? Or was it used by the people to address a person in power? Its evolution appears to be the consequence of all these propositions. In ancient times, the title of Raja was ritually solemnized by a priest after a ruler achieved a conventionally qualifying status, progressively with higher decorations like Maharaja, *Maharajadhiraj* and *Chakravarti*, and carried a kind of ethical sanctity of guardianship over the subject people. However, in medieval times, the title exuded more of a power of control. In the sixteenth century, the priest appears to have gone backstage; with the powerful king aspiring to assert his suzerainty over a territory, either by assuming the title on his own or by bestowing it on friendly chiefs.

This happened with the Huseypur ruler when Akbar decorated him with the title of 'Raja', and successive emperors reaffirmed the honour with additional titles of 'Maharaj Bahadur' and 'Sahi' to the later Kalyanpur-Huseypur successors. This fact is likely to have helped them maintain friendly relations with the Mughals, almost as allies rather than vassals.

However, since the British were in the process of establishing themselves as Raja (monarch), they sparingly used the term 'Raja' for others, because, traditionally, it implied an autonomous status with certain privileges and moral obligations as a protector of the subject people, which they were not inclined to accept. Instead, they generally called them zamindar. This was one of the earliest instances of the use of language and social mores as tools of the colonial empire. Small wonder then that their ambitions to assert suzerainty incited a violent retort when they tried to lord it over Fateh Sahi. We will soon return to see how.

Whatever the truth, the lineage of the royal bards, legends and folktales of the region believe in this long antiquity of the Kalyanpur-Huseypur rajas, and continue to sing of the olden days of the dynasty and the deeds of its illustrious kings. The claim of Fateh Sahi's descendants and that of the cadet line keeps the issue of origin alive. Under the circumstances, even a conservative estimate may privilege them to be among the oldest and, probably, unbroken royal lineages of the Indian subcontinent.

With this assumption, let us pick up the strands of our story again, from a period where we have more concrete evidence. In the middle of the seventh century CE, when the last centralized empire in north India broke down with the demise of king Harsha, local chiefs started emerging. The non-Aryan aboriginals, such as Cheros and Bhars, carved out small chieftaincies in the region, by clearing jungles and creating settlements along the Ghaghra-Saryug and Gandak rivers. With the Muslim conquest of northwest India during the eleventh and twelfth centuries, migration started eastward. As a result, Rajputs entered the area, and in coalition with reigning Muslim chiefs, they drove the Cheros out.

The Bhumihar Brahmins entered the arena around this time; and, together, they displaced local aboriginal chiefs. Thus, this UP-Bihar junction became a buffer zone between the spheres of influence of the Delhi sultans, the independent kingdom of Jaunpur, and the rulers of Bengal. This helped these émigré chiefs flourish and increase their power unhindered. Rajputs settled at Manjhi, Amnour and Majhauli. The Bhumihars gained predominance at the village and pargana levels and established several zamindaris. The Muslims gained hold in scattered pockets.[19]

Arabic-Persian sources indicate a long-standing Muslim presence in *Sarkar* Saran and *Subah* Bihar since the Turko-Afghan period. They immigrated on a large scale in the thirteenth century when Afghan traders and Sufi saint-warriors settled in the plains of south Bihar and engaged in agricultural colonization. The Sufi warrior Malik Ibrahim Bayu defeated the Kol chiefs, hostile to the local Muslims, and conquered their territories. The Kharagpur Raj in Munger was originally controlled by Rajputs, but after a failed rebellion by Raja Sangram Singh in 1615, his son converted to Islam. The Faujdars of Purnia created an autonomous territory in Eastern Bihar around 1700. The Pathans broadly comprised two groups: the descendants of Pashtun settlers, and the second, local converts from upper-caste Hindus.[20] Numerous villages with Muslim names and others with sizeable Muslim populations in the province still testify to this historical reality. The presence of the *dargah* of the *Pirs* (Sufi saints) and various relics are living testimonies of Hindu-Muslim cultural interaction at the village level till now.[21]

In Saran, the Muslims were clustered particularly around Siwan (headquarters of the modern eponymous district). Two Muslim mercenaries settled there on land grants received from the Majhauli Raj in return for their services in rescuing its zamindari. One of them, Raja Ali Baksh, a contemporary of Fateh Sahi, flourished in the mid-eighteenth century. The ruins of his fortress, Purana Quila, are still extant in the town, and a memorial plaque registers his support for the construction of a mosque there. The town itself was named after him as Aliganj.[22] To a few others, such as an Afghan at Burharia, interposing in the Fateh story, we will return later.

Notably, most of these Muslim chiefs belonged to non-Mughal stock. Many were of Afghan origin, and their history may be traced to the Mughal-Afghan conflict of Humayun and Sher Shah, and the latter's brief rule in the region. Therefore, the Indian converts could be genuinely loyal neither to the Mughals nor to the English. Even though these chiefs were Muslims, their interests conflicted with that of the Mughals, and most of them tried to resist any imperial control until the end of Mughal rule, and subsequently, that of the East India Company. This naturally placed them on the side of local Hindu chiefs, like those of Huseypur or the Raja of Benares, even though their mutual disputes were not unheard of.

During the Mughal period, we find references to a large number of territorial chiefs in almost every part of north India. Locally, they were called Raja, *Rana*, *Raís*, *Rawat* and so on; but in contemporary Persian sources, they are referred to as zamindar and *marzaban*.[23] They were fully or semi-autonomous chiefs, ruling over their respective territories for long lengths of time, and played important roles in medieval polity. They commanded a considerable portion of the economic and military resources of the empire. One-sixth of Babur's total revenues as well as soldiers of his army came from them.[24] According to Arif Qandhari, a historian contemporary of Akbar, about two to three hundred of these chiefs possessed their own forts. Each of them commanded their own armies, consisting generally of their clansmen, whose total number Abul Fazl estimated at 47,00,000.[25]

W.H. Moreland was the first modern historian to draw attention to these chiefs in 1929. He defined them as 'vassal chiefs', who existed in territories outside the direct control of the Mughal state, except in Bengal.[26] However, Irfan Habib believes that they were present all over the empire.[27] S. Nurul Hasan has categorized them as autonomous, intermediary and primary, according to their status.[28] These studies deal with the Mughal Empire, but none looks at Bihar. Even so, they underline the significance of these zamindars in the empire. Hasan's categorization of 'autonomous zamindars' lends support to Fateh Sahi's position in the political matrix of the time, and explains why he revolted when the British tried to bring him under their control.[29]

It is against this long and expansive backdrop that the Mayyur lineage emerged in the region. Mayyur's son, by his Bhumihar wife, received a share from his father's estate that later developed into the Kalyanpur-Huseypur Raj. Its descendants believe that Raja Beer Sen laid the foundation of the dynasty in the region, then a part of ancient Kosala. However, in the absence of tangible evidence, we do not have any detailed and concrete information about its rulers until the time of Akbar and only scanty references, prior to Fateh Sahi.

Prelude to Power

Before we return to Fateh Sahi, let us take a look at his neighbouring zamindars, especially those of his caste, who would become potential allies in his rebellion against the East India Company in the years ahead. Close to Huseypur, a branch of Bhumihars had gained a foothold in southern Saran by the end of the sixteenth century. Jagarnath Dikshit, a scholar and traditional healer from Hastinapur, was invited by a local raja to treat his ailment, so goes the legend. On being cured, he rewarded Dikshit with a jagir, in which Dikshit settled in the village of Eksar near Ekma in Saran. Over time, his four sons settled in new villages, where they founded several zamindaris in four generations, the major ones being Manjha, Parsa, Chainpur, Rusi, Khaira and Bagoura. In the course of time, some descendants moved eastward into Tirhut and established zamindaris there. The initial expansion of Dikshit's descendants may be attributed to the abundance of male heirs that compelled them to disperse, and the inability of the State to restrict their expansion.[30] But their internal disputes restricted them from developing into major estates. Nevertheless, they wielded considerable control over the local society and skilfully managed to deal with the Europeans in such a way as to act freely in their estates. Incidentally, they did not clash with the Bagauchhias of Huseypur in their pursuit of territorial expansion. Later, they entered into marriage relations with them, as also with the Raja of Benares and other notables of the region, which added to their influence and power, and enabled them to resist the newly introduced British control. This helped in creating an anti-British platform over time.

In fact, several chieftaincies of the caste emerged around this time in the region from eastern Uttar Pradesh to Bengal. Besides Benares, the Kalyanpur-Huseypur Raj and the Dikshit line discussed above, their clan fraternity included the estates of Betia, Tikari, Sheohar, Madhuban, Maheshpur (Sultanabad estate), Pakur and Dhanwar in Bihar, Lalgola in Murshidabad, Singhabad near Malda and Mahishadal in east Midnapur in Bengal.[31] Most of them had originally migrated from eastern Uttar Pradesh and Bihar; and some were also relations of the Huseypur rajas.[32] This league increasingly harboured grievances that fuelled a widespread anti-British resentment among the landed aristocracy in the eastern regions.[33] This would have definitely empowered and emboldened Fateh Sahi to challenge the Company.

In view of the vast expanse of the country, the Mughal emperors and their governors had actually never been able to rule without the help of such local chiefs. Realizing this, the British collaborated with them and used them as links with the indigenous society. These 'intermediaries provided a solid foundation for Pax Britannica, extending its reach into the society lying outside the grasp of its formal structures of rule. Thus, the overarching authority of the British Raj was able to encapsulate even the most distant hinterlands in its political system.'[34] A system of consultation and control was erected in the Permanent Settlement of 1793 that defined the 'legal and administrative framework within which agrarian relations were determined … until the zamindari abolition acts of the 1950s.'[35] In the parganas of Kalyanpur Kuari, Sipah and Chaubara, the Raja of Huseypur held most of the land in the first two and of

Majhauli in the third. But their settlement was deferred because of their recent rebellions against the British. Instead, their holdings were leased out to private revenue farmers. Jagmohan Mukherji leased Huseypur for a revenue of Rs 1,39,209 (almost 15 per cent of the district's total revenue).[36]

These circumstances had paved the way for the Huseypur family to rise to power from Kalyanpur in Saran, from the sixteenth century onwards.

Mughal Recognition

The first reference to the Kalyanpur family occurs in 1539 CE when Raja Jay Mull (f. c. 1525), the eighty-third Raja of the dynasty, helped Humayun after his defeat at the Battle of Chausa (1539). This was an age of unrest and disorder. The last of the Lodi kings fell at the hands of Babur in the Battle of Panipat (1526), allowing him to control an extensive territory from the eastern limits of Persia to the western boundaries of Bengal. The Pathans attempted to establish a new kingdom at Jaunpur under Darya Khan Lohani, but Babur defeated him. During his expedition, Babur took possession of Benares and Patna, and left prince Humayun to tranquilize Awadh. Bihar was under Mahmud Lodi, who had made himself its ruler in 1529. Babur defeated him and appointed the grandson of Darya Khan to govern Bihar.

Some years after this, the historic battle between Humayun and Sher Shah Suri took place, resulting in Humayun's flight following the battles of Chausa and Kannauj. Sher Shah ascended the throne at Delhi in 1540. This turbulent phase offered ample scope to exhibit military genius and it was at this time that Jay Mull, Fateh Sahi's ancestor, appeared on the scene. He provided Humayun with food and fodder for his troops. Probably around this time, he assumed the title of Mull (or Mall, meaning 'duel' in Sanskrit, synonymous with his roots with Mall warriors). But after Sher Shah established his control over north India, he took stern action against Jay Mull, who fled into the surrounding jungles, from where he engaged in rebellion for a long time. Once Humayun reinstated himself, he rewarded Jay Mull's grandson Raja Jubaraj Sahi with four parganas.[37] Thus, friendly relations between the Kalyanpur family and the Mughals continued. Circumstances would bring them together, again and again.[38]

In the neighbourhood of Kalyanpur, the Afghan chief Kabul Muhammad of Barharia was a constant irritant both to the Kalyanpur family and the Mughal emperor. Kabul had set himself up virtually as an independent ruler in the area and had been constantly encroaching on the Kalyanpur estate.[39] He was a supporter of Daud Khan, the ruler of Bengal, who had raised the standard of revolt against Akbar. The Mughal forces were unable to contain Kabul. Therefore, towards the end of his regime, Akbar presumably asked Kalyan Mull for help, who attacked and killed Kabul Muhammad, and captured and destroyed his fort in the early seventeenth century. Pleased, the emperor honoured Kalyan Mull, eighty-sixth in line, with the title of 'Raja' and allowed him to retain pargana Sipah, conquered from Kabul.[40] The remnants of Kabul Muhammad's huge, sprawling fort are still visible on the west side of the Siwan-Barharia Road in the present Siwan district. Though its moat is drying up and the fort is camouflaged under wild growth, its high relief audaciously overlooks the surrounding plains.

This victory over Kabul Muhammad added considerably to the status of Kalyan Mull, who emerged as an illustrious king in his line. The emperor also presented him a *danka* (drum) and a flag with the insignia of the fish crest of a *mansabdar*.[41] Kalyan established his capital at a place subsequently named after him as Kalyanpur, and the surrounding pargana was named Kalyanpur Kuari.[42] In all likelihood, Kalyan Mull was active in 1600, in the latter part of Akbar's reign, when the financial expert Raja Todar Mal was the viceroy of Bengal and Bihar, when the division of the country into parganas was undertaken after a general survey. Probably, Kalyan Mull helped Todar Mal in the survey, in recognition of which Akbar seems to have decorated Kalyan Mull with the title of 'Maharaja'. The remnants of Kalyan's capital and a large well of 50 feet in diameter existed there up to the beginning of the last century.[43] Today, there is little left of the old fort at Kalyanpur, except mounds of bricks overgrown with wild plants and the moats that might have once surrounded the fort are almost flattened and dried now.

The relations of the Kalyanpur Raja and the Mughals with Kabul Muhammad's family remained strained for a long time, as Kabul's descendants continued to intrude wantonly into the allies' territories. Consequently, the allies had to act repeatedly with regard to the Sipah pargana. Jubaraj Sahi regained the disputed territory after a tough fight. A legend says that he was defeated by the Burharia chieftain several times. After his last defeat, when he was fleeing through the jungle with a handful of followers, it is said that Goddess Bhavani appeared before Jubaraj Sahi in a dream and encouraged him to fight again. She promised him help and explained that the minute he set out on his journey, he would see a jackal on the left and a serpent on the right. She advised him to bow to the jackal and kill the snake. The Raja acted accordingly and triumphed over his enemy at the battle of Ramchandrapur, a mile east of Thawe.[44] After this victory, Emperor Jahangir re-conferred the title of Raja on the eighty-seventh Raja, Kshem Karan Sahi, and added other appellations of 'Maharaj Bahadur' and 'Sahi' on his successor, the eighty-eighth Raja, Bhupati Sahi.[45]

These honorifics have continued with successive rulers of the line. This added to their status and they enjoyed autonomy under the nominal suzerainty of the Mughals. The ninety-eighth Raja, Sirdar Sahi, is said to have invaded the Majhauli Raj and destroyed its fortress. Thus, Huseypur gained ascendency over its founding line.[46]

In order to situate Huseypur against the political backdrop of the time, a brief glance at the administrative structure of Bihar under the Mughal Empire may be helpful. In the time of Akbar, Bihar consisted of seven *sarkars* (districts)—Tirhut, Saran, Champaran, Monghyr, Bihar and Rohtas—and 199 parganas. Of these, the first four sarkars were situated to the north of the Ganga. They constituted most parts of the old kingdom of Mithila (Tirhut), which disintegrated after the downfall of the Qiniwar dynasty into small principalities under their own chiefs.[47] Abul Fazl mentions the zamindar of Champaran (Udai Karan Singh of Betiah) and that of Kalyanpur (Kalyan Mull).[48]

Saran was integrated into the Mughal Empire when the Afghan ruler of Bengal, Daud Khan, was defeated and Patna was captured in 1574. In the 1582 settlement, the district was described as having seventeen parganas.[49] Nevertheless, Saran was not under any unified control. Despite its amalgamation with the Mughal Empire, it was ruled by several chiefs.

Another reference to Kalyan Mull occurs in connection with revolts in the eastern provinces in the early 1580s. According to Abul Fazl, when Mughal forces and the allies chased the rebels (Masum Khan Farakhudi, Noor Mohammad and Khwaja

Abdul Gafoor), Gafoor sought shelter with Kalyan Mull, but he refused to oblige.[50]

Such a gesture by the Kalyanpur rajas must have warmed their relations with the Mughals. Sources suggest that the eighty-seventh Raja, Khem Karan Sahi, established cordial relations with Emperor Jahangir and helped the imperial government consolidate its rule in Bihar. In appreciation of his services, Jahangir honoured him with the titles of Maharaj Bahadur and Sahi, which enhanced his status. He shifted his capital from Kalyanpur to Huseypur, about three miles away, and built an extensive fort on an imposing site at a commanding position on the confluence of the Jharhi and Shiahi rivers. When Fateh Sahi ascended the throne, he enlarged its precincts by adding another fort called Naya Quila. Huseypur remained the seat of power until it was destroyed by English forces during Fateh Sahi's encounter with them in 1767.[51]

There is little information about Saran after Jahangir's reign until Peter Mundy, an English traveller, referred to the Raja of 'Kalianpur'. In the course of his visit to India (1628–34), he stopped in Patna briefly.[52] Giving an eyewitness account of his stay, he recounted how the Raja of Kalyanpur was received with fanfare by Mughal provincial authorities at Patna and was granted a robe of honour. However, soon after, he was thrown into prison and his properties plundered. The reason is not clear. The Raja's wife and his supporters rebelled against the authorities, and created so much disorder that special assistance had to be dispatched to restore calm. Mundy does not provide any further information about the incident.[53] Apart from these brief and occasional references, there is virtually no more information about Kalyanpur during the reigns of Shah Jahan and Aurangzeb. This absence of information is meaningful, as it may suggest a dwindling control of the Mughals over the Huseypur rajas and their precarious relation with the provincial authorities at that time.

Moving forward, we meet Sirdar Sahi, father of Fateh Sahi. Sirdar Sahi seems to have lived till 1747. He is known for invading the principality of Majhauli in Gorakhpur district and demolishing its fortress. The Majhauli rajas were of considerable influence during the Mughal rule. They were called 'Tilakdhari Raja', i.e., the raja empowered to install others as rajas. One of the conditions on which Sirdar Sahi made peace with them was that they would not display the *nishan* (flag) and danka ensigns of rajaship, until they had retaken them after defeating the Huseypur rulers. These insignias are still in the possession of the Tamkuhi Raj family.

Such things could happen only during a total collapse of imperial control, which ensued after the invasion of Nadir Shah in 1739. The Marathas were the masters of the Deccan, and they extended their depredations to Bengal and Bihar, exacting *chauth* under the leadership of Raghuji Bhonsle. Malwa and Gujarat had separated from the empire; and the Sikhs had grown powerful in Punjab, while the Rohillas were virtually independent in the foothills of the Himalayas northwest of Ayodhya. Thus, the Mughal Empire existed only in name, and the local chiefs in it were fighting each other with impunity.[54] With Mughal control on the wane, its governors became equally independent.

But by far the most general political change, which affected the whole of eastern India from Allahabad to Bengal around this time, was the consolidation of the agrarian castes, the Rajputs and Bhumihars in the region. Since Mughal rule in eastern India had always been superficial, these local changes became consequential. They were the tip of an iceberg—that of the slow process of settlement, which set the main features of land control from the borders of Awadh to Bengal.[55]

Initially acting as the revenue collectors of Awadh, the Gautam Bhumihars became the rajas of Benares during 1739–1760.[56] These populous clans of warrior-cultivators enhanced their local sway in various ways. They suppressed pockets of resistance among aboriginals, tribals and nomads living in the wild terrain, and pushed cultivation into the forest zones north and south of the great plains. The lower-caste farmers were reduced to agrarian dependence in the process. These consolidations occurred in three great swathes—in north and south Awadh; south of Awadh, in the fertile riverine rice-growing area of Benares, Gorakhpur and Bihar; and on to the fringe of Bengal, the Bhumihars strengthened their sway. In the hilly borders of central India, the Baghel, Bundela and Gaharwar Rajputs conspicuously gained most from the decline of Mughal control and expansion of arable land.[57]

The success of these princelings may be credited to their strong clan organization. There were perhaps as many as one lakh Bhumihar clansmen backing the power of the Benares rajas in what later became the districts of Benares, Gorakhpur and Azamgarh. This proved a decisive advantage when the dynasty faced its rival and a nominal suzerain in the Nawab of Awadh. The Benares ruler mounted an exhausting guerrilla war against the Awadh camp using his clan levies, and forced the Nawab to withdraw his forces. To the east again, it was the presence of more than two lakh militant and closely organized men from their community that allowed the Huseypur and Betia rajas to consolidate themselves virtually as independent rulers. Efforts by the imperial Muslim power to crush them slackened after the Maratha invasion of Bengal in the 1730s. The rise of the Rajput notables to the north and south of the Bhumihars proceeded along similar lines.[58]

These developments would have considerable implications for Fateh Sahi's struggle against the British in the years to come. Among these chiefs, the Huseypur rajas were the oldest line of rulers in the region. It was in this era of turbulent transition and instability that Fateh Sahi was born—the only son to Sardar Sahi. As his successor, his life was fated to be equally unstable and bumpy, if he challenged the overpowering British regime. But the geo-ethnic legacy that he inherited emboldened him to assert his autonomy and defy the diktats of the British.

Not all the chiefs of his time were so daring—and that makes Fateh Sahi stand out.

3

At War for Freedom

1767–1772

Luckily, both for Fateh Sahi and for the course of history, his maternal side proved to be of help. His mother was born into a family of Bhumihar Brahmins at Lilkar in the present Balia district of Uttar Pradesh. Khwaja Jahan, the founder of the Sirqui kingdom of Jaunpur, had given their ancestor Shivraj Dev a jagir of six parganas in the eastern districts. Of this line, Rakad Dev had kept eastern Uttar Pradesh free from the oppressions of Sikandar Lodi. However, Babur had attacked the family citadel at Mandarpur (Kanpur) in 1527 and destroyed their fortress. In the eastern part, the family faced similar onslaughts from the Nawab of Awadh, Safdar Jung and Muhammad Shah's commander, Salawan Khan Bakshi. Yet they managed to hold on. Since the people of Lilkar used to loot British cargo passing through the Ganga-Yamuna waterways, Hastings attacked and demolished their fort (*garh*) at Lilkar. However, they did not yield, and seem to have supported Fateh Sahi during his rebellion.[1]

The World Around

In 1750, seven years before the Battle of Plassey and fourteen years before the Battle of Buxar, Fateh Bahadur Sahi ascended the throne on the eve of the foundations of the British Empire in India, as the ninety-ninth Raja of Huseypur. Robert Clive had joined the East India Company as a clerk in 1744; he was appointed the first Governor of Bengal in 1757.

We begin with the immediate concerns of the Huseypur Raja and the circumstances that shaped the nature of his opposition to the East India Company. When he rose to challenge British imperialism, it was in its earliest days. Even then, it was a fight between unequal opponents. The Company from the start was a private business firm, with huge financial resources, backed by rich and powerful investors with a considerable say in their home government in Britain. Additionally, it had a large, well-equipped and well-trained army. Fateh Sahi was no match for the Company, except, perhaps, in terms of his courage and his people's support.

He was a hereditary raja, who had inherited a poverty-stricken, backward territory, where the socio-economic conditions had deteriorated under declining Mughal rule. The penetration of European traders into the region deepened the crisis, which was further aggravated once the Company acquired financial and administrative powers after the battles of Plassey and Buxar, and the grant of Diwani rights (right to revenue collection). However, Fateh Sahi seems to have made use of the situation. A glance at the prevailing conditions in the subcontinent provides some understanding as to the reasons for his acting the way he did, and for the rationale behind the long operations that kept the English on their toes for as long as he lived.

India had been a centre of attraction for people from faraway lands since time immemorial. As an important part of the Gangetic heartland with its long history, Bihar had attracted many foreign travellers, explorers and religious missionaries. In modern times, the prospects of trade and economic gains lured the Dutch, Danes, British and French traders, especially to Sarkar Saran and the adjoining areas. After a series of wars and diplomatic manoeuvres, the East India Company triumphed over its geopolitical rivals.[2] Sarkar Saran was part of the Mughal Empire, though with decreasing control when the Europeans entered the region.

Peter Mundy had visited Bihar in November 1632. He stopped over in Patna and wrote about the life in the city: a market with about 200 grocery shops along a thoroughfare lined with trees. It was the end of autumn and beginning of winter. Boats laden with merchandise were being ferried up and down the Ganga, running along the northern fringe of the city. The river appeared to be a hub of commercial and social activities. Mundy spotted luxury boats used for pleasure trips on the river. There was no system of hotels for visitors then; so, he stayed in *sarais* that were something like modern-day hotels. He names a few of them and many more en route his westward journey. He also writes about some wrongdoings in them, probably by the agents of local officials, and hints at the tyranny of the local faujdar, which forced Mundy to move from one sarai to another.

During his stay, Mundy saw the Raja of Kalyanpur, who had come to meet the faujdar, with some unique gifts—an elephant, antelopes and hawks, among others. Mundy was pleasantly surprised. This indicated the affluence and status of the Kalyanpur Raja, who was well received by provincial authorities and presented with a ceremonial robe. But in a surprising twist in events, the Raja was soon arrested and his property plundered. His wife and supporters rebelled against the outrage, creating bedlam, which forced local authorities to dispatch law enforcement personnel to restore order.[3] This episode shows that the relations of the Raja with the provincial government were precarious—an indication of the struggle for autonomy of the Kalyanpur rajas. Mundy does not provide more details of the episode.

The hectic commercial activities on the Ganga in Patna at the time provide some clue as to future developments. This was the beginning of the extraction of India's resources. Patna was a major hub for European commercial activities, as by this time, the Dutch, the French and the Danes had all established their local presence. Indeed, the main trading office of the Dutch in Patna, known popularly as the Dutch Building, still stands majestically on the banks of the Ganga in the city. Today, it houses Patna College, the forerunner of Patna University, and one of the oldest premier institutions of the country. It was from Patna that the Europeans, particularly the Dutch and the French to begin with, sailed to the west and northward, into the northern plains.[4]

The Europeans started from Hooghly, Murshidabad and Calcutta in Bengal and sailed to Bhagalpur, Monghyr (Munger), and then to Patna. From Patna, they cruised westward to Buxar, Benares, Mirjapur, Jaunpur, Kanpur and Allahabad. From Allahabad, they continued on the Ganga further up towards its origins in the Himalayas; whereas River Yamuna, on the other hand, would allow them access to both Agra and Delhi—then two major centres of power and trade.[5] Likewise, from Patna, they penetrated into the interiors of north Bihar and eastern Uttar Pradesh via the rivers Ghaghra (known as Saryug upstream), and the Gandak, both perennial rivers originating in the sub-Himalayan ranges. The traders entered with limited merchandise initially, but stumbled upon rich deposits of the raw material of saltpetre, muslin, hides and varieties of the region's forest products. They found its fertile alluvial soil most suitable for the cultivation of opium, indigo and other commercial crops, already in demand in the European market. Saltpetre was required for the production of gunpowder, urgently needed for wars for colonial expansion in Europe and elsewhere. Indigo was in demand for the production of blue dyes for the textile industry, heralding the Industrial Revolution in Britain, while opium was an important item of British trade with China.

The Ghaghra-Saryug and the Gandak rivers almost flanked the Huseypur territory from the west and east, respectively; in the north, it was enclosed by a deep stretch of dense forests. In this uneven wild topography, these water routes proved a boon, in conjunction with the auxiliary river networks, like that of the Jharahi along Huseypur in the west and smaller tributaries of the Gandak in the east. Together, they facilitated internal movement and transportation for foreign traders, and would soon turn into vital channels of military supply and political control. Their importance lay in the fact that they served as arteries to the great Ganga, fast emerging as the highway of European trade in India and finally of British power.[6]

The Company: A New Master

It was against this background that Fateh Sahi seems to have first come into direct confrontation with the English East India Company, probably in 1763. The immediate provocation came from the failed Seige of Patna. In the course of the ongoing tussle between Mir Kasim, the Nawab of Bengal, and the East India Company during the dual system of government, the overall conditions were vitiated. Robert Clive introduced dual government in Bengal in 1765. Accordingly, the administration was divided into two parts—Diwani and *Nizamat*. Diwani, the right to collect revenue, was given to the East India Company, and Nizamat, the responsibilities of administration, was left with the Nawab. When the Company started misusing its trade permits and privileges rampantly, Mir Kasim took measures to assert his authority. The deputy of Henry Vansittart (Governor, 1762–64), Warren Hastings, wanted to have a good working relationship with Mir Kasim in view of the future prospects for the Company in Bengal, but there were many in the Company circle who had opposite views, vested interests and personal stakes in the local trading and operations.[7]

Mir Kasim suspected that William Ellis, the chief of the English factory in Patna, was fomenting a rebellion against him. Ellis had lost a leg at the siege of Calcutta in 1756; whereafter, he hated everything Indian, and almost sadistically disregarded Mir Kasim's sovereignty and independence. In the beginning of February 1762, Ellis decided to arrest Mir Kasim's senior Armenian official, Khoja Antoon, which the Nawab objected to strongly. Meanwhile, Mir Kasim had assembled a new army to consolidate his position. Both Warren Hastings and Vansittart watched the developments;[8] but alarmed at the goings-on, the officials decided to deal with Mir Kasim firmly. James Amyatt, a friend of William Ellis and an aggressive member of their circle, was deputed to put Mir Kasim in his place. But the Nawab was in no mood to yield. He abolished certain customs duties that deprived the English of their unfair advantages over local traders.[9]

Soon after, on 11 March 1763, armed clashes broke out between Mir Kasim's men and the Company. Backed by his new army, Mir Kasim's supporters hit back in Dhaka and Jafarganj, leading to gunshots and killings. Across Bengal, British boats carrying goods of private Company traders were blocked and their merchandise—saltpetre, opium and betel nut—mostly sourced from Bihar (Saran in particular) was seized. As the situation grew more tense, on 23 May, James Amyatt rushed to Monghyr to force Mir Kasim to revoke his free trade order, but one of Amyatt's boats was found hiding 500 matchlocks, destined for the Patna Factory. The Nawab's Armenian commander, Gurgin Khan, wanted to impound the vessel, but after a standoff and a great deal of parleys, it was allowed to leave.[10]

This was the time when William Ellis planned to seize Patna by force. He readied 300 Europeans and 2500 sepoys, and, on 23 June, the anniversary of Plassey, they were marched under Wolf to Patna. Frantic preparations continued on the 24th, and at one o'clock on the morning of the 25th, the English forces began their assault on the city which was still asleep. They attacked the Mughal fort, and the retaliatory actions resulted in heavy casualties on both sides. But the English prevailed for a while, when they ransacked the bazaar and looted whatever they could find on the way.[11] The Nawab, however, already had intelligence of the planned coup and so he had force-marched his troops from Monghyr under General Markar, one of his senior Armenian commanders. They soon outnumbered the Company forces, beat them back and forced them to flee on all sides. Victory was declared for Mir Kasim. With the English factory surrounded and besieged, Ellis abandoned his position and fled with his men (about three platoons), through the water gate and sailed westwards, hoping to escape into a neutral territory bordering Awadh.[12]

But when they reached Chapra, their boats were attacked allegedly by the faujdar of Saran, whom popular memory identifies with Fateh Bahadur Sahi. Soon after, Mir Kasim's German commander, Walter Reinhardt Sombre (popular as Samru), also reached there with a few thousand of his sepoys' force, marched from his encampment at Buxar. Surrounded and outnumbered, the Company forces surrendered. They were taken prisoner and brought shackled to the prison within Monghyr fort in Patna; and on Samru's orders, all of them were killed. Among the dead was also James Amyatt, the envoy sent by the Calcutta Council. By the end of the week, of the 5000 Company troops in Bihar, 3000 had been killed, arrested or had gone over and joined Mir Kasim's army.[13]

This could have been the beginning of Fateh Bahadur's contact with Samru in the coming years, to whom we will return later.

Thus, across Bihar and Bengal, the provincial Mughal elite rose as one behind Nawab Mir Kasim in the last desperate bid to save their collapsing world from an alien usurper. A week later, on 4 July 1763, the council in Calcutta formally declared war on Mir Kasim.[14]

For the local chiefs and people, however, the wilderness and extremes of the tropics, especially the humid summers, erratic cyclones, heavy rains and the recurrent flooding, creating extensive swamps and marshes, acted as a natural protection against the intruders. South of the Ganga, defences were provided by the craggy hills of the Camur Ranges—the sprawling eastern end of the Vindhya Mountains.[15]

Against this background, the present-day Revelganj emerged as an important inland port at the junction of the Ganga and the Ghaghra, about seven miles to the west of Chapra in Saran. In 1788, Henry Revel established a factory here in order to manage the thriving opium trade. Increasingly, he became involved in the local society, worked for its welfare and decided ultimately to live and die there. His grave lies at the place subsequently named Revelganj in his memory. To date, he is fondly remembered by locals. His fellow feeling, kindness and generosity towards them projected a happier side of colonialism, which has been well portrayed in the Bhojpuri novel *Phoolsunghi*.[16]

As European trade thrived, Chapra became a trading hub that would emerge as the centre of the Saran district. Both Tavernier and Bernier, who visited Bihar in the 1660s, had referred to the Holland Company trading in saltpetre in Chapra. Close to Chapra town, Karinga was in the possession of the Dutch till 1770. The *District Gazetteer of Saran* of 1960 recorded the presence of a cemetery at Karinga dating back to 1712; and of the mausoleum of the Dutch Governor Jacobus Van Horn at Chapra was reminiscent of the importance of Saran.[17]

On the eastern side of Saran, the Europeans entered the north Bihar plains via the Gandak River, another tributary of the Ganga, at Sonepur on the left and Hajipur on the right—both across Patna situated in the south, on the other side of the Ganga. They proceeded upstream, northward via Lalganj, Sattarghat and Govindganj to Bagaha where the Gandak descended from the Himalayas on to the plains of Champaran, at Bhaisalotan (Balmiki Nagar). The upstream ports brought these traders into the Betia and Huseypur Raj territories.[18] A branch of the Gandak, called Budhi Gandak, flowed eastward through Sitamarhi to Khagaria, assuming different names as it streamed further, facilitating access to the remaining parts of north Bihar. This whole stretch would later develop into a bastion for European planters and Christian missionaries.

Apart from their immediate business interests, the Europeans were lured by the prospects of long-term economic gains from the region: its rich alluvial soil was ideal for the cultivation of opium and indigo, both of which they tried their hand at successfully. The region was full of extensive water bodies, and varied flora and fauna. Going by Renell's survey and map, this natural wealth was in abundance in the eighteenth century.[19] The chain of enormous oxbow lakes thriving with rich marine life, artisanal wells and hot springs in the midst of lush green tropical flora, lapped by the Govardhana and Someshwar ranges of the Himalayas to the north, would have been an enticing prospect. On clear days, these newcomers could see the snow-capped Himalayas, especially the Annapurna ranges.

Many Europeans settled in this region in the decades to follow. An Englishman, Alfred Augustus Tripe, settled at Dhang, a village at the foot of the Himalayas in Champaran bordering Nepal, in 1845. He acquired considerable land, married a local girl and the family lived there happily until the 1934 earthquake destroyed their home. Her family was another example of a colonizer's love for their new homeland: when they were given the choice of choosing to stay or leave India in 1947, they opted to stay back. Happily, the great-granddaughter of Alfred Augustus Tripe, Sylvia Dyer, has lived long enough to share her memories of that 'fairy-tale world of picturesque beauty' in her *Spell of the Flying Foxes* (2011).[20] Sylvia's husband continued to serve in the free India's army and fought for India in the Indo-China War. There were also others who arrived before or after this family; you may meet their descendants blogging their endearing nostalgia for the place on various media portals.

A sizeable portion of the local population in the area were aboriginals, living a primitive way of life. This encouraged Christian missionaries to carry forward their civilizing mission. The first Catholic missionaries arrived in 1740 and established their first mission in 1784 at Betia in Champaran, then part of Saran. The Western interest in the region became so compelling that clusters of Europeans flocked to settle there and carry on business. Betia, Motihari, Muzaffarpur and the whole of the Tirhut area developed as their hub. Opium and indigo plantation farms gradually sprang up all around, including in the vicinity of Huseypur. A European Club was started at Muzaffarpur in 1885; and in order to cater to the needs of the Western settlers, a stud farm and later an agricultural institute were established in 1905 at Pusa, close to Muzaffarpur. When the noted American humorist and satirist Mark Twain (1835–1910) visited the area in 1896, he was especially charmed by the gorgeous spread of poppy flowers and groves laden with red litchi fruits around Muzaffarpur.[21]

By now, the English stake in the region extended not only to everyday trading but also to long-term economic concerns and social responsibilities arising out of the increasing presence of Europeans in the region. Political and military contingencies were heightened by rivals and adversaries, as some with connections to anti-British European cliques were present around Huseypur.

This scenario, with its disparate players, events and issues, may help one understand the significance and intricacies of the apparently simple and isolated events in and around Huseypur, in the broader history of Indian resistance to British rule.

After acquiring the grant of the Diwani of Bengal, Bihar and Orissa by the Treaty of Allahabad in 1765, the officials of the East India Company were gung-ho and excited about tasting political power and financial bounties. Their operations in north India started from Bengal and spread to its outlying areas. Soon, the earnings of the Company increased substantially, but it also led to bureaucratic corruption, anarchy and lawlessness. Robert Clive described it thus:

> Such a scene of anarchy, confusion, bribery and corruptions and extortion was never seen or heard of in any country but Bengal nor have such and so many fortunes been acquired in so unjust and rapacious manner. The three provinces of Bengal, Bihar and Orissa producing a clear revenue of £30,00,000 sterling have been under absolute management of the Company's servants, ever since Mir Jafar's restoration to the Subhedarship; and they have, both civil and military, exacted and levied contributions from every man of power and consequence from the Nawab down to the lowest zamindars.[22]

The arrival of Europeans into Saran's interiors vitiated the situation. Later accounts discuss slavery and criminal activities such as *thuggee* and looting in the area. The Europeans used slaves as domestic helps and in their business activities as well. Thugs, on the other hand, presented a common menace. In the absence of any gainful means of livelihood, thuggee had become an occupation. As trading picked up and the movement of merchandise through neighbouring river channels increased, it attracted the attention of pirates, who often attacked boats and looted goods. This hints as much at the thriving European trade in the district as it does to the growing local resentment and animosity against the extraction of local resources by outsiders. But trading stakeholders did not give up. The East India Company deployed guard boats of fourteen oars each on the Ganga between Hajipur and the western extremity of Sarkar Saran.[23] While famine, epidemics and flooding remained a perpetual problem, the raids of sanyasis and Marathas, highway hold-ups and looting worsened the situation.

The Company could not alleviate this condition. Indeed, it was aggravated by its agents, who freely carried out extortion and oppression. Most of these agents were semi-literate and belonged to the lower and middle classes. With no experience in public dealings, but backed by Company support, they treated themselves as second only to their masters and never hesitated to encroach upon the privileges of the traditional aristocracy. This bred widespread discontent against Company rule.[24]

The new regime was concerned solely with amassing wealth from the people in the form of taxes, presents, trade profits and the like, without caring for their welfare. In 1760, the thirty-five-year-old Clive returned to Great Britain with £234,000 from his Indian exploits (£23 million pounds today). He came back to India in 1765, and two years later, he returned to England with a fortune estimated at £400,000 (£40 million now).[25] This was unlike the traditional native rajas and zamindars who had cared for the welfare of their ryots. But as these chiefs succumbed to growing British power, they started retreating from the scene. Under Company control, both agriculture and cottage industries—the mainstay of the self-sufficient village economy for ages—declined.[26] Famine-like conditions arose in many parts of Bihar and Bengal, a prelude to the infamous famine of 1770. The initial increase in tax returns of the Company dwindled suddenly. When higher authorities pressed for increasing tax collection, their subordinates resorted to all types of cruel methods, and the old zamindars connived at paying their dues.[27]

The situation became so nasty that many Englishmen within the Company establishment felt morally hurt. They felt helpless as they could not relieve people's suffering and regretted the British policy of trying to collect taxes and rule over the payees without any responsibility for ensuring their welfare. This was quite contrary to their tradition at home in England.[28] Richard Bechar, the Company's Resident at Murshidabad wrote on 2 June 1770:

> The scene of misery that intervened and still continues, shocks humanity too much to bear description. Certain it is that certain parts of the living have fed on the dead and the number that has perished in these provinces that have not suffered is calculated to have been within these few months as six is to sixteen of the whole population.[29]

The sting of the tragedy deepened due to the selfish conduct of many Company servants in Bengal who turned the public distress into a source of private profit for themselves, the Court of Directors conceded in their letter of 28 August 1771.[30]

The internal correspondence among Company officials at various levels speaks volumes about the maladministration, insubordination, corruption and bribery prevalent at all levels within their system, not to mention the gross indifference towards the security and welfare of the taxpayers.[31] Robert

Clive, his immediate successors and others from the revenue and intelligence departments continuously complained about the state of affairs, but to no avail. Clive initiated measures to set things right, but with little success; and, later, he himself was found to be not above board. After the Battle of Plassey in 1757, in return for supporting Mir Jafar as ruler of Bengal, Clive had been granted a jagir of £30,000 (equivalent to £4,300,000 in 2021); and when he left India in January 1767, he carried home a fortune that made him probably the richest person in Great Britain.[32]

Initially, the British wanted to maintain the administrative traditions of the Mughals and retain their local officials who had been previously associated with administration. They were, however, rampantly corrupt and inefficient, but they were easy to handle with petty lures. In such a scenario, the Company's newly emerging Indian workforce—tax collectors, clerks, gomastahs and the like—exploited and extorted people unashamedly.

After the Battle of Buxar, the administration of Bihar was carried forward by Mirza Muhammad Kazim Khan, brother of Mir Jafar, assisted by Deputy Governor Dhiraj Narain. After two quick successions, James Alexander was designated supervisor of Bihar in 1769. Meanwhile, Dhiraj Narain was removed from office and Sitab Rai was made the sole *Naib Nazim* of Bihar, with his son Kalyan Singh acting as his deputy. Sitab's place as the agent of the Mughal emperor was taken by Munir-ud-Daulah.[33]

Clive also acted to control and organize the army, especially in the north-west corner of Bihar, against the inroads of the Marathas and Ahmad Shah Abdali. On hearing of a mutiny of European soldiers in Monghyr, Clive rushed there on 15 May

1766, and after suppressing it, he subdued another sepoy revolt at Manjhi near Chapra in Saran. Back in Chapra, he convened a convention attended by General Carnac, Shuja-ud-Daulah (nawab wazir of Awadh), Munir-ud-Daulah (the minister and envoy of the emperor), Raja Balwant Singh of Benares, a Jat raja and the Rohilla chiefs. Thus, the foundation of a treaty was laid among them for mutual defence against a Maratha invasion.[34] Shuja-ud-Daulah was entrusted with the task of managing territories with the approbation of the president of the council in Calcutta. In September 1766, a brigade was cantoned at Sasaram and Colonel Barker was dispatched to the banks of the Karmnasa River. Thus, Bihar became 'the watch tower of the English' during this ongoing political turmoil.[35] There was a garrison at Monghyr, a brigade at Patna and a battalion at Karmnasa, besides the pargana sipahis. These troops were, however, a nuisance for the local society. While the locals had to supply them food and other consumables, the soldiers harassed them in many ways. Moreover, these troops were also used to realize arrears of revenue from local zamindars, or to bring them under the effective control of the Company.[36]

Thus, once at the helm of affairs, the Governor targeted big zamindars. On 24 July 1765, he asked Raja Jugal Kishore Singh of Betia to resume the payment of the Rs 6 lakh or 7 lakh that he earlier used to pay into Mir Kasim's treasury but had lately stopped. The Raja was directed to pay the balance immediately and guarantee its regular payment in future. In case he failed, the English army would settle the issue, the Governor warned. When Jugal Kishore did not respond, Sir Robert Barker was sent from Patna to Betia early in 1766 to demolish his forts, and also reduce the other turbulent zamindars in arrears of revenue to obedience.[37] The Raja escaped to Bundelkhand for safety.

In his absence, the management of his estate was entrusted to Krishna Singh of Sheohar and Abdhut Singh of Madhuban, the two younger brothers of the Betia Raja. However, this did not work; so, Jugal Kishore was reinstated in his zamindari, on condition that he paid the revenues regularly in future. But, in 1772, he defaulted yet again, upon which the Company took over his estate and pensioned him off. He died in 1783/84.[38]

The Court of Directors rejoiced at the success of the Betia expedition. Barker wrote to the council in Calcutta highlighting that Betia would be of considerable consequence to the Company from the viewpoint of trade, in several local products like fir, timber, musk, ivory and many more.[39] In response, the council employed Simeon Droz to collect detailed information of its produce. One of the objectives of Captain George Kinlock's unsuccessful expedition to Nepal in 1767 was to explore the possibilities of trade with Betia and Nepal. This expedition had been commissioned following a message from Golding, the Resident in Betia, to Thomas Rumbold, chief of the English factory at Patna. The Calcutta Council recommended strict measures to enforce the payment of arrears by zamindars in Bihar, but it was not equally emphatic about the south Bihar zamindars.[40] This may be attributed to the huge economic prospects of north Bihar and its importance in warding off potential security threats from the northwest.

In terms of Mughal control, three emperors—Ahmad Shah, Alamgir and Shah Alam II—were contemporaries of Fateh Sahi. Ahmad Shah witnessed five invasions of the empire by Ahmad Shah Abdali, and Alamgir II ruled at the time of the Battle of Plassey. Shah Alam II had lost the Battle at Panipat (1761) and most of the eastern part of the empire at the Battle of Buxar (1764). At Buxar, his coalition with the nawabs of

Bengal and Awadh had lost collectively to the East India Company, making Shah Alam II the first Mughal pensioner of the Company.

The consequences of the breakdown of the Mughal administration and the local economy manifested in some curious social developments, such as the emergence of sanyasis and *fakirs* in north India. As the Mughal durbar and establishments of the nawabs and zamindars declined, their armies were disbanded and countless people lost their livelihood and their living became precarious. The famine of 1770 worsened the economy and life in a way never seen before. A multitude of people had no home or work, and many took to crime. The most important of these groups that concern this account were the sanyasis and fakirs.

These mendicants moved in groups of hundreds and thousands, apparently on pilgrimage; but they were armed and collected forced levies from people living on their routes. Whenever they were met with resistance, they resorted to violence and did not spare even the state authorities. They projected their assembly as a religious congregation but indulged in plunder and loot. They comprised two groups, sanyasi and fakir, and a third category—the *Nagas*—was actually a sect of Hindu sanyasis. These wanderers were active mostly in districts of Bengal, Bihar and Awadh. Some sources hold that they came from western India and became notoriously active in its eastern part, due to the chaotic conditions prevailing there.[41]

The Naga sanyasis had a long history of resisting foreign invasions during the medieval times. They are known for their aggressive temperament and love for freedom.[42] They lived naked and continue to do so. Traditionally, these wandering mendicants were revered as holy men. In happier times, they were voluntarily offered contributions by zamindars and others, as long as the donors were better off economically.[43] But with a dwindling economy and administrative controls in the eighteenth century, such charities dried up. Consequently, these groups started collecting their alms forcefully in the name of traditionally sanctioned obligations.[44]

The exploitative control of the Company upset them considerably. Over time, many sanyasis had acquired property as rent-free land grants from the zamindars and entered into the business of moneylending and trading in goods. Usually, they purchased merchandise from Bengal and transported it to Mirzapur where they sold it to traders from the Deccan. Their articles included raw silk, piece goods, opium, copper and spices. The raw silk came from Murshidabad and woollens from Kashmir, and their operations extended in the north up to Nepal and Tibet. In this trade circuit, Mirzapur (about 186 miles from Tamkuhi) emerged as a major centre, where the sanyasis were chiefly concentrated in its Chaurasi and Upraudh parganas. In Bengal, they were active in Murshidabad, Malda, Dinajpur, Rajshahi and Mymensingh districts.[45] In the course of time, they also gained a hold in south Bihar. Their leaders, called 'Mahant', often possessed enormous wealth, landed property and even private armies that they lent as mercenaries to the local rulers and chiefs in return for cash or kind. But now, the Company's land revenue policy threatened their traditional privileges on land grants, while its trading endangered their business prospects.[46] This proved to be a major cause of conflict between the two, which made it imperative for them to ally with partners like Fateh Sahi, who had risen against the British.

The Marathas were probably the first to hire the Nagas as mercenaries during the raids on Bengal in 1760, but in many instances, they were also used by local chiefs to sort out domestic disputes. In later years, these wanderers directly clashed with the English, and captured and ransacked their factories in Bengal. Subsequently, they fought as a wing of an anti-British coalition under their leaders Anupgiri and Umraogiri, during the siege of Patna in 1764.[47] They participated in the Battle of Buxar, in which Fateh Sahi, too, is believed to have fought on the side of the allies. This is likely to have forged his relations with the Nagas as future allies in his wars against the British.[48] No wonder, Mirzapur being their prominent centre close to Huseypur, their clustering in and around Huseypur was frequently reported now onwards.

The Raja Revolts

It was in these circumstances that, on behalf of the East India Company, the revenue collector of Saran finally sent his officers to Fateh Sahi to collect revenue from him at the end of 1767. This was outrageous for the Raja. He refused to obey orders and asserted his hereditary rights over his territory as its ruler, challenging the legitimacy of the Company to have any control over him or his people. He was so provoked that he instantly mobilized his forces against them. He took to his fort and succeeded in keeping the Company forces at bay. Caught in the crisis, the Company agents contacted the higher authorities in Patna and sought an urgent dispatch of troops for help. Hectic consultations followed and, on their advice, especially of Raja Sitab Rai, the Indian member of the council in Patna, forces under Captain Wilding were rushed to Huseypur.[49] The adversaries clashed and Fateh offered strong resistance, but he was dislodged after a fierce fight. Tactically, he beat a retreat into the adjoining Bhagjogni jungle, lying between Saran and Gorakhpur—partly in Saran but mostly under the control of the vizier of Awadh.[50]

He was, however, not reconciled to his plight at all, and was constantly on the lookout for an opportunity to attack Company forces and return to his citadel. The gravity of the situation is fleetingly reflected in the contemporary official correspondence, but a later inquiry into the episode by Samuel Charters, ordered by Governor-General Warren Hastings, provides many details of the rebellion. On 25 June 1782, Charters submitted his report, in which he tried to explain the causes of Sahi's rebellion and the reasons why the rebel was able to sustain it until then. Charters also looked at those who supported the Raja as well as those who sided with the Company government, and at various related issues.[51]

Based on Samuel Charters' report, one can visualize the scenario, and the gaps in the story can perhaps be filled with feedback from popular memory, empirical knowledge and, finally, with a little 'historian's imagination'. It was mid-winter towards the end of 1767. Due to shorter days, there was little activity in the countryside. The weather was foggy, reminiscent of the Eighteenth Brumaire of the French Revolution.[52] In view of their successive victories at Plassey and Buxar recently, the fierce retaliation by Fateh Sahi must have come as a jolt for the British. Earlier, Sahi had fought against them on behalf of the allies at Buxar, but then he was only one of many collaborators, unlikely to have been identified individually. But now it was a direct confrontation. The British could not have expected such violent resistance from a local ruler. So far, they had subdued their adversaries, individually or in alliance, from Plassey to Buxar, on their own terms, but this time, the Raja's retaliation was audacious and shocking for them. He was to be defeated and destroyed at all costs. So, they put everything at stake, reinforced their army and pulled in all possible resources to check the enemy.[53]

In no time, the royal palace burst into a loud commotion and a volley of gunfire boomed intermittently. There were shouts and screams all around. Within minutes, soldiers lay dead and bleeding around the entrance of the palace; some cried for safety but others shouted to attack. The Raja had to decide what to do right away, and he chose to retreat instead of surrender. He would return soon and avenge his loss, he thought.

By now, his followers were already assembling around the Raja. Armoured for cavalry manoeuvres, he finally decided to escape on the elephant of Soobans Mishir, a staunch supporter and a *malguzar* of Soonwal. Tall and massive as he was, the Raja was a formidable sight on the elephant—sitting straight, with his head covered with a helmet, a spear in his hand, and a matchlock and a sword hanging on the sides of his armour. A little idol of Satwahini Durga sat above the *dhal* (shield) on his back. His erect posture and hard gaze exuded his determination to encounter and annihilate the enemy soon. A long crowd of soldiers trailed him—cavalry, peons and others, shouting the battle cry—'Jai Bhavani . . . Jai Bhavani . . .'—that tore through the quiet of the countryside. Small hamlets passed by intermittently before the convoy entered the canopy of arching trees leading to the forest—his future home.

But he was worried about the safety of the family he had left behind at Huseypur and about the marriage of his daughters. Suddenly, a long line of gallant ancestors appeared in his mind—Beer Sen, Kalyan Mull and Jubaraj Sahi—who had prevailed over their enemies. He recalled Jay Mull who, too, had retreated into the forest and continued his rebellion against Sher Shah Suri when the latter tried to subdue him. Perhaps Fateh was marching on the same track to the jungle! It was not a defeat, nothing to worry about, the Raja reassured himself; it was a short respite before retaliation. He would rise once again like a colossus and pound the enemy to dust, he thought, and commanded the mahout to speed up the giant elephant. War cries continued but became feeble gradually, as the convoy marched ahead and disappeared into the jungle.

Back home at Huseypur, Fateh Sahi's zamindari was taken over by the East India Company under its direct management, and, for revenue collection, it was farmed out to one Govind Ram. After a year, it was to be passed on to Basant Sahi, the rebel's cousin. This was an effort by the Company to create a controlling mechanism for tax collection from estates that refused its control.[54]

However, what the Company did not realize was that Fateh still held some portion of his original zamindari under his own control, along with the wild stretch of land connecting it with his hideout, situated in the pargana of Sidhua Jobna, within Subah Awadh.[55] Later, Fateh Sahi's family also shifted to his jungle hideout; and from there, he remained active and in touch with his people who were not willing to pay taxes to any new masters. The unsettled state of the country, his easy access to the territories of an independent Awadh Nawab, where Company troops could not pursue him, and the impenetrable forest surrounding his refuge—all facilitated his plans. The collusion of the agents of the vizier of Awadh and, above all, the attachment of the people to their expelled Raja and their dislike for the new Company revenue farmer proved a major advantage for him. Thus, he kept the country in a state of terror and the Company authorities on the alert constantly.[56] The Gorakhpur sanctuary served him well because of his long family ties with its leading notables like the Majhauli Raja. Actually, Sahi's presence in the area was welcomed by all with any stake in the area, also as a 'powerful bulwark against Banjara raids.'[57]

As the Mughal imperial authority hit an all-time low and lawlessness and chaos spread everywhere with the grant of Diwani, the Maratha and Banjara infestations in Bihar became a nagging problem. Maratha raids became recurrent, and Banjaras operated like thugs and the Pindaries of central India, cheating people or robbing them outright. The Banjaras were trading nomads who might have had origins in the Mewar region of Rajasthan. Gradually, they spread across many parts of the country. They became a menace in Tirhut and bordering districts, as they started collecting mandatory contributions as a levy and other favours from the local people, so much so that Ali Vardi Khan had to send a special taskforce of Afghans under a new Afghan chief named Abul Karim Khan.[58] Even if some British officials praised the trustworthiness of the Banjaras as carriers, they finally declared them a Criminal Tribe in 1871 (to continue up to Independence).[59] In the socio-political context of the eighteenth century, they acted like mercenaries similar to the sanyasis.[60] It is possible that Fateh Sahi used them as couriers, spies and soldiers.

Around this time, about 5000 sanyasis entered Saran. The faujdar in Patna sent two companies of sepoys after them. Captain Wilding rushed from Patna to control them since they were terrorizing people in the countryside and disrupting revenue collection. The next year, the Diwan of Patna, Raja Sitab Rai, complained that Fateh Sahi had endangered the country by creating disturbances with the help of a body of Naga sanyasis. Captain Wilding rushed to the site again, dispersed them and took over the Huseypur fort.[61]

In early 1770, a Company officer had to resist 5000 fakirs forcing their way into Awadh by crossing the Ganga. In June, Captain Gabriel Harper, commanding officer at Faizabad, reported their arrival with lots of English arms and ammunition. This was a small contingent, but they seemed to be members of a larger group that had plundered the Gorakhpur area before moving towards Rohilla country.[62] In October, according to Brigadier General Robert Barker, about 10,000 armed sanyasis gathered in Benares, intending to pass through Bihar on the way to Bengal, but the next month they turned towards Mirzapur.[63] The next year, Barker informed Nawab Suja-ud-Daulah of Awadh that about 6000–7000 Nagas had crossed the Yamuna River at Kalpi on 29 April 1771 and had proceeded towards the Ganga through the confines of Kora. They claimed to have *parwana* from the Nawab to cross the Ganga and pass through his territories.[64] But nothing was heard of them afterwards.[65] In December, the superintendent of Saran reported to the Patna Council that about 4000 Nagas were encamped within 16 to 20 miles of Huseypur in the territory of the Nawab of Awadh, intending to cross River Dewah. Necessary steps were taken to repel them,[66] but they appeared to have taken an alternative route through the Betia Raj. Nothing was heard of them again.

Even though there aren't many direct sources to support the collusion of Fateh Sahi with these mendicants, its truth is a foregone conclusion. By now, besides the Company's trading, its exploitative policy had started affecting the interests of these groups, too.[67] The newly introduced land revenue policy of the British deprived them of the privileges of not paying rent on their holdings and the Company's vigorous trading in silk and similar items brought them into direct competition and conflict with each other. Since the Company regime privileged the new landlords over these mendicants in the land control management, the latter became hostile to these zamindars and often clashed with them. Thus, they naturally fell on the side of the peasants and became a part of the mainstream anti-colonial plank.[68]

The resident sanyasis entered into independent fiscal relations with the peasants and zamindars. Trading and business created a sense of camaraderie among members of the sanyasi groups. That is why when fighting the Company forces in Bengal, they frequently receded to the upper provinces of Bihar and Awadh for fresh recruits for their forces and money from their brethren. Thus, eastern UP and Bihar were closely linked with Bengal for both economic and strategic reasons.[69] Many villages in the Saran area still have descendants from the sanyasis, with their ancestral surnames like Bharati, Gosain, Giri, Puri, Parvat, etc., and have certain traits of their forefathers.

Of the Muslim fakirs, the Madari (or Madar) sect was active from Awadh to Bengal. Its leader, Majnu Shah, had his headquarters at village Makhanpur near Kanpur. He entered Bengal for the first time probably in early 1771, through the Purnea District of Bihar. The journey was disguised as a pilgrimage to Mahasthan Garh, the site of the dargah of a Muslim saint in Bengal. His real intention, however, was to plunder and levy contributions on people residing on the route, and to create difficulties for the British authorities, whom he loathed. But despite countless bloody encounters, his forces were pushed out of Bengal. Majnu Shah never forgot this insult and always wanted to take revenge.[70] It was, perhaps, a destined possibility that his group came into contact with the Huseypur Raja as his forces shuttled between Makhanpur and Mahasthan Garh via Saran.

In later years, these groups of wanderers captured and looted many English factories in Bengal.[71] During the famine of 1770, the poor and destitute joined them in hordes. The increase in their followers led to a corresponding increase in their rapacious behaviour. By now, working as a mercenary had become a profession. In 1766, *sanyasis* had been hired by the Bhutias to help in their war of succession. Thus, their presence around Huseypur at the time leaves little doubt that Fateh Sahi was colluding with them.

The easy access of Fateh Sahi to the territories of friendly Awadh and the complicity of its functionaries helped him succeed in his mission. The British troops could not pursue him to Awadh. More importantly, it was an endless stretch of tropical forest full of bushes and undergrowth, water pools, marshes and wild animals.[72] No stranger could venture into it. Fateh Sahi must have had ample knowledge of its topography and considerable assistance of the local people in this regard. He could not have survived without their support and loyalty, for whom, too, the British were a common enemy.

In the higher reaches of Champaran, I have heard folk songs recounting the oppression of state agents in the distant past. One of them referred to the excesses of the *Kotwal*, presumably from the preceding century. The song was moving enough to appear as a *bhajan* (devotional song), presented by Tharu villagers before the deity in a temple. This was at Sahodra near Bhikhnathori, which, was selected as a hunting site when George V visited India in 1911. In Done, I met with a tribal group who recalled similar past excesses. This indicated the chaos and oppression in the region, which might have attracted the local people to Fateh Sahi as a potential liberator.[73]

All this offered Fateh Sahi an environment to rise, and emboldened him to embark on his incursions. His audacity to challenge the British authorities in a fierce engagement in 1767 and his unrelenting attacks against them and their supporters thereafter, project him as the liberator the common masses looked for. His hereditary status as the Raja of the territory, his family relations with several neighbouring chiefs like that of Majhauli, Padrawna and Benares, and the support of his clansmen and Muslim feudatories around Huseypur added to his clout. He was also firmly in league with the Nawab of Awadh, in whose territory he had encamped.

The possibility of any rivalry with the next-door Muslim chief had already been largely dealt with by Fateh Sahi's grandfather Jubaraj Sahi, when he defeated the Afghan chief of Barharia and had wrested Sipah pargana from him. Nevertheless, the Barharia family had not reconciled with their fate. They were unwilling to accept any further control by the British. Thus, they transformed into a primary opponent against the British in the area. The private ownership of the fort was deemed an embarrassment for the Company and politically crucial for future consolidation of their authority. In case of disturbances, Barharia was likely to fall into the hands of the enemy. It was situated towards the borders of the Company's possessions and open to Shuja-ud-Daulah's country.[74] Moreover, the Barharia chief's family resided in Awadh and refused to hand over charge of their fort. It was a rebuff for the Company officers; nevertheless, they sought to overcome the problem cautiously, for fear of driving him into Fateh Sahi's camp. Ultimately, in May 1771, Company forces besieged the fort and compelled its owners, Sheikh Abdullah and Imamam Baksh, to surrender.[75]

These developments, including the recent episode of Betia Raj, are likely to have cautioned the zamindars of the region, because all of them were equally threatened. This was enough to frighten the fledgling British establishment and force it, in turn, to fight the rebel Raja of Huseypur tooth and nail. They established an army station at Baragaon, close to Huseypur, to keep watch on him and encounter him whenever needed; and, they stormed the royal fort to rubble. Its ruins are still visible. The location of the military station is now known as Line Bazar, indicating its association with the military line (cantonment).

Why was the Company's control over Fateh Sahi and Saran so urgent and crucial? The Europeans had entered this region over a century ago and by now they were fully acquainted with its commercial potentials and its strategic location. It was a great source of saltpetre, opium, indigo, sugar, cotton, piece goods and the like, for the Company's trade both in India and abroad.

Although the EIC was a fast-emerging power, its important rivals and enemies—the Portuguese, the Dutch and the French—already had a foothold in Saran. Even as they were overpowered and sidelined by the British gradually, their commercial activities and interaction with the local society, especially with zamindars and rajas, continued. This was a concern for the British; in the circumstances, local opponents like Fateh Sahi needed to be eliminated or reconciled with, to prevent any future coalition between them and the European opponents. The increased demand of saltpetre, opium and other items and the presence of the Dutch trade in Saran made the district crucial for the EIC. During the end of the seventeenth and early eighteenth century, Saran was the centre of attraction for the European trading companies for saltpetre.

In that, once the Company was able to sideline its European contenders and crush most of the indigenous adversaries, gaining sway over eastern India, the defiance by Fateh Sahi was a disconcerting challenge and real concern—his elimination was a top priority.

The emergence of the Ganga with its tributaries, such as the Ghaghra-Saryug, Gandak, Budhi Gandak, Bagmati, Kamla Balan, Mahananda and Kosi, as a highway of European trade and navigation in north India encouraged the British to prioritize their political control, especially north of the Ganga, simultaneously with consolidation of their trade. This swath opened up a vista of the Gangetic plain up to Delhi and Agra, and provided a gainful trade route to Nepal, Tibet and China in the north, and to the Deccan in the south.[76]

On the southern fringe of the Indo-Gangetic plain, the rivers originated from central India, and as they flowed eastward across the Vindhya Mountains through the craggy and rocky terrain of the Kamur Hills, they became unfit for navigation. Most of them dried up in summer, but during the rains, they turned into rapids. They carried with them sand and not the soft alluvial soil in their silt that could promote agriculture, thus depriving the region of many agricultural products then in demand for European trade. The value of minerals that occurred in its south-east were yet to be appreciated. Such a topography could not lure the European traders or travellers.

In the circumstances, the country north of the Ganga emerged as the prime location for the Europeans to capture. Meanwhile, as Chait Singh of Benares inclined to submission, the nawabs of Awadh postured alike and the grassroots local resistance subsided, the existence of a small but audacious rebel Fateh Sahi in this power arena was a great challenge for the English, as much for their trade as for their political enterprise.

Before the coming of the Europeans in Bihar, some of the important river-born trading centres on the south-eastern periphery of Saran were Chapra, then touched by the river; and Doriganj, 7 miles east of Chapra. Facing Patna across the Ganga in the south and situated on the Ganga-Ghaghra confluence, almost opposite the rivers Sone and Arrah, it was once a large market, with considerable river-borne traffic. Chirandh had an impressive antiquity spread over centuries; but all of these centres gradually lost their status on account of the shift in the position of the Ganga and Ghaghra rivers.[77]

With the arrival of the Europeans, new trading centres emerged on this route. A mile over the Ganga-Ghaghra junction, Godna emerged on the Ghaghra's north bank. Soon, a customs office (*chauki*) was established there by Henry Revel, the customs collector, and later named after him as Revelganj (1788). It developed as a major entrepot dealing in varieties of goods, exchanged between eastern India, the Western Provinces, Central India and Nepal. By the 1870s, it was the 'most important centre of trade in north Bihar'. Its trade with Calcutta alone was estimated in 1872–73 at a total tonnage of 37,000 kg (or over 1 million maunds).[78] However, as the two rivers later shifted to the east, Revelganj declined in its commercial status.*

Twelve miles north-west of Revelganj on the river, Manjhi was a thriving market in the late eighteenth century,

* SDG: 489–92

but it declined soon. Farther upstream, Darauli continued to prosper as a major transit point for exchange of merchandise between Saran and the North-Western Provinces.[79] The other inland ports and trade centres that developed upstream of the Ghaghra-Saryug were Siswan, Barhaj and Barhalganj.[80] Most of the inland ports on Saran's south-west boundary faced the western provinces and Awadh and served as entry points to them. They are all likely to have aided Fateh Sahi's mobility and resourcefulness. Since a considerable volume of English trade was carried on this river route, it became a site of crimes—looting of English boats and forced collections by local toughies from them. The involvement of Fateh Sahi's men in these activities cannot be ruled out, as it was an easy way of procuring stores and supplies for his military operations. The Charters Report refers to the instances wherein Sahi focused on procuring resources and denied the enemy access to them, by ensuring complete evacuation of villages during the English raids. This was his earliest version of an economic warfare the English practiced later, especially through the Scorched Earth policy during the Second World War.[81] The menace became so grave that the Company had to take up special measures to deal with it (discussed elsewhere).

A little away from Sahi's eastern boundaries, north to south downstream, Bagha, Gobindganj, Lalganj, Muzaffarpur and Hajipur developed as another line of inland ports along the Gandak, and with smaller ones in the interiors.[82] In the course of time, they helped the Europeans enter the interiors of Saran, Champaran and Tirhut that would soon turn into their foremost stronghold.

In the absence of steamships, which were introduced in the 1830s, and the railways that came into the region in 1860, overland transportation was an important means of circulating trade items. Its volume can be presumed by some random data: In the peak months, December to April, as many as 8000 carts and an equal number of bullocks and ponies operated by well-known Banjara pack-bullock traders passed daily over the roads along the Ganges.[83] However, this Banjara channel of trade, without a glance at their notoriety in the region around the time, may remain incomplete. Going by their past records, did they in any way help Fateh Sahi in his military operations?[84]

Unlike the Ganga's southern tributaries, its northern counterparts were far better suited for navigation, agriculture and trade. Rising from the Himalayas, perennial and abounding, they aided to the fertility of the host soil, making it highly productive for a variety of commercial produces needed by the European traders. Later accounts refer to the flourishing trade of grain and related goods and the occurrence of cattle fairs in the Ganga-Ghaghra stretch, the largest *mela* taking place at Sonepur. The raw material for saltpetre occurred abundantly in this region.

Saran, in fact, the whole of the Bhojpuri-speaking adjoining region, seems to have remained defiant of any outside authority for ages (discussed in Chapters 2 and 3), which was well testified by the revolt of Fateh Sahi and many others in the following centuries. In the nineteenth and twentieth centuries, some of the big zamindars from this region immensely contributed to India's freedom movement. The establishment of the Khadga Vilas Press in Patna by Rajkumar Ram Deen Singh of Balia in 1880 provided an important platform for the promotion of nationalist ideas in the freedom struggle. Mangal Pandey's exploits of 1857 and Chitu Pandey's most daring open revolt in 1942 were burning examples. No wonder the British believed that the region was defiant of their rule, and so, they paid extra attention to its administrative control. They would station, in the coming days, one of their most loyalist troops, the Gorkha Regiment, at Gorakhpur.

Thus, though forced to retreat into the jungle, Fateh Sahi continued his raids and depredations, and incessantly clashed with the Company's agents and forces. He was also thrashed, but he always returned. He was not the only one disgruntled with the British regime. The old aristocracy, Hindus and Muslims, was unhappy with the treatment of the Company's officers and local agents, whose avarice and corrupt practices were unacceptable to them. Consequently, opposition against the British stiffened because of political and economic incompatibilities, maladministration and personal disaffection. An undercurrent of resistance was visible throughout India, as seen in the revolts of Chait Singh of Benares, Vazir Ali of Lucknow, Hyder Ali of Mysore, the rajas of Malabar, insurrections in Assam, the Killahdars of Bundelkhand and Vijay Singh of Rohilkhand.[85]

Indeed, Fateh Bahadur Sahi was among the rare few, if not the only one, who grasped the value of independence and the disastrous consequences of foreign rule. No wonder, he would not just revolt violently, but remained in a state of war for the rest of his life.[86]

4

Raids from the Jungle

1772–1795

The takeover of the Huseypur Raj by the East India Company and its transfer to Basant Sahi for management after the 1767 clashes left Fateh Sahi deeply embittered and enraged. Immediately, he started planning from his jungle hideout how to undo the damage. He organized a sizeable army, and appears to have spread a network of spies to report on the goings-on in and around Huseypur. A large section of his ryots remained loyal to him and they paid him revenue even in exile; but now it was time for him to be articulate and tactful if he wanted to counter an enemy who had greater resources and military prowess. This needed the cooperation of other zamindars in his neighbourhood in eastern Awadh and Bihar, who had grievances against the new regime. The Nawab of Bengal had already challenged the British at Plassey, but without success. In 1764, a coalition of the nawabs of Bengal and Awadh and the Mughal emperor confronted the Company at Buxar. Yet again, they lost. It was demoralizing for all those opposed to the expansion of the East India Company in the country; however, things could not stay this way forever. Grievances against the Company surged over time. Fateh Sahi's was not the only case of defiance. An undercurrent of resistance was running throughout India. Soon, Chait Singh would revolt in Benares, and Vazir Ali in Lucknow. Both these revolts were closely connected to Fateh Sahi's rebellion that outlived them both.[1] But we will come to that later.

After the grant of Diwani, the East India Company came to power in 1765, opening the gates for vested interests to act at will. India's problems were compounded when the Company's individual employees and agents began to indulge in personal trading. The socio-economic life in the country had not been much better in the preceding years, but it grew grimmer under the Company's system of dual government. Referring to the situation in Bengal, the Select Committee wrote to the Court of Directors in February 1767: 'We beheld a presidency headstrong, divided and licentious; a government without nerves, a treasury without money, and a service without subordination, discipline or public spirit.' It continued, '. . . amid a general stagnation of useful industry, and of licensed commerce, individuals were accumulating immense riches which they had ravished from the insulated Prince and his helpless people, who groaned under the united pressure of discontent, poverty, and oppression.'[2]

Pillage and Chaos

Robert Clive left for England on 29 January 1767, and under the brief tenures of his two immediate successors, Verelst and Cartier, confusion intensified. A few days before leaving office, Verelst wrote to his successor-designate on 16 December 1767:

> Our circumstances impelled us forward, and the grant of Diwanny (. . .) became as much an object of necessity as it was of advantage. Thus we insensibly broke down the barrier betwixt us and government, and the native grew uncertain where his obedience was due. Such a divided and a complicated authority gave rise to oppressions and intrigues unknown at any other period; the officers of the government caught the infection, and being removed from any immediate control, proceeded with still greater audacity. In the meantime we were repeatedly and peremptorily forbidden to avow any public authority over the officers of government in our own names, and enjoined to retain our primitive characters of merchants with the most scrupulous delicacy.[3]

As advised by Verelst, supervisors were appointed in 1769 to augment the collection of revenues. But they could not bring about any improvement and so, their powers were withdrawn. Subsequently, the council in Calcutta appointed revenue councils at Patna and Murshidabad. The council of Bihar consisted of James Alexander as president, and Robert Palk, George Vansittart and Sitab Rai as members. Rai was in the lineage of the Mughal emperor's representative in Patna. He and his son were already involved in cases of corruption and were enmeshed in conspiracies that haunted the corridors of power at the time. They were not alone. There were plenty of others, often from previous local administrations, who were past masters in fraudulence and conspiracy. They thrived on sycophancy and favours and were now busy consolidating their powers under the Company regime. Acting against other Indians was an easy way to prove their loyalty to the new masters. It is, therefore, unsurprising to discover that Sitab Rai was instrumental in advising the authorities in Patna to send in the army against Fateh Sahi.[4]

Far from removing the manifold abuses in internal administration, the divorce of responsibility from power under the dual government produced many more. The consequent breakdown of the administrative system and governance, the oppressions of the amils and the revenue farmers and the harsh treatment of the local manufacturers by Company agents, such as the gomastahs, hastened the economic decline. Various trade abuses contributed to escalate the anarchy in the province. When the famine of 1770 ravaged Bengal and Bihar, the miseries of the people knew no bounds. But this misery did not arise all of a sudden. It had been coming for quite some time.

Official correspondence and contemporary tracts tell horrifying stories about the calamity. They recount people begging in the streets, parents selling their children for food and sustenance, and people dying of hunger and disease by the hundreds every day in Patna, Purnia and other places. The hungry stooped to cannibalism, cremation grounds were crammed with dead bodies and pestilence devastated crops in several parts of Bihar.[5] The massive Goleghar, hurriedly built to store the grain required to fight starvation, still stands conspicuously on the southern bank of the Ganga in Patna. It is a rare reminder of the monstrosity of the calamity of the 1770s.[6]

The widespread shortages and absence of livelihood during the famine led to unusual social activities—large-scale demographic displacement, loot, thuggee and plunder by sanyasis and fakirs. Pressed under the new obligations of the Company, native chiefs and notables reacted angrily and the common masses harboured a general dislike for its agents and agencies. Traditionally, local masters had always protected their subjects in hard times, by exempting them from many feudatory obligations, including land revenue. They often launched public welfare projects like digging ponds and wells, and building roads and dams that provided employment for the poor and the unemployed. Cottage industries stood them in good stead. But the new regime was not at all concerned about their sustenance and welfare. Small wonder, then, that the local people were on the lookout for a liberator.

Here, let us take a closer look at the presence of the weird wanderers in and around Huseypur. Fateh Sahi was in touch with them and continuously used them in his fight with the English. His descendants confirm that he visited the Mahakumbh Mela at Allahabad in 1775, in order to get help from militant Naga sanyasis. After the conclusion of the Kumbh Mela, their movement became frequent through the Gandak to Mahananda, in the long tract between the Bhagjogni jungle in Gorakhpur to Purnia in east Bihar. Another route was via the Pakur, Khargadiha and Rajdhanvar estates in present-day Jharkhand. Jagannathpuri in Odisha was a sacred complex to which their visit from Bengal was quite common. The Dasnami Nagas attached to various *akharas* of Allahabad and Benares travelled to Bengal along these routes. They had established their stronghold also in Nepal and Bhutan, and their presence could be seen up to Assam.[7]

The most important leadership position of the Dasnami sanyasis was that of the *mahanth.* In the time of Fateh Sahi, this position was held by Raja Himmat Giri Bahadur, who had considerable influence in the region of Awadh, Prayag, Bundelkhand and Kashi. Fateh Sahi met him and won his trust in the course of his military coalition with Chait Singh during the Banaras Rebellion. This must have helped Sahi in gaining Naga support for his attacks on the Company. Himmat Giri had several pontiffs active in royal services in central India. For example, Kanchan Giri served in the army of Samsher Bahadur, the son of Mastani and Baji Rao, the ruler of the Banda region in Bundelkhand.[8]

Fateh Sahi began with the Nagas in his early clashes with the English; subsequently, he is believed to have also enlisted other groups of sanyasis, fakirs, vagabonds and destitutes, even bandits. Their loyalty and dedication to him seems to have emanated from the fact that they did not have any better option for livelihood before them. In happier times, people offered them alms voluntarily; but as the general economic condition deteriorated, all such sources dried up. Thus, these groups started indulging in activities that helped them survive. Already deprived of a normal social life, they had nothing to lose. Being a man of strong religious disposition, Fateh Sahi could have also fanned their religious sentiments against the English. The Nagas and *Nathpanthis* were traditionally known to be relentless warriors for freedom and protectors of Hinduism. We know about the role of the Nagas in Fateh's rebellion, but not about the Nathpanthis, whose prime centre was Gorakhpur, from where they operated in the neighbouring districts of UP and Bihar. All of them seem to have added to the strength of Sahi's militia.

Displacement of people in the eighteenth century, caused by natural calamities (floods, famines and epidemics), wars, and disturbed law-and-order conditions was a common phenomenon. The raids of Fateh Sahi greatly contributed to migrations from the villages, when hordes of their residents joined his militia because there was nothing else for livelihood at hand there, and many deserted to avoid recurrent raids and clashes in their area. This continued almost throughout the entire period of Sahi's prolonged struggle with the British, as evidenced by the large numbers of abscondings taking place in 1792.[9] These desertions are indicative of many things: the scale and intensity of Sahi's operations and the Company's failure to contain them, the recurrence of the natural calamities and all the factors helping Sahi enhance his fighting power by incorporating the masses. Finally, this suggests he was militarily active even in the 1790s.

It was at this juncture that Warren Hastings (1732–1818) entered the scene in April 1772, as the Governor of Bengal and the de facto first Governor-General of India.[10] He took matters seriously, and hectic changes were made in revenue administration during 1772–80. Diligent and plain-living, Hastings was an Indophile who, in his youth, fought hard against the loot of Bengal by his colleagues.[11] He sought to reform every branch of administration—revenue, justice, law and order and the economy.

The most mismanaged was the revenue administration and revenue farmers were very often in arrears. Early in 1772, Raja Sitab Rai, the Indian member of the revenue council in Patna, was summoned to Calcutta to answer the charges of corruption and mismanagement against him. Somehow, his son Kalyan Singh managed to get him acquitted and reinstated in office, though he was not destined to hold it for long. Sitab Rai fell ill soon after, so, when in 1773, Hastings came to Patna and wanted to take him to Benares, he could not accompany him. Yet, Sitab used the opportunity to impress upon Hastings to look on his son as successor to all offices and jagirs held by him and to extend similar favours as had been shown to Sitab Rai.[12]

However, by the time Hastings returned from Benares, Sitab Rai had passed away. Hastings visited Kalyan to offer his condolences. The next day, Kalyan was appointed to all the offices that had fallen vacant on the death of his father. On the Governor's orders, Kalyan was escorted with pomp and show from Bankipur to his residence in Patna City and installed on the Nizamat in the Diwan-e-Khana. Kalyan was about twenty-one years old then; so, Sadhu Ram and Kheali Ram were to act as his naibs to help in his official work. Thus, initially, the British tried to operate under the façade of the Mughal administrative structure and traditions to hide their foreignness, while consolidating their power in India. For that, they tried to take along those who had degenerated morally during the declining years of the Mughals, because they were malleable to the lures of money and power.[13]

Ghulam Husain, the author of *Siyar-ul-Mutakharin,* holds that Hastings appointed Kalyan just to ensure that nobody suspected Hastings's malice towards Sitab Rai. Otherwise, Kalyan's immature age aside, his weaknesses of character blotted his official conduct, and he soon lost the confidence of the revenue council.[14] The government reduced his stipend; and gradually he lost the jagirs of his father in UP, Delhi and elsewhere. The disloyalty of his naibs added to his woes. He lost control over the departments of *Kotwali* and *Faujdari* in Bihar. Revenue arrears to the Company piled up and in order to pay them off, he sold his property and personal assets. He personally went to Calcutta to plead before the Governor-General to pardon his lapses, but to no avail. When Kalyan finally returned home, after twenty-four years of stay in Calcutta, he was penniless, and lived in penury in a rented house at Pathri Ghat in Patna City. He went back to Calcutta again in 1812 and died there in 1822.[15]

While this was going on, Saran was created as a separate district in 1779, and Charles Grome was appointed as its Collector. William Maxwell, the senior-most member of the revenue council in Patna, was appointed the revenue chief of Bihar. Kalyan still continued to be part of the administration, but he was not on good terms with Maxwell, because their relationship was not defined, as Kalyan had been appointed on orders directly from the council in Calcutta. Such internal conflicts and corruption in administration, besides all-pervading oppression, led to chaos and confusion, and catalysed a widespread opposition to the Company's rule.[16]

Stir in the Ganga Valley

Soon, many rose to challenge the Company regime in the Gangetic plains, from Awadh to Bengal. Although the region was a flatland, its wild and marshy terrain had historically provided an obstacle to external control. The few groups that had managed to enter and had naturalized themselves in the region over time now resisted the penetration of the Company. Of these groups, two Bhumihar Brahmin families—one of Benares and the other of Huseypur in the Bhojpuri-speaking tract—emerged as formidable adversaries for the British. They enjoyed the support of their kinsmen who held zamindaris in the region. South of Huseypur across the Ganga, Rajput chiefs put up resistance in south Bihar. The Muslim zamindars were generally reticent, but they preferred to support leading Hindu rebels against a common enemy—the British. Fateh Sahi had many collaborators and sympathizers from these groups.

Of these, Raja Chait Singh (reigned 1770–81) of Benares was the most important. He instigated almost all the rebellious groups in the swathe from Awadh to Bengal. His ancestors had a long history of being independent rajas with nominal allegiance to the Mughals, but later, they became feudatories of the Awadh nawabs.[17] Soon after the death of Nawab Shuja-ud-Daulah, his son Asaf-ud-Daulah signed a new treaty with the East India Company in 1775 as a pre-condition to his accession. According to this Treaty of Faizabad, the sovereignty of Benares was transferred to the Company, thus making Chait Singh a vassal, obliged to pay Rs 22 lakh annually. Besides, he was forced to contribute cavalry and maintenance grants for the Company's sepoy battalions. However, it was specifically laid down in the treaty that beyond the stipulated tribute, 'no demand shall be made upon him . . . of any kind or on any pretence whatsoever, nor shall any person be allowed to interfere with his authority or to disturb the peace of his country'.[18]

The Raja refused to accept the terms and began to secretly correspond with the enemies of the Company in the hope of breaking the arrangement forcibly. But the plan was discovered and he was placed under house arrest, pending an interview with Warren Hastings, who had his own designs.[19] His government was faced with financial stringency around this time, arising out of its engagement in war with the French, Dutch, Marathas and Hyder Ali of Mysore.[20] This added to an enhanced need for money, which drove him to extort it from Chait Singh, in violation of the terms of the 1775 treaty. In 1778, Hastings asked him for an additional Rs 5 lakh as a war levy. In fact, he was determined to plunder Chait Singh and planned to demand larger and larger contributions until he remonstrated, which Hastings would take as defiance and a crime, and confiscate all his possessions.[21]

When Chait Singh did not respond, Hastings made the demand twice. In 1780, the Raja eventually sent him

Rs 2 lakh, and wrote an apologetic letter requesting him not to repeat the demand any more. This infuriated Hastings, who proceeded to Benares to punish him. In order to pacify him, Chait Singh personally received him with all courtesy at Buxar and begged his pardon. However, Hastings refused to discuss the matter until he reached Benares. He reached there on 14 August 1781, but he did not allow any interview with the Raja, who was keen to settle all contentious issues to the satisfaction of the Governor-General. Instead, Hastings charged him of 'disaffection and infidelity to the Government', along with a long list of allegations, which Chait Singh kept denying in a most submissive manner.[22] But this did not satisfy Hastings, who emphasized the 'spirit of Independency which the Rajah had, for some years past, assumed'.[23] Hastings had, in fact, already made up his mind to act against Chait Singh. He directed Markham, the English Resident in Benares, at 10 p.m. on 15 August, to arrest the Raja the next morning and keep him under custody until further orders.[24] He also ordered two companies of sepoys to rush to the scene in case the Raja retaliated. Hastings cleverly selected the early hours of the day for the arrest, in order to pre-empt any local support.

Early next morning, Markham arrived at the royal palace at Shivala Ghat. Chait Singh quietly submitted to his arrest, promising to obey the orders of the Governor-General, and placed his assets at Hastings's disposal. The guards of the palace were disarmed, except for a few who were left to attend to the Raja. Markham returned to Hastings with a letter from Chait Singh, seeking an amicable settlement of all issues.[25] But Hastings was equally determined to humiliate him for his earlier defiance.[26]

News of Chait Singh's arrest spread like wildfire. Locals began gathering around the Shivala Palace and across the river in his support. Resentment hung thick in the air. Hastings sent a message to Chait Singh to forbid his supporters from indulging in retaliatory violence. The failure to heed this, he warned, would be treated as a crime against the Company, for which the Raja would be held responsible. The messenger, Cheitram, a *chobdar* of Markham, delivered this message to the Raja in a manner rude enough to provoke his supporters to kill Cheitram.[27]

Events now took an ugly turn. By 10 a.m., a large crowd gathered around the palace. Tactically, the Company troops on duty there were not armed in order to avoid provocation. But to deal with the latest situation, they frantically asked for immediate reinforcements of troops and ammunition. By now, all routes of supply were blocked by the king's supporters, and, by the time help reached, a cold-blooded massacre had already taken place. The Company forces put up a feeble resistance and almost all of them were hacked to pieces.[28]

Taking advantage of the chaos and confusion, Chait Singh escaped from the palace. He killed the guards on duty; and tying his turbans together, he went through a window and down the wall, into a boat waiting for him in the river below. He sailed to the opposite bank, followed by his supporters. Now he made an impassioned appeal to the chiefs of the region for their support against the British. His forces were not willing to tolerate the indignities heaped upon their master; instantly, a pitched battle ensued.[29] By midnight, the Raja left Ramnagar with his family and effects for Latifpur, ten miles from Chunar.[30]

Without losing time, Hastings focused on the collection of revenues and the consolidation of his control over the city.

He looked to the enemies of the Raja and appointed Ausan Singh as the naib. Ausan Singh was a former officer of Chait Singh, but now his arch-enemy. Hastings ordered troops to march on Benares from Chunar, Mirzapur and Danapur. A large contingent arrived from Mirzapur on 19 August 1781. They marched towards Ramnagar the next morning, but were intercepted in the narrow streets of the city and most were killed. Captain Mayaffre's severed head was held atop a spear and displayed as a trophy in procession in the city.[31]

Clashes continued, and the Raja's forces and followers blocked the supply routes to the town and *dawk* with other places. The movement of anything on the rivers likely to aid the Company's operations stopped completely. North of the Ganga, the rebellion of Chait Singh afforded an opportunity to Fateh Sahi to renew his attacks against the Company on behalf of the Benares Raja. Chait Singh not only gave him money but also encouraged him to kill Europeans and their sepoys. Resistance to local authorities increased as many more zamindars refused to cooperate, and some of them even killed the Company emissaries. Every day, the Saran Collector encountered instances of determined disposition among the inhabitants to throw off all subjugation of his authority.[32] Allying with the zamindars of Majhauli, Perrouna and the Narrowneys, Sahi fielded an army of 8000 men and six cannons.[33] Colonel Williams informed the government on 7 September 1781 that Fateh Sahi, Ghia Rai and Ajit Mall of Saran had crossed the Manjoli River with their men on the invitation of Chait Singh and, in league with Zalim Singh and others, they were terrorizing the surrounding country. Williams suspected the complicity of Sadat Ali and the begums of Awadh in the matter.[34]

The forces of Chait Singh and his allies, led probably by Fateh Sahi, put up a tough fight against the Company forces. Together, they defeated Warren Hastings, the supreme commander of operations, and forced him to flee the battlefield. He is said to have been briefly imprisoned; others say he took shelter in the house of a local businessman. However, he managed to escape; and routed completely, he left Benares for Chunar on the night of 21 August. The state of his desperation and nervousness at the time has been vividly captured in a folk saying that recounts how, while fleeing in panic and confusion, he ordered a howdah for the horse and a saddle for the elephant:

'Ghode par hauda, hathi par jin,
Bhaga, bhaga Warren Hastin'

Hastings reached Chunar at daybreak the next day. But he was now cut off from the eastern provinces; and going by the correspondence among Company commanders, the prospects of assistance from anywhere were grim. Chait Singh's forces had prevailed so completely that Hastings was now looking at a substantial loss of credit, having no money or food. Somehow, Lt Col Blair raised Rs 2500 from a Chunar *shroff* and some food by extortion.[35]

Following their supreme commander, the English army vacated Benares on 23 August 1781, leaving it at the mercy of the followers of Chait Singh.

Diplomacy was the best option before Hastings, now. In order to recover Benares and consolidate his position, he approached the opponents of Chait Singh and other vested interests, and mobilized the Company's forces stationed at different locations in the country. Chait Singh's forces and followers fought bravely, but they were routed. He was deposed, and his minor nephew Mahip Narayan Singh (1756–1795), son of his sister Padma Kuwar, married in Narhan Estate in Darbhanga (now Samastipur District), was installed in his place on 14 September 1781. The new Raja agreed to make an annual payment of Rs 40 lakh to the Company, in place of the Rs 22 lakh previously agreed upon by the treaty of 1775. However, the traditional animosity of his predecessors with the British continued and they, in turn, declared him unfit to govern.[36] On 27 October 1794, they transferred his four revenue districts (sarkars) to the direct control of the Company, leaving only the family domains under him. In return, he was given Rs 1 lakh annually in compensation and any surplus revenue arising out of the sarkars. He died a year later and was succeeded by his eldest son, Udit Narayan Singh.[37]

An episode occurring in 1791 may be recalled to understand the complex and ambitious considerations guiding the Company's moves, played out with the Benares Raja. Having been seriously dented in his territorial status and authority, Raja Mahip Narain was not comfortable and insisted on the reversal of the Company's recent decisions. In the spring of 1791, the issue of the marriage of his son seemed to bring his relationship with the Company to a flashpoint. On 2 March, Mahip Narain informed Duncan, the Company Resident in Benares, that he was soon to celebrate the marriage of his son, for which he sought the latter's permission. Duncan did not show any objection and wrote to the government to contribute as much as possible to the expenses of the marriage, as it would prove extremely gratifying to the Raja and his family and strengthen their mutual relations.

Meanwhile, Duncan came to know that the bride was the daughter of Fateh Sahi, the dreaded rebel zamindar of Bihar, who had supported Chait Singh during his rebellion. So, he did not approve of 'the improper choice' of the marriage, and just seven days before the celebrations, he asked the Raja to postpone the marriage for fourteen days, while he solicitated directions from the government. The Raja mentioned that the bride had no connection with her father, Fateh Sahi, because, since the death of her mother, she had lived with her maternal grandfather Pahalwan Singh, a zamindar of Benares. Eventually, as the government did not apprehend any bad outcome from the match, the Resident permitted the marriage, and it was consummated on 17 June 1791.[38]

Meanwhile, Chait Singh's fight with the Company forces continued outside Benares. He strengthened his forts at Latifpur and Patteta with impregnable fortifications and massive troop deployments with efficient artillery. His troops fought gallantly, but the disclosure of his strategy by a local of Chunar helped the British pre-empt his plans. The Raja was forced to flee Latifpur. He reached Bijaygarh on 21 September, but did not stay for long. After instructing the *kiladar*, he left his family and dependents there, and hurried with his treasure and convoy to the Agoree fort on River Sone closer to his territory.[39]

Hastings had always set his eyes on Chait Singh's enormous wealth, a good portion of which he was now carrying with him. According to Hastings, the Raja left Bijaygarh with 1 lakh gold mohurs, Rs 15–16 lakh in silver and an unknown amount of precious jewels.[40] Khairuddin informs us that the treasure was carried by twenty-five elephants, fifty camels, 1500 bullocks, 1000 coolies and 200 *bungy bardars*.[41] The British forces pursued him until he turned towards Bundelkhand for safety.

Back at Bijaygarh, the Company army intensified its attacks on the fort and eventually forced the besieged Rani to agree to negotiations for peace, resulting in a settlement. It granted her limited rights to the fort, with an option to reside in the province or leave to go to her son and husband. Peace was restored with the imposition of the Company's control over Bijaygarh; but as soon as its fort came under their possession, Major Popham captured its treasure and distributed it among the troops as their prize. The treasure amounted to Rs 23 lakh and even the subalterns received Rs 20,000 each. Hastings was exasperated at this indiscriminate loot.[42] On 21 September, Major Crab took possession of the pass and the fort of Latifpur.[43]

These victories made it easy for Major Balfour to capture Ramnagar on 22 September. Heartened and emboldened, Hastings left Chunar on the evening of 25 September, and reached Benares on the morning of 28 September.

On 29 September, he issued a proclamation revoking with immediate effect the rights or interests of Chait Singh, Sujan Singh and their dependents in the zamindari of Benares.[44] Thus, Benares became a part of the Company's territories. The news of the plunder of the Benares Raj treasury spread like wildfire, evoking strong local reactions. In Faizabad, the begums of Awadh ordered guards placed at their city gates in order to prevent the entry of the British, and the forts of Gorakhpur, Ballia and Dumrigunj were captured by the zamindars and the amils of the Nawab.[45]

Ousted from Benares, Chait Singh and his supporters do not seem to have reconciled with their destiny. They continued efforts to regain Benares. The revolt of Jagat Singh was one of them. A relation of Chait Singh, Jagat Singh conspired with Company sepoys and others in 1799 to free the city from the

Company's control. However, his plan was leaked to the enemy, and he could not hold his ground for long. He was arrested, tried and sentenced to death; but fearing the possibility of a violent and widespread rebellion in his support, Company authorities commuted his sentence to transportation for life to a far-off place. In order to hide their fear, the British took refuge in an obscure local law that forbade the hanging of a convict if he was a Brahmin by caste.[46] Saint Helena, a British Overseas Territory, was chosen for the purpose, a remote volcanic tropical island in the south Atlantic, reserved for the most dreaded enemies of the British. Napoleon Bonaparte would be imprisoned here over a decade later.

Thus, an East India Company ship named *Asterley* was readied, with the highest security arrangements and meticulous planning. Advanced directions were transmitted to the Governor of St Helena, intimating him about the permanent stay of Jagat Singh there, with instructions to provide him with everything to keep him comfortable and happy. When the ship was to depart from Bombay, Jagat Singh was reported to have consumed poison the night before his departure to escape the ignominy and passed away.[47] Or, was he poisoned by the British? This is yet to be probed. The enormity of the fear of him among the British reminds one of their arch-enemy Napoleon Bonaparte, who met with a similar fate at their hands over a decade later, when he was imprisoned at the same St Helena where he died, supposedly of slow poisoning by his captors.

Jagat Singh was connected with Fateh Sahi via Tekary Raj. Today, a colony of Benares is named after him as Jagat Ganj.

Once out of Benares, Chait Singh received a jagir from Mahadaji Scindia near Jhansi in Gwalior, where he lived until his death.[48] He died in Gwalior on 28 March 1811,[49] leaving three sons whose descendants are settled there. His *chhatri* (memorial structure at the cremation ground) is still present in Gwalior and a road is called Kashi Road.[50]

Although most native rulers had not responded to Chait Singh's initial call, with the exception of Fateh Sahi and his allies, the rebellion in Benares was not for a lost cause. This was the time when the expansionist policy of the East India Company entangled it with Indian and European rivals. This resulted in constant clashes and wars in the south, which encouraged the zamindars in north India to rally round Chait Singh, in apprehension of a similar fate waiting for them. Gradually, many of them, such as Reza Quli Khan, the ex-amil of Sasaram, Pitamber Singh, a relative of the Raja of Tikari, Buniyad Singh of Chainpur, Narain Singh of Seris and Kutumba (Gaya), Akbar or Akbal Ali Khan of Naraht Samai (Gaya), Saugand Roy and Gaj Raj Roy of Palamu, the rajas of Ramgarh and Nagpur and a number of Ujjainia Rajputs, revolted in their respective territories.[51]

Word of the uprisings poured in at Company establishments, with reports from civil servants and army commanders alike, especially in Shahabad, Ghazipur, Balia, Mirzapur, Gaya, Hazaribagh and Jungle Terai. These rebels had common problems and almost identical grievances, related principally with land revenue and the Company's infringement upon their privileges and autonomy. This united them into an undeclared solidarity, and, in many cases, into covert cooperation. The scale, nature and intensity of their rebellions may be estimated by the size of their fighting forces, the speed of their operations and the intensity of their assaults. Typically, their army comprised individually up to 15,000 soldiers, with significant numbers of matchlock men, guns, cavalry and peons. The increasing participation of the common people in their operations was a striking feature across the entire range of the Kaimur Hills with intermittent passes and the forest tracts stretching towards the east via Gaya and Hazaribagh.[52]

The office-bearers and agents of Chait Singh were involved in several of these uprisings. Since the non-payment of land revenue arrears was behind most cases, the rebels evaded payment and incited others to stop their own.[53] The whole of Ramgarh region rose in revolt and its communication was cut off with Patna. The zamindar of Narwada, ruling over the Jungle Terai Division, took up arms and instructed the inhabitants of the region to withhold their payments to the Company. He also summoned influential locals to join him to settle revenues afresh. His followers attacked the Collector of Ramgarh, who escaped miraculously. The Raja of Nagpur evaded payments and raised troops, acting in tandem with Chait Singh.[54]

The supporters of Chait Singh disrupted all communications between Patna and Benares. J.L. Ross, the revenue chief at Patna, wrote to the council in Calcutta that communication by dawk had been cut off between the two cities, and any intelligence had been rendered impossible. Similar difficulties were experienced by Major Moses Crawfurd, the commanding officer, 28th Regiment at Dildarnagar. Rebels clustered at several locations to clash with Company forces, as on the Ghaghra river at Ghazipur and in Balia, where they lined the riverbank waiting to shoot if any British parties sailed past.[55] These locations on the western bank of the Ghaghra were situated just opposite the territory of Fateh Sahi on its eastern bank.

This shows the extent of the popular wrath seething among the common people. Cooperation and coordination were perceptible even among those who later surrendered to the British.[56]

On receiving intelligence of the disaffection of the zamindars of Bihar, J.L. Ross took stern measures to deal with everyone suspected of acting against the Company. He took into custody Hussain Ali Khan, the renter of Arwal and Masowrah, who acted as an emissary of Chait Singh.[57] Ross asked Kalyan Singh, Rai-Rayan of Subah Bihar, to instruct his zamindars and subordinates to assist the Company government against the insurgents. He also dispatched private messengers to the Resident at Lucknow and military commanders at Gorakhpur and Kanpur, and to Colonel Williams on the border of Saran, to caution them against rebellious zamindars.

General Giles Stibbert requested the authorities at Fort William to send more sepoys to maintain peace in Bihar.[58] Accordingly, the Calcutta Council dispatched a regiment from Behrampur (Bengal) and troops were posted at different places in Bihar. Major Moses Crawford was at Dildarnagar to intercept Chait Singh's forces. In August 1781, he was joined by Major James Crawford. At this point, the British also succeeded in eliciting some support from local zamindars.[59]

However, the rebellion of Chait Singh was suppressed eventually. This acted as a dampener on the spirits of the zamindars, and peace was restored in the region. No uprising of an equal proportion took place for a long time. This shook the confidence of Chait Singh's sympathizers and supporters. Many of them gradually became loyal to the English, essentially to save their zamindaris at the forthcoming Decennial Settlement of 1790.

Nevertheless, the rebellion of Chait Singh marked an important phase in the early resistance by the Indian aristocracy to the British rule. Although it was put down, providing the Company with a stronger foothold in the Gangetic plains, it inspired others at the same time to rise against the British in the years to come.[60] Moreover, the handling of these revolts by Hastings tarnished his image as a diplomat and an administrator, leading to his impeachment by the British Parliament.

In this interlude, Fateh Sahi kept the flames of revolt burning from his jungle hideout since 1767. Other Saran zamindars, including Sheikh Muhammad Ali of Siwan and the zamindars of Bagoura and Chainpur, who did not take up arms against the British, assisted Fateh Sahi secretly and created obstacles for his enemies.[61] Others to rise in his support were zamindars Bijay Sahi of Pargana Pushlak and Govind Narayan of Pargana Nal. Udwant Roy and the zamindars of Bikmah too recruited soldiers to help Fateh Sahi.

For the British, the next target was Awadh, one of the wealthiest of the twelve subahs of the Mughal Empire and the granary of north India. It was strategically situated for the control of the Doab, the fertile plain between the Ganga and the Yamuna rivers, and a bulwark against Maratha and Afghan raids. Broadly, it covered most parts of the United Provinces and portions of Nepal. Around 1555, it had been annexed to the Mughal Empire by Humayun, and administered until 1719 by its governors called subadhars, later designated as nawabs. But, with the decline of the emperor's power, they became practically independent rulers of their territories and exercised supreme power over their subjects.

Saadat Khan, a Persian adventurer, was the first Nawab of Awadh. He laid the foundation of its capital city at Faizabad (1722), which prospered under the third Nawab, Shuja-ud-Daulah, as the hub of the composite culture of North India. However, he fell out with the British after he aided Mir Qasim, the fugitive Nawab of Bengal. Shuja-ud-Daulah was defeated by the Company troops at Buxar, forced to pay heavy penalties and cede parts of his territory that expanded with the passage of time. Yet, the Company was not keen to outrightly capture Awadh, because that would bring them face to face with the combined might of the Marathas and the Mughals. The fourth Nawab, Vazir Ali Khan, ascended the throne with the support of the British in September 1797; but within months, they accused him of being unfaithful and replaced him with his uncle Saadat Ali Khan II.[62]

Vazir Ali was granted a pension of Rs 3 lakh and shifted to Benares in February 1798; but he was not reconciled to his fate. In September 1798, he had a secret meeting with Jagat Singh of Benares to revolt against the Company rule, but the plan leaked, and Jagat Singh was tried and punished, which we have already discussed. Subsequently, the Company decided to move Vazir Ali still farther from his territory to Calcutta. When British Resident George Frederick Cherry conveyed this order to him during a breakfast meeting on 14 January 1799, the Nawab became furious. In the ensuing argument, he struck Cherry with his sword and his security guards killed Cherry on the spot, along with two more Europeans. Immediately thereafter, the guards attacked the residence of Samuel Davis, the magistrate of Benares. Davis somehow managed to defend himself with just a spike on his staircase until he was rescued by Company troops. This episode is known as the Massacre of Benares. Instantly, Vazir Ali assembled an army of several thousand men, challenging the Company forces. However, he was pushed back and forced to flee to Rajputana, where he got asylum at Jaipur. On the request of Arthur Wellesley, the Jaipur Raja handed over Vazir Ali to the Company, on the condition that they would not prosecute him. He was brought to Calcutta in December 1799 and placed in confinement at Fort William. He spent the rest of the seventeen years of his life in an iron cage and was buried in the Muslim graveyard at Kasi Baghan in Calcutta.[63]

Saadat Ali Khan II, on the other hand, acted as a puppet and ceded half of his territory to the British under the treaty of 1801. He also agreed to disband his troops in favour of a hugely expensive army under the Company's control. Consequently, a portion of Awadh became a vassal of the East India Company, though Mughal suzerainty continued over it nominally until 1819. The treaty proved extremely beneficial for the British. They were able to use Awadh's vast treasury for low-interest loans, earned hefty revenues for running its armed forces and Awadh acted as a buffer state against their potential adversaries. Thus, the nawabs remained merely ceremonial rulers enjoying pomp and show, while the Company controlled their administration and resources. However, the Company now became impatient to control the province directly. The nawabs gave them the opportunity as they signed an agreement to change the status of Awadh into a British protectorate in 1816.[64]

Some of these Awadh nawabs were contemporaries of Fateh Sahi, whose estate adjoined theirs. Sahi watched the loot and persecution carried out by the Company in his neighbourhood, first in Benares and its neighbouring south Bihar chieftaincies, and then in Awadh. He was not just friends with the Benares Raja, but also his relative; and his exile in Awadh was based on mutual consent. Appalled at the situation, Fateh Sahi decided to pay the British back in their own coin. He resolved to continue his attacks with more vigour and ruthlessly. Blood for blood![65]

During the disintegration of the Mughal Empire, many adventurers and mercenaries entered India. The mercenaries belonged mostly to the countries hostile to Britain; hence they easily found employment in the armies of its adversaries in India, such as Hyder Ali, Tipu Sultan, Mir Kasim, the Marathas and Ranjit Singh. Walter Reinhardt Sombre (1723–1778), a mercenary from Luxembourg, and his collaborator, George Thomas (1756–1802), an Irishman, operated in north India around this time. Gloomy and cold, Sombre was ruthless, but he was quick to adapt to the local manners and could speak many local Indian languages. Maybe all this helped him come close to the local rulers. He fought on behalf of Mir Qasim, Nawab of Bengal, and butchered hundreds of the Company's captive soldiers during the Patna Massacre.[66] He also fought against the Company at the Battle of Buxar, in which Fateh Sahi is believed to have participated from the side of the Indian allies.[67] There is every likelihood that Sombre helped Sahi during his rebellion. Sombre's wife, Joanna Nobilis Sombre (1753–1836), alias Begum Samru, originally a Muslim courtesan of Kashmiri origin, commanded a huge mercenary force after the death of her husband, and was probably one of the greatest powerbrokers of her time. She is said to have led her troops in the battlefield in her typical battle gear, and was rumoured to cast a hypnotic spell on the adversary, forcing them to surrender.[68] Together, the couple helped with their forces many opponents of the Company; but after her husband's death, Samru also entertained some of the highest Company functionaries, including the commander-in-chief, Lord Lake. How is it possible that the couple was unaware of Sahi's rebellion and his concerns?

A different case from the Company circles was that of George François Grand (b. sometime after 1750 – d. 1820) and his wife Catherine.[69] George Grand was a Company civil servant of French-Swiss-Huguenot descent, who worked as the first Collector of Tirhut, headquartered at Muzaffarpur.[70] A brief but highly scandalous affair involving his wife Catherine Noël Grand (1762–1834), and Sir Philip Francis (1740–1818), a member of the supreme council and the Governor-General himself, in 1778, seemed to imperil the fate of them all. Grand sued Francis for trespassing into his house to seduce his wife. The eyewitness account in the court apart, Grand has himself given in his biography a fairly detailed description of the episode: Francis had planned the escapade well. Having a couple of accomplices with him, he had secured a folding rope ladder and put on a black outfit before proceeding on his mission. It was about 10–11 o'clock at night when Catherine was alone and in the house, that Francis scaled into the premises and tried to barge into her room. But the guards encountered him in the nick of time and a furious scuffle followed. He was overpowered, apprehended and tied up. But he whistled to his accomplices to signal a crisis, and they rushed instantly and rescued him. But one of the accomplices, Mr Shee, was not that lucky. Grand, who was having supper with a friend nearby, was immediately informed of the matter. When he reached home, he saw the culprits fleeing, but Mr Shee bound to a chair and struggling to break free. It was an utterly bizarre scene involving some top men of the Company in an unusual crime—a member of the supreme council of the Governor-General and a would-be member of British Parliament, and the other, a future knight and peer of the realm! When Grand tried to interact with Francis hiding in a nearby house, he declined to oblige.[71]

Grand did not meet Catherine that night, as he spent the night awake with a friend nearby. The next day he confronted her. Implicitly, she accepted her connivance. Grand pitied the immaturity of the sixteen-year-old girl that she was; but he could not be kinder. He called for her sister and brother-in-law and sent her with them with a promise to bear her expenses.[72] Moreover, he filed a case against Francis for trespassing into his house to seduce his wife. The Supreme Court found Francis guilty and fined 50,000 sicca rupees to be paid to Grand as a punishment.[73]

Philip Francis had been hostile towards Hastings ever since he arrived in Calcutta. Now it was Hastings's turn to use the incident against Francis. Hastings raised it in the supreme council, and their acrimonious relations worsened further. Soon, they were involved in a gunfight, in which Francis was seriously wounded. Although he recovered, he felt so humiliated that he left for England and started plotting the impeachment of Hastings. In India, the Grands' marriage floundered and finally broke off (1778). Catherine, too, left India for Europe. As a great beauty of her time, she immediately became popular in the elite circles of London and Paris. In Paris, she became friends with Charles Maurice de Talleyrand, the noted diplomat and the first prime minister of Napoleon Bonaparte, who finally married her with Bonaparte's persuasion (1802).[74] In June of that year, George Grand visited Paris and he knew where Catherine resided, but it is not clear if they met.[75]

In India, Hastings faced a surge of rebellions, prompted by the revolt of Chait Singh of Benares in 1781, which stirred most parts of the eastern provinces. In the midst of these disturbances, in 1782, Hastings appointed George François Grand to the highly coveted position of the first Collector of Tirhut, to administer revenue and justice in Tirhut and Hajipur—two important districts of Bihar. Grand was in touch with Hastings for a long time and he was also part of his entourage to Benares and Chunar. Intriguingly, it was at a morning breakfast on ship returning to Calcutta, that Hastings appointed him the Collector of Muzaffarpur and Hajipur, just after a brief chat.[76] Was this Hastings's magnanimity, or an effort to win over Grand to his side, apprehending the lurching threats from Philip Francis in London? The circumstances hint at a strong possibility of the latter.

However, Hastings relinquished the post of Governor-General soon after (1785), and the new regime, feeling alarmed at Grand's growing influence in north Bihar, started curtailing his powers. Finally, he was transferred from Muzaffarpur in 1787, which dented his private business considerably.[77] When Catherine came to know of the sorry plight of her former husband, she rushed to his rescue. In fact, they were not divorced yet, and she hadn't snapped her ties with him, even though she was comfortably settled in Paris, where Talleyrand provided her with enough resources for lavish living. Thus, she helped Grand financially with money received from Talleyrand.[78] On his part, aggrieved with the top management and perceiving the rebellious situation in the region, heightened now by Chait Singh's revolt, Grand befriended the local zamindars around Muzaffarpur, to recover from his personal crisis.[79] Most of them were Fateh Sahi's clansmen or, in some cases, relations, such as Betia Raj and its two offshoots, Sheohar and Madhuban. In Saran proper, his other clansmen, especially the Eksarias of Parsa Garh, Chainpur, Manjha, Bagaura and Gavirar, had already fought in the Battle of Buxar on the side of the Indian allies, claim their descendants.[80] Could not this equation have generated support for the rebellion of Fateh Sahi? Grand's recollections in his biography (1814) indicate that he was fully aware of the contemporary political situation in Bihar and the United Provinces.

Away from these goings-on, Fateh Sahi had never reconciled to the Company's assault on him and his dislodgment from Huseypur. He continued to raid his ancestral territory and obstruct the collection of revenues by Company officials. In 1772, he marched into Huseypur and killed Govind Ram, the Company-appointed revenue collector of the district. Incessant incursions followed. Afraid of him and fed up with his recurrent raids, the Company gave up the idea of reining him in. Instead, they resorted to diplomacy. Efforts were made to keep Fateh Sahi in good humour. The district collector of Saran, Golding, recommended his pardon in the Govind Ram murder case, and permission to return home to Huseypur. The Company agents engaged in negotiation with the Raja and eventually, he was persuaded to meet the Governor in Patna. In 1772, Golding himself accompanied him to the meeting, during which Sahi denied his involvement in the murder. In order to buy peace at any cost, the authorities did not question it and meekly accepted it prima facie! Govind Ram's murder was pardoned, and Fateh Sahi was offered a monthly stipend of Rs 300, with a promise of cessation of military action against him. He was to have full autonomy within his territory in lieu of a payment of Rs 25 lakh tenure and permission of the Company to circulate British currency in it.[81]

The proposal does not seem to have ever been formalized or implemented. Apparently, Sahi did not react to the offer, but agreed to remain peacefully with his family at Huseypur. He maintained a low profile, and used the truce to manage his family affairs, including the marriage of his daughters. However, his turbulent disposition did not allow him to remain quiet for

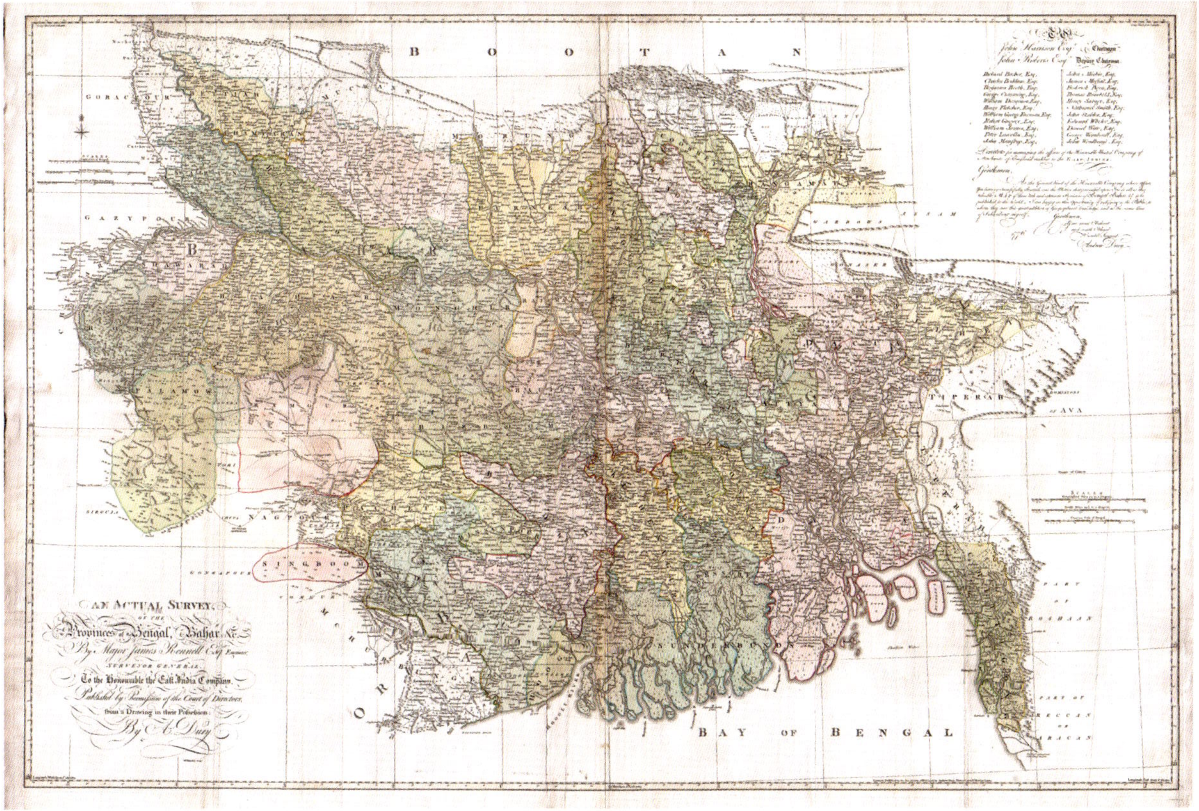

An Actual Survey, of the Provinces of Bengal, Bahar &c.
By Major James Rennell Esq. Engineer, Surveyor General.
To the Honourable the East India Company.
Published by Permission of the Court of Directors, from a Drawing in their Possession:
By A. Dury

BOOTAN

BAY OF BENGAL

SINGBOOM

Map of eastern India in the eighteenth century

Source: National Archives of India, New Delhi

Map of Saran district and its vicinity in the eighteenth century

Source: National Archives of India, New Delhi

Courtesy: Tamkuhi Raj family, Tamkuhi

Remnants of Fateh Sahi's fort at Tamkuhi

Courtesy: Tamkuhi Raj family, Tamkuhi

Sheesh Mahal surviving from the Fateh era at Tamkuhi

Courtesy: Tamkuhi Raj family, Tamkuhi

A portion of Fateh Sahi's fort surviving at Tamkuhi

Courtesy: Tamkuhi Raj family, Tamkuhi

Another portion of the old fort at Tamkuhi

Courtesy: Tamkuhi Raj family, Anapur House, Allahabad

Weapons used by Fateh Sahi

Courtesy: Tamkuhi Raj family, Anapur House, Allahabad

Large sword used for animal sacrifice in Fateh Sahi's time

Source: 'Golghar', Wikipedia, https://commons.wikimedia.org/wiki/File:Golghar_%E0%A5%AA.jpg

Golghar at Patna (completed 1786), a gigantic granary that survives as a reminder of the famine of the 1770s in Bihar and Bengal

Source: 'Patna College', Wikipedia, https://en.m.wikipedia.org/wiki/Patna_College#/media/File%3AWide_Angle_view_of_Patna_College.jpg

The Dutch Building, constructed in the seventeenth century as their commercial office, now home to Patna College, one of the oldest colleges of the country

Genealogical Table of Huseypur-Hathwa-Tamkuhi Raj Family

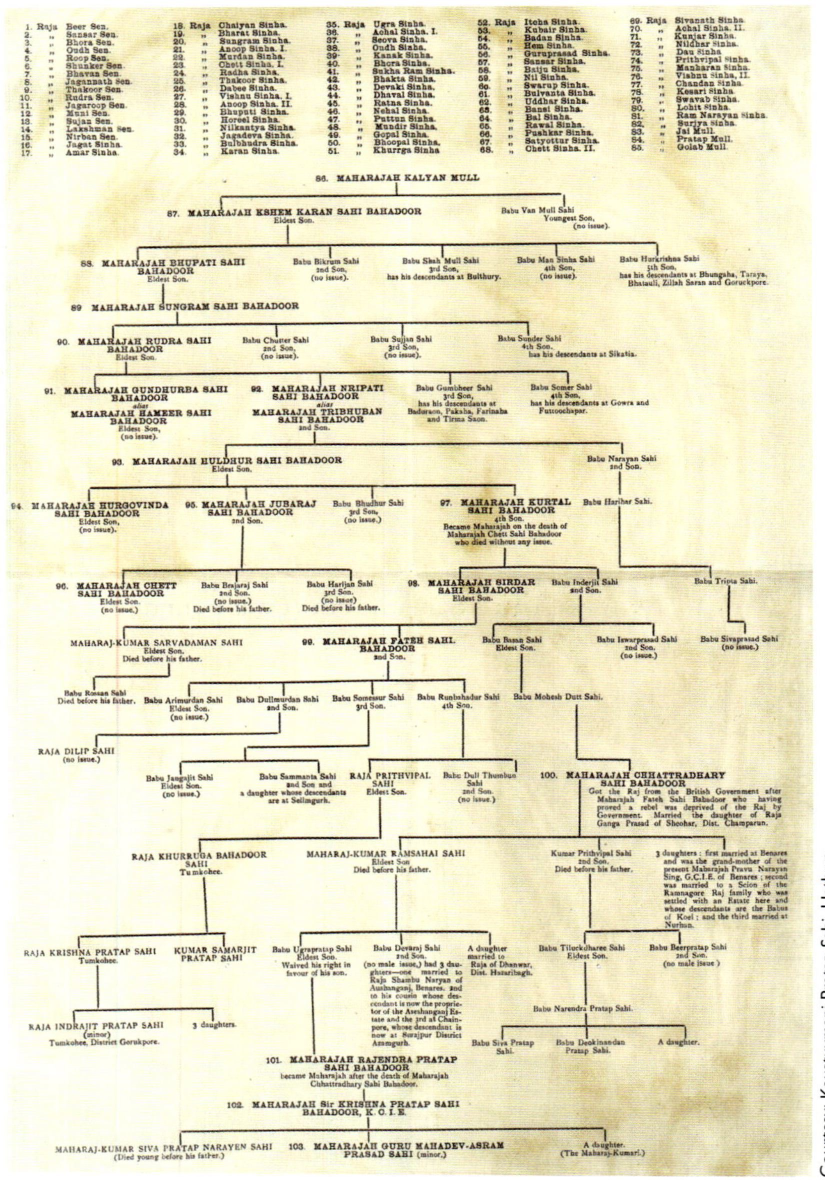

Courtesy: Kaustuvmani Pratap Sahi, Hathwa

Source: D.N. Dutt, *A Brief History of The Hatwa Raj*, 1909, Appendix

long. Within two months, he returned to his jungle hideout and chose to be at war against the British forever. His depredations resumed once again, which were constantly reported by the local revenue officers to their superiors.[82]

Meanwhile, in place of Govind Ram, the Company appointed Syed Jamal Mahomed (popularly known as Mir Jamal) of Bokhara as the superintendent of the Huseypur revenue, and took it under its direct management for a year. Thereafter, the estate was farmed out to Fateh Sahi's cousin Basant Sahi.[83] In order to strengthen his hand, Basant Sahi sought a marriage alliance with the family of Raja Chait Singh of Benares, who also became his financial guarantor for the Company's share of revenue. However, Chait Singh candidly admitted to Golding that he would be always regarded as a 'usurper'. Thus, notwithstanding Golding's attempts to effect a reconciliation with Fateh Sahi, the effort was bound to fail as the rebel was unwilling to give up his claim over Huseypur.[84]

Like Fateh Sahi, the Narrowney Rajput zamindars rebelled in 1773. They held villages in pargana Pachlakh, adjoining Gorakhpur. When the Company agents sought to recover revenue arrears from them, they were attacked by the zamindar, who killed a gomastah and his servants and fled into Awadh territory.[85] In 1774, they marched into Saran with 500 men bearing matchlocks and killed several petty officials while demanding financial contributions from local zamindars. They were in touch with Fateh Sahi and were also linked to the Raja of Majhauli, who allowed them to camp in his Gorakhpur territories. Disaffection escalated in the region when, in 1774, Ajit Mal, the Majhauli Raja who had not, until now, taken up arms against the Company, openly resisted the attempts by the amil of Gorakhpur to collect revenues. Fateh Sahi and the

Perrouna zamindar Gennoo Rai did the same. All three resorted to the familiar tactic of crossing over to Bihar whenever Awadh officials pressed them for revenue.[86]

Meanwhile, the Company authorities tried to negotiate peace with Fateh Sahi, and they chose Basant Sahi, his cousin sympathetic to them, to mediate. As planned, they reached Fateh Sahi's camp; but once they reached there, things changed suddenly. Fateh Sahi was not present there, but the interaction that followed vitiated the situation and the Company men attacked the hosts and probably killed one of the rebel's sons. Except for oral sources, there is no documentary evidence to authenticate the incident.[87] A few suspect the connivance of Basant Sahi in the matter, but the sequence and swiftness of events at the time call for a closer look: Does the absence of Fateh Sahi on the occasion suggest that he was apprehensive of foul play? However, the popular memory is silent on any further role of Basant Sahi in the killing, suggesting that he was kept in complete darkness about the ulterior motives of the English, which Fateh Sahi seems to have anticipated. Thus, they ditched all sides in the matter, and used the meeting to execute their plot. The sequence of developments around the time strengthens the presumption. Whatever the reality, it estranged relations with his cousin and shaped his future course of action.

Raids from the Jungle

Aggrieved and vengeful, Fateh Sahi bided his time in his hideout in the jungle of Charakhia. In the beginning of May 1775, he marched once again into his hereditary domain in Saran. In a pre-dawn swoop, he reached Jadopur (a village 5 miles to the north of present Gopalganj) near Huseypur, 12 miles from Baragaun, with 1000 men on horseback.[88] It was still dark. They galloped to the spot where Mir Jamal and Basant Sahi were camping. The victims had not expected any attack at that hour. Just the previous night, they had received a letter from Fateh Sahi, letting them know that he was within 6 miles of their camp but they need not feel any danger from him, because he was just returning to the Bhagjogni jungles to meet his family. As a result, tired and relaxed, most of the victims and the guards were fast asleep when the raiders stormed the camp, taking them aback.[89]

In a face-to-face fight, Fateh Sahi killed Mir Jamal and his own cousin Basant Sahi. Some attribute the killing of Basant Sahi to a loyal soldier of Fateh Bahadur. It is said that when Fateh Sahi saw his cousin Basant in the camp, he became emotional and withdrew all of a sudden. Seeing him retreat, one of his soldiers screamed, 'Why do you spare him?' Fateh retorted impulsively, 'But who stops you? Is he your son-in-law?' Incensed, the soldier killed Basant Sahi. Another legend has it that when the two brothers met face-to-face, Basant Sahi cried, 'Is the raj so important for you that you are bent upon killing a brother?' Fateh became sentimental for a moment and began to withdraw. He paused momentarily, but impulse overwhelmed him the next moment and he shouted, 'Yes, for freedom! I can sacrifice many brothers.' He then struck his cousin down.[90] Most of those present at the camp were killed; the raiders ransacked the site, looted whatever they could get and escaped before the occupants knew what had actually happened.[91] Later, in his petition to the Company, Syed Golam, the younger brother of Mir Jamal—the victim—approximated the rebels' troops as 'a body of 1000 horsemen and peons', who carried off whatever they found—horses, camels, ready money, effects and part of the government treasure.[92]

It is said that Basant Sahi's severed head was sent to his wife to remind her of the cost of her husband's sympathies with the English. Shocked, she committed sati with her husband's head in her lap, along with thirteen aides whose husbands, too, had died in the attack. Before dying, she forbade her family from ever partaking of any food or water with Fateh Sahi or his relatives.[93]

The relations between the two families did not normalize for decades. The Hathwa Raj family still refrains from taking food or water while travelling through the Tamkuhi area, though today, it is more by way of a traditional ritual than any gesture of enmity, says M.P. Sahi, the head of the Hathwa family. The two families do have amicable relations now, and are proud of the sacrifices of their common ancestors. The fourteen *stupas* containing the ashes of the satis still exist at Huseypur and are annually worshipped by Basant Sahi's Hathwa descendants. With the passage of time, this story has assumed a kind of spiritual sanctity as a symbol of conjugal love, martyrdom for freedom and the good of all. A mela is held there every year when people from all communities and creeds assemble to seek blessings for their well-being, from the souls enshrined in the monument.[94]

This was an unfortunate episode, upsetting for all concerned. On receiving the news, the provincial council in Patna sent two companies of sepoys, under Lieutenant Erskine of the 16th Battalion of Bengal Sepoys, in pursuit of the rebel. But by then, Fateh Sahi had a trained body of horsemen and matchlock men with him, along with a medley of followers including fakirs and bandits. The entire region around the

Bhagjogni jungles were brought under his control. Lieutenant Erskine informed the council in Patna that unless a body of troops was deployed to drive him out of the jungle, Fateh Sahi would prove to be a pest. But there were so many entrances to the jungles that it would take a battalion of sepoys to block them all and capture the rebel. In its letter of 14 June 1775, the council recommended to Hastings that since Fateh Sahi had taken the protection of Nawab Asaf-ud-Daulah of Awadh, it wouldn't be practical to seize him in person. Thus, the council suggested that Hastings write to the Nawab through the offices of Bristow, the British Resident in Awadh, to seek his help in the matter. But despite some initial compliance with this request, nothing seems to have been done to arrest the Raja.[95]

Subsequently, Lieutenant Hardinge was sent to pursue the rebel, with a body of sepoys from the 5th Battalion. He was instructed to cooperate with Syed Muhamad, the faujdar of Gorakhpur, in order to arrest Fateh Sahi but 'on no account to act as the principal [party]'.[96] Hardinge and his detachment spent seven days in the faujdar's camp, expecting to come in close quarters with the rebel. But when Hardinge persuaded the faujdar to march within 150 yards of the rebel's entrenchments, Muhamad's troops stopped suddenly and would not advance a yard forward. At this juncture, the faujdar informed Hardinge that the attack was deferred till the next morning. Afterwards, Hardinge came to know that the faujdar was actually engaged in settling his revenue matters with Fateh Sahi. In disgust, Hardinge returned with his detachment to the Baragaon military station.[97]

However, Hardinge wrote to the chief of the council that Fateh Sahi's position was so strong that, in order to ensure success, he needed a backup with guns. But the season of the year was too far advanced to dispatch military reinforcements to Hardinge's aid. Instead, Hardinge 'was instructed to surprise him [Fateh Sahi], if he possibly could, and to issue a proclamation offering a reward of Rs 10,000 to any person who could either apprehend him or point out the place of his residence.'[98]

In this way, the growing string of his successes in the midst of increasing public disaffection emboldened Fateh Sahi to go for another assault. In early 1777, he attacked the Company's Baragaon military station, which had been especially established to suppress his rebellion. He tore down the officers' quarters and *kachcheri* (office) and placed his own men in charge of the buildings. In a daring feat, he also rebuilt his Huseypur fort and openly reasserted his right of rent collection. A frantic message from the Company's tax farmer at Huseypur reported that the rent collectors of every *tuppeh* (a revenue circle) had appeared before the rebel Raja and they had pledged one-fourth of the produce to him, and were now acting accordingly.[99]

To add to the troubles of the British, the same year (1777), the Raja of Majhauli, Ajit Mal, also refused to pay revenue for the Bihar portion of his holdings. The Company, however, treated his case cautiously, and even refused to assist the Gorakhpur authorities in their efforts to compel the rebels to return to their territory. Ironically, the Patna Council refused to see any similarities in the actions of Fateh Sahi and Ajit Mal; instead, it pronounced Fateh Sahi 'guilty of the atrocious crime of premeditated murder and rebellion' and Ajit Mal guilty of 'no offence', because he had merely 'relinquished his hand in Gorakhpur on being unable to pay the rent charged on them'.[100] Nor were the authorities eager to apprehend Gennoo

Rai, the zamindar of Padrauna, who had absconded into Saran. The authorities feared that an invitation to the Awadh forces to pursue him into the district, or their own attempts to mobilize troops into battle, would disrupt 'peace and obstruct the collections of a large district'.[101]

But, this 'passivity was quickly transformed into accommodation', when a nawabi detachment entered Company territory in pursuit of the Majhauli Raja. In a turnaround of the earlier position, the Patna Council asked Saran officials and local military commanders to assist the nawabi forces, as the Gorakhpur authorities had agreed to join the fight against Fateh Sahi, once the expedition against Ajit Mal was successful.[102] Right from the start, the Patna Council had sought the cooperation of the Awadh authorities in order to counter Fateh Sahi's tactic of retreating to Gorakhpur whenever he was confronted in Saran. They did not have, in fact, any administrative infrastructure to replace the networks of control and support that Sahi had created in Huseypur.

However, this 'alliance of convenience proved to be short-lived'.[103] The joint forces of the Nawab and the Company did not succeed against both the Rajas. Once pressure from the highest authorities continued to be put on the Awadh Nawab, he too complied, yet 'little changed to upset the balance of the seesaw contest. Rather than wage war against Fateh Sahi, the Nawab's representatives in Gorakhpur found it more expedient to compromise with him'.[104] In spite of a secret agreement signed between Warren Hastings and the Nawab in 1779, even Major Alexander Hannay, the revenue farmer of Gorakhpur, was unable or unwilling to displace Fateh Sahi. 'To the Calcutta Council, he attributed his failure to the fact that the rebel evaded the Awadh forces by crossing into the

Huseypur side where he enjoyed the support of the Company's Indian coadjutors.'[105]

Clearly, both the Nawab and the Company recognized the advantages that the rebels had acquired when they sought safety in a foreign territory. But none of them 'was willing to renounce the politically expedient strategy of collecting revenue at the minimal costs possible'.[106] Consequently, neither side committed itself fully to expelling these fugitives from the other side. 'Cooperation was therefore, at best, transient, because just as Company officials weighed questions of joint efforts against the potential damage to their primary goal of extracting revenue, so did the nawabi officials. Therefore, neither side could win against enemies who availed themselves of the escape option.'[107]

In October 1781, when Company forces were withdrawn from Baragaon during the Benares rebellion, Fateh Sahi took advantage of the situation. He arrived with his allies, Ajit Mall and other zamindars from around Gorakhpur, with a body of 12,000 (other sources estimate it at 20,000) at Munjoora, 6 miles from the Company military station at Baragaon, the head cutcherry of the district. A very obstinate engagement with Major Lucas's regiment followed. They fought a pitched battle with Company troops and plundered the military post. This happened in spite of the vigil of two companies of sepoys stationed in the neighbourhood under Lieutenant Erskine to subdue Fateh Sahi. Sahi was, however, defeated, and having lost everything in his camp, he fled to the jungle and his troops dispersed.[108]

But once the Company regiment went back to Dinapore, Fateh Bahadur returned with his party to his camp at Ramnagar, situated on the outskirts of an extensive thicket.[109]

This development alarmed Company authorities, who sought help from the Patna Council as well as the supreme council in Calcutta, which rushed in men and material to deal with the crisis with the utmost urgency. News of the situation was conveyed to the Governor-General as well, and he ordered Samuel Charters, a member of the Patna Council, to proceed to Huseypur with the mandate to gather information and submit a comprehensive report on Fateh Sahi's revolt, its causes, his ability to sustain it and suggestions on how to contain it.[110]

By the time Charters reached Huseypur, Saran Collector Charles Grome had procured accurate information on Sahi's location, and a joint expedition was planned with the faujdar of Gorakhpur, to surprise Sahi at Ramnagar. Mirza Abdool Beg, the vizier's faujdar in Gorakhpur had been persuaded to join the English forces. A part of Major Lucas's regiment was still at Baragaon, which Charters was authorized by the Governor to use in the mission. Charters directed Dirgoo Sing, a veteran known for his bravery in the earlier battle at Manjoorah, to join with his 500 men (*bircundas*). Thus, several parties from different stations moved towards Ramnagar on 17 February 1782. But Sahi was closely tracking the movement of the enemy's forces. He was probably not worried about the Gorakhpur faujdar's forces as he expected his complicity in the matter, but he could not overlook the forces present at Baragaon. Therefore, he left the place the night before the day of the planned attack. He proceeded towards Purrawna to dodge the other parties looking for him.[111]

Having apprehended such an eventuality, the Company authorities had already alerted the two companies stationed at Bagaha (now in West Champaran) under the command of

Lt Lally to track the rebel's movement. The intelligence reported the possibility of his arrival in the evening; so, Lally marched all night through the jungle, led by his guides, until he reached within musket range of Fateh Sahi. But, as soon as the first shot was fired, the fugitive fled into the jungle and marched alone without troops throughout the night across the long stretch of dense forest approaching Baharaich.[112]

A letter of 19 October 1781 from Major General Lucas from Huseypur to the Commander-in-Chief Giles Stibbert has given graphic details of the occurrence—of the British worries, their encounters with Sahi and the overall state of affairs prevailing at the time: Proceeding from Patna, Lucas crossed the Ganga and reached Chapra, where he stayed for a few days to take stock of the situation. Even though he had only recently defeated Fateh Sahi thoroughly enough to disrupt his plans, the rebel was reassembling his militia, reported Lucas's informers, and the fear of him was perceptible in the area. When Lucas marched from Chapra, his troops faced a violent storm. A further journey was also marred by heavy rains, lasting for several days. The downpour flooded the entire tract and rendered all roads utterly inaccessible. Consequently, Lucas was forced to halt at Siwan. It was a large town but 'totally Deserted', states the letter. Its zamindars had openly assisted Fateh Sahi, but were now afraid of the consequences. Lucas sensed the widespread popular support for Sahi among the locals, along with the fear of reprisals if anyone acted against him. Lucas tried to dispel this apprehension and promised them peaceful times ahead. On 14 October, a new zamindar was appointed to take control of the situation there. Finally, Lucas arrived at Baragaon on 15 October. More forces joined him the next day, and at daybreak on 17 October, they proceeded to confront Fateh Sahi, entrenched within a few miles of the jungle's borders.[113]

This was a difficult terrain, consisting of dense forest and water bodies, especially a canal that obstructed easy passage. As Company troops advanced, a volley of gunfire showered over them from behind large trees, bushes and trenches. The Company forces fired in return, and the jungle reverberated with gunshots. Lucas was happy as, at last, he was in close proximity to the fugitive who had frightened the Company for so long. Now, it seemed as though Fateh Sahi would finally fall into their hands. But even as they closed in, the retaliating gunfire suddenly fell silent, and when they reached the rebel's entrenchment, there was nothing left to indicate his presence there, except some dead bodies. Fateh Sahi had escaped once again!

With a bastion about 14 feet high, the entrenchment lay unfinished. It appeared to have been intended for a fort; there were only a few temporary hulls within, and no magazine of any kind. The total strength of Sahi's soldiers at the time appeared to have been between 5000–6000 men; around 200–300 of them had been killed or wounded. On the Company's side, the casualties numbered one sepoy, two subadhars, one havildar naik and two peons killed, sixteen sepoys wounded and about fifty peons lost. Here, Company casualties appear to have been projected in a way to minimize the psychological effect of their total losses. For himself, Lucas was happy that no European had been killed in action, even though balls fell incessantly around them, implying that those who suffered were Indian sepoys. He was also happy that not much property had been seized by the enemy. Nonetheless, there was always the fear of Sahi's return. Therefore, Lucas requested Warren Hastings to maintain sufficient fighting forces at Huseypur to deal with this eventuality.[114]

Panicked and helpless, Saran Collector Grome approached the anti-Fateh clique of the cadet line for help. A long-time associate and well-wisher of the estate, Dhujju Singh, was already in the good books of Company authorities since the killing of Basant Sahi, when Dhujju had been appointed the guardian of Basant's minor son. In this role, he tried to do his best, especially when he realized that the Company was the child's sole protector. During Fateh Sahi's incursions, Dhujju Singh was always cautious, often traversing the surrounding woods with Captain Coxe as his aide, in pursuit of the rebel. This made the Company rely on him. Coxe requested the higher authorities for reinforcements and that Dhujju Singh be recognized for his services. He also recommended that Dhujju Singh be made the diwan of the estate, and some villages be added to his own *taluka*, but this was not approved.[115]

Now, the Company authorities approached him once again to join against the fugitive rebel. Soon, Dhujju Singh assembled over 1000 of his supporters, and together, they fought a fierce battle against Fateh Sahi non-stop for eighteen days, in which Dhujju Singh and his son were severely wounded. Fateh Sahi too suffered huge losses and was again compelled to retreat to the jungle.[116]

Major Lucas commended the bravery and contributions of Dhujju Singh in the campaign in his report to the government. Dhujju Singh was called by the Governor-General to Benares where he was decorated with a khillat of gold cloth and bestowed with many other marks for his distinguished services. He was also granted a monthly pension of Rs 200 and promised other favours.[117] The British, however, did not dare punish any of

Fateh Sahi's supporters, fearing a mass revolt in the area. This gesture reveals the depth of the popularity that the deposed Raja still held among the masses. Even two and a half centuries later, this episode remains engraved in the annals of popular memory. One of their locations is now called Mudkatwa Bagh, and the nearby cemetery with tombs of the Company's soldiers stands as testimony to the bloodshed that went into the making of the British Empire.

For Fateh Sahi, his ability to strike at will testified to the control and support he still enjoyed in Huseypur. His repeated incursions crippled revenue collection, making it virtually impossible for the newly appointed revenue farmers of the zamindari, let alone allowing them to establish alternative networks of control. Prospective revenue farmers, who were tempted to tap the riches of the large estate, were frightened away by the ever-present threat of assassination by Fateh Sahi. Unable to stop his raids, the British had already taken the precautionary measure of relocating the minor heir of the late Basant Sahi to Patna, in 1776.[118]

The Charters report, tuppeh-wise, listed eighty-eight Fateh Sahi supporters from Huseypur and Saran who participated in the rebellion with resources. However, some entries refer to groups and communities, which would multiply the total manifold when the numbers within the group were taken into account. Moreover, this counting relates only to the leaders and not their followers. Of them, Keesdeat Misser (Krishnadut Misir?) and Bawanny Pattock (Bhawani Pathak?) supplied Fateh Sahi with money since the beginning of his revolt, and stood security for amounts of bonds for loans taken by Sahi from Bonyram (Beniram?) and other petty malguzars. Shaikh Mahomed Aly, zamindar of Juvan, obstructed grain supply to the Baragaon military station, and his men fired upon the sepoys retreating there. On the approach of troops under Major Lucas, Aly fled and was never heard of again. Abdulally, zamindar of Decsare, who managed the taluka, was instrumental in opposing the sepoys so as to help Fateh Sahi, and in prevailing upon the ryots to quit the country, in order to starve the English forces of food, revenue and other supplies.[119] This tactic seems to be a common strategy adopted by Sahi throughout his successive wars—a precursor of war tactics used centuries later in modern warfare, including in north-east India during the Second World War.[120]

Sahi's supporters were malguzars, renters and common men, and belonged to different castes and creeds, including Muslims and tribes from far-flung areas; whereas the majority of the Company's supporters were government employees like amils, or those associated with the cadet line of Basant Sahi (such as Dhujju Singh), while the rest were under property litigation, looking for government favours. This suggests Sahi commanded wide support in Saran and beyond. There are indications that his supporters died fighting for him; a few others returned to their villages after their leader's rout; but many never went home, supposedly staying on with their rebel leader. Elaborating upon the major supporters of Fateh Sahi, Charters has given details about some of them, such as Geenoo Roy, zamindar of Padrawna (whose annual jumma amount was Rs 34,000), Ajeet Mull, zamindar of Mangowlah (annual jumma amount of Rs 81,000) and Fateh Sahi himself (with jumma of Rs 31,000), who had zamindari in Joogney Baunk situated contiguous to the above-mentioned zamindars. Ajeet Mull held the zamindari of Chowbarrah of Sarkar Saran, was actively associated with Fateh Sahi before the battle of

Munjoorah, and Sahi had accompanied him to Gorakhpur where he now lived. In order to contain him, Charters directed Grome to attach his zamindari of Chowbarrah, as well as that of Siwan belonging to Shaik Mahomed Ally until further orders. Geenoo Roy was expelled from the zamindari of Padrawna by Lt Colonel Hanny; thereafter, he was instrumental in Sahi's plan of attacking Baragaon.[121]

Joogney Baunk was in Fateh Sahi's possession, and he had lately concluded a settlement on its revenue with Mirza Mogul (son of Mirza Abdullah Beg of Gorakhpur). They met in a conference and Sahi offered him 'considerable' presents. The settlement was concluded in the name of Fateh Sahi's diwan, with a reduction of Rs 7000 in the jumma. Besides, Mirza Mogul stationed Downd Sing, a friend of Fateh Sahi, in command of 5000 horses and two companies of sepoys at Gungooah in Joogney Baunk, serving virtually as a guard and protector of Fateh Sahi.[122]

Thus, even after his exit from his citadel, Fateh Sahi continued to be a force to be reckoned with, with many advantages.

Samuel Charters wrote in his report:

> As it may appear extraordinary to the Honourable Board that this man [Fateh Sahi] should be enabled to raise and subsist such formidable bodies of men, and to support his rebellion so long against the Company's Government, I was particular in my enquiries on the head as time and opportunity would admit of.
>
> It is certain that the Causes of the Subsistence of this Rebellion essentially consist in the aid and protection afforded to Futty Saw by some frontier zamindars in

> Goruckpore, as well as by the inhabitants of Houssipore, which last though not in the degree of the former have greatly contributed towards his subsistence. There is an apparent attachment of the inhabitants to his person and interests, but I am inclined to believe it may arise greatly from a fear of his power, since they have seen him maintain his situation so long, and I have such frequent opportunity of pushing those who may have shewn attachment to Government, which he has always done with rigour, the circumstances of his being a Brahmin may also be a cause which restrains the inhabitants from taking part against him.[123]

The Charters report indicates that Fateh Sahi was a nagging and complex problem for the Company, which is amply corroborated by the numerous letters and official notes exchanged between the Company authorities in Saran and Patna and the office of the Governor-General and upward, between them and the board of directors in London.[124] The Raja might have been a fugitive, but he was deeply rooted in the local society. He had managed to sustain his revolt for this long only because of support from the locals as well as the big zamindars. Charters provided in his report a list of eighty-eight zamindars and others belonging to different classes of society, with brief introductory notes against their names indicating the nature of their association with Fateh Shai. This includes Hindus of both upper and lower castes, tribals, Muslims and homeless people (as there is no mention of any village against their names), coming from different parts of Saran and eastern Uttar Pradesh. Some of them financed Sahi's operations and provided logistics support, and many joined his militia and participated in his raids.[125]

Charters has also listed details of fourteen natives who were attached to the government. Some were agents of the Company (as amils), while others were zamindars and renters displaced from their land rights, or those in need of some kind of administrative favour from the Company government.[126] All this explains Fateh Sahi's widespread popularity and the extent of the influence of his rebellion territorially.

In such a situation, Charters put forward a few measures, short and long term, for consideration by the government: He did not perceive the revolt by Fateh Sahi and collaborators to be occurring in isolation from the widespread popular dissatisfaction against Company rule. He noted that local people were accustomed to the rule of local zamindars and rajas, and they were not in a mood to accept any overarching, external control, such as that of the East India Company. Charters therefore advised Company authorities to work to alleviate common grievances, in order to wean popular support away from Fateh Sahi. Secondly, he suggested the opening of negotiations with the Nawab of Awadh, in order to prevent Sahi from launching any assaults from within the Nawab's territory, where he had been camping for a long time. Thirdly, as a long-term measure, he advised the government to bring a major part of the Bhagjogni jungle under cultivation, so that the rebel lost his sanctuary within it. In all cases, Charters suggested the maintenance of a strong military presence in Huseypur and the adjoining areas.

However, in his advice and action, Charters clearly refrained from the idea of attacking Sahi afresh or arresting him and his supporters, because that would lead to a mass uprising in the area, and would encourage people to desert to him. The report gives an idea of a puzzling situation in which Charters appears to be hesitant and doubly cautious about suggesting or initiating any aggressive and retaliatory measures. He cites the representation of Ramchund Pundit, a Sudder renter, who urged that any arrest at that time would be followed by the ruin of revenue for the year, which Pundit had been obliged to place in the charge of people who had been associated with the recent insurrections of Fateh Sahi, because they were not more inclined to Sahi's cause than the rest of the people. Moreover, he had received similar assistance from them on earlier occasions. As such, the repercussions of arrest or any aggressive measures might extend to almost every man in the district and incite a widespread revolt.[127]

Acting in accordance with his suggestions, the Company requested the Nawab of Awadh to farm out the portion of the Huseypur zamindari falling under his domain in fair and equitable valuation to the farmer with whom the rest of the zamindaris situated in the British territory had been settled. Additionally, Captain Coxe, then commanding a battalion at Bagaha, was directed to hold himself ready to march with his battalion to Gorakhpur to collaborate with nawabi forces to apprehend Fateh Sahi, and also install and stabilize the Huseypur zamindaris, as decided by the Nawab. But nothing appears to have been done in this regard, and at the end of 1784, Fateh Sahi was still at large. However, he could not regain the power to strike at will into the district or mount any major campaign after the October 1781 war, although his periodic incursions continued sporadically even after 1785. According to official records, he raided Champaran for the last time in 1795, when he carried away 1600 heads of cattle from the Gandak riverine.[128]

Charles Cornwallis (1738–1805) was at the helm of affairs around this time. He had been appointed Governor-General and Commander-in-Chief of India in 1786, with instructions to avoid conflict with the Company's neighbours. As such, he immediately initiated certain conciliatory diplomatic moves and was soon known for his reforms. This seems to have reduced the provocation from the Company's side for Fateh Sahi; and, thus, an atmosphere of comparative peace prevailed for a time.[129] This gave the rebel Raja enough time to consolidate his possessions and power at his jungle hideout.

The reverses Fateh Sahi suffered in the 1780s were indicative of the overwhelming military supremacy that the Company had acquired in the region. It also indicated its growing willingness to use military force to defuse threats to its authority. Its success on the battlefield was accompanied by its rising advantages on political and diplomatic fronts Indeed, in the initial years after the grant of Diwani, it was difficult to overcome any adversaries with tenacious strongholds in the interiors. But in the years to come, these adversaries slowly proved to be less formidable, as the Company improved not only its revenue collection mechanisms, but backed it up with considerable firepower. This deprived recalcitrant zamindars of their major source of income—their land.[130]

This change in the balance of power between regional authorities and local controllers is epitomized in the different strategies the Company used to suppress the Huseypur Raja during the 1770s–80s. 'In the earlier decade, although he virtually crippled revenue collection on a number of occasions, his "loyalty" was still sought. In the 1780s no effort was made to reinvite his support.'[131] In contrast, local officials tended to bypass his customary claims by acknowledging Mahesh Dutt, son of his slain cousin, as the proprietor of the estate. Mahesh Dutt personally met Warren Hastings at Benares in 1782 and accompanied him to Patna, when the Governor-General recommended his entitlement to the Patna Council.[132] Although his right was not granted at the Decennial Settlement when the estate was leased out to revenue farmers, the Company officials at least approved of his designation as the 'next heir'. But they seem to have deferred this recognition almost immediately out of fear of inciting Fateh Sahi into taking drastic action against revenue collection and endangering the life of the sole male survivor of the loyal cadet line.[133]

Mahesh Dutt died before his claim was accepted in 1790, and his minor son Chhattaradhary Sahi was made 'proprietor' of the estate.[134] As he was just four years old then, he was placed under the guardianship of a Company-appointed manager until he attained majority in 1802. Symbolizing a new beginning, Chhattaradhary Sahi decided to relocate his headquarters to Hathwa, where he built his palace and fort. Thus, the cadet line ascended to the rajaship, while the senior line emerged as Tamkuhi Raj at Fateh Sahi's jungle retreat in Gorakhpur.[135] Meanwhile, Fateh Sahi's family did not give up its claims to the original estate of Huseypur. His wife continued to press for his title and rights through intercessions and petitioned to appeal against the 'unequal liberality of the English government'[136], suggesting favourable treatment to the Hathwa line and denying it to her family. She begged the Company to consider her plight and that of her daughters 'left destitute of a resource or even the means of a poor subsistence'.[137]

The triumph of British authority in Saran was thus accompanied by the transformation of the rebellious Huseypur zamindari into a loyal Hathwa estate. Hathwa became an important political imperative of the system of colonial rule in the region. Although other zamindars were also incorporated into the system as permanent 'connections', they would not be considered important. 'In the nineteenth and early twentieth centuries, these relationships served as the foundation of the developing pattern of collaboration between the British Raj and the local controllers in the district.'[138]

Political and financial considerations explain why the British were not willing to take action against Fateh Sahi's followers in Huseypur, even after his rout in the 1781 battle and a thorough probe into his rebellion subsequently. The arrest of his Saran supporters, it was feared, 'might extend almost to every man in the District, or that the seizure of particular persons would so much alarm the inhabitants that they would again desert to Futtee Saw'.[139] 'In the Raja of Huseypur, the Company had acquired an adversary who was firmly anchored in local society as a territorial magnate with control over both land and its inhabitants.'[140]

These rebellions showed that the British were yet to build an effective local system of control to supersede the pre-existing zamindari networks. Indeed, the events of the 1780s had undermined the delicate balance that characterized the uneasy standoff between the emerging colonial state and contentious local zamindars. That is why Fateh Sahi and his fellow travellers of Majhauli, Padrawna and Narrowney were able to persist in the face of stronger forces. They remained beyond the reach of regional authorities because their resistance was localized to the areas where they enjoyed strong popular support. Besides, as the Company had already become a formidable regional power by then, such local challenges were no longer serious enough to warrant unlimited resource commitment. 'Nor did the British have the capability to make their full power felt expeditiously and inexpensively at the local level. Thus, the loyalty of rebels had to be frequently reinvented, despite their contravention of authority.'[141]

Increasingly, the financial and administrative burden of containing these rebels was escalating. Revenue collections fell sharply, while the expenses of beating them back rose fast. Military expenditure and disruptions caused by Fateh Sahi adversely affected revenue collections in Huseypur. By 1768, Rs 9,00,000 had been lost on account of his rebellion.[142] In the following years, this amount escalated substantially. The situation demanded decisive action, and the Company doubled the reward for his capture to Rs 20,000.

The uprising of Chait Singh added a new dimension to the rebellions against the Company, because it threatened to link with recurring unrests at local levels and turn them into a major regional conflagration. That contingency loomed large as Chait Singh was related to many Bihar zamindars by kinship and caste ties, and he was actively seeking their help. Within the district, resistance to Company authorities increased as many more landlords refused to obey orders. Some even assaulted the emissaries of the Company. Every day, the Saran Collector encountered 'fresh instances of a determined disposition in the inhabitants . . . to throw off all subjection of my authority.'[143]

This discontent spread beyond Saran and extended into Bengal. Nearby, the Raja of Betia in the east, the zamindars of Chainpur and Bagaura in the south and Tikari and others south of the Ganga, did have clan connections with the Huseypur family. A branch of the Huseypur family, the descendants of Maharaja Kalyan Mull and his son Maharaja Kshem Karan Sahi had migrated to south Bihar, in the course of the recurring political turmoil in their native place. They settled at Sakho Bansdih in Kharagdiha in the present Giridih district, where they later acquired Gadi Ledo. This was a feudal tenure position for quasi-military services introduced under the Mughals. Its holders were responsible for maintaining law and order in their territories and also for collecting revenue in some cases. Their only obligation was to acknowledge the supremacy of the raja of their region, as of Kharagpur and Kharagdiha. In the course of time, they became hereditary and almost autonomous. The arrangement existed primarily east of Hazaribagh, and they came into prominence in the context of countering Maratha invasions. Finally, they established themselves around Hazaribagh and Deoghar, as Ghatwal, Gadi and Mulrayati.[144] Subsequently, they became independent zamindars who wielded considerable power in their territories and were treated as such when the Company undertook to parcel out land in the settlements of 1793.[145] There is all likelihood of their having lent support to Fateh Sahi.

A little further to the east, Rani Sarveshwari Devi of Sultanabad (Maheshpur Raj) in Santal Parganas rose in revolt, in alliance with some hill chiefs during 1781–82. The Company government dispossessed her of zamindari and sent her out of Sultanabad, in May 1783. A humiliating pension of Rs 100 (later reduced to Rs 50) per mensem was granted and she spent her last days in Bhagalpur jail where she died on 6 May 1807.[146] This episode must have had angered many in the native aristocracy of the region.

There were several others in Bengal, with their roots in Awadh and Bihar, likely to have anti-British feelings and sympathies for Fateh Sahi. The founder of the Betia Raj was a general of Akbar and a Mohiyal Brahmin from Punjab. People migrated over time in search of gains and livelihood. During the socio-political instability in Mithila, many migrated to Bengal, moving to the region of the Santals, to Pakur, Malda, Murshidabad and Midnapur. Some established major zamindaris there.

Of them, the Lalgola zamindars of the present Murshidabad district of West Bengal seem to have taken the Fateh saga to Bengal. Originally migrants from Ghazipur, they founded a prominent zamindari at Lalgola and, later, served as a link between the earliest onslaughts of Fateh Sahi against the East India Company and the emergence of nationalism heralded by Bankim Chandra in the country. The story began at Berhampur, the district headquarters of Murshidabad, where Bankim Chandra was posted as a deputy magistrate. On 15 December 1873, he was crossing the Barrack Square Ground in his palanquin as usual, when suddenly Lt Colonel Duffin stopped him from following that route. When Bankim protested, Duffin forced him to alight and manhandled him.[147] Furious at the insult, Bankim filed a criminal case against the colonel, and named the Lalgola zamindar Jogindra Narain Roy as a witness. Local lawyers rallied behind Bankim and refused to appear for Duffin. Apprehending the backlash, authorities persuaded Bankim to withdraw the case, which he did grudgingly, but only on the condition that Duffin apologized to him in the open court. Duffin did so, though reluctantly.[148] This did not go down well with the British militia stationed at Berhampore Cantonment. Sensing the situation, Bankim went on long leave and, fearing a physical assault on him, the Lalgola zamindar took him away to his palace for safety. This was among the early instances of the Indian zamindars supporting the anti-British camp in the nineteenth century, and an extension of the legacy of Fateh Sahi.

It was during his stay here that Bankim conceived the story of his novel *Anandamath* and began working on it. It is believed that he heard from the Lalgola zamindar the story of Fateh Sahi's revolt occurring nearly a century ago in Bihar, and adapted it as the broader theme for his novel, embellishing it with details of the ambience, people and artefacts of the Lalgola Rajbari.[149]

More recently, Kishan Chand Bhakat of Lalgola has closely examined the Lalgola-*Anandamath* connection and has authenticated its truth. The description of the palace, temples, deities, *poojari*, surrounding places and some landmarks in the novel closely resemble the current ruins at Lalgola.[150] The two sets of the images of goddess Kali at its Rajbari temple particularly merit attention: in the first, Kali appears in a pitiable condition—naked, chained and sunken in gloom—presumably suggesting the miserable condition of the country as depicted in the novel; and, in the second, as Jagatdhatri, the protector of the world—triumphant and blissful, shining in the radiance of the rising sun—probably a reflection of Bankim's aspirations to see the country liberated and prosper in a similar ambience, as shown in the novel. Bhakat identifies many characters of the novel with those then living at the Lalgola Palace.[151] Pradip Bhattacharya, a former district magistrate and, later, commissioner of Murshidabad, has probed the issue further. He claims to have visited the Lalgola Rajbari and the surroundings, where he found many pieces of evidence corroborating the *Anandamath*-Lalgola link.[152]

At the Kali temple, Bankim is said to have seen an old *tantrik* chanting a mantra before Kali, whose words appear to have lent expression to Bankim's *Vande Mataram*. Bhakat believes this happened on the full moon night of Maagh (31 January–1 February) 1874. Bankim refers repeatedly to this as 'Maghi Purnima', when the death anniversary of zamindar

Rao Ramshankar Roy was observed at the Lalgola palace where sadhus assembled from as far as Benares.[153] At the Raghunath temple, Pradip Bhattacharya found piles of *Shivalingas* and *Saalgraams* allegedly kept there since the Sanyasi Rebellion of 1772–73.[154] This suggests that the idea of nationalism was quietly incubating at the Lalgola Rajbari, and the sanyasis were conspiring against the British around it.

The ruins of the ancient Vihara nearby, once the abode of Buddhist goddess Kalkali, and the adjoining rivulet named Kalkali after her, are both mentioned in the novel. Its white-haired, white-robed ascetic appears to be the royal priest Kali Brahma Bhattacharya. It is said that he used to meet groups of Bir and Shri sects of warrior tantriks at the confluence of the Kalkali-Padma-Bhairav rivers and taught them how to fight with the British. A tunnel from the Kali temple goes straight to the Kalkali river, whose banks in the past were dotted with temples that sheltered these tantriks.[155]

What brings us still closer to the Fateh story is the identification by Bhakat of village 'Padachinnha' in the novel, with Diwan Sarai and the burning *ghat* at Basumati in Nashipur, which were frequented by Bhojpuri-speaking tantriks, who received spiritual initiation from Kali Brahma. Figuring in the novel as plunderers and sepoys, they were initially brought by Lalgola zamindars to serve as soldiers and domestic caretakers and help. Bhakat himself claims to have descended from them.[156] They used surnames like Mishra, Pandey and Rai, which were common among Sahi's clansmen, and Bhojpuri was the mother tongue of his region. Despite the time-gap between Fateh Sahi and the Lalgola episode, this finding reinforces Sahi's influence on *Anandamath*, especially when matched with his jungle retreat, his religiosity, devotion to Kali and association with the sanyasis.

Had the predecessors of these sanyasis joined Fateh's army, or did they come to Lalgola after his army was disbanded?[157]

Rakesh Roy of the Singhabad (Tilasan) estate family claims that his forefathers were among the earliest immigrants from Ghazipur in the area, who came in direct contact with the sanyasis and witnessed their anti-British activities in the surrounding forest—as depicted in *Anandamath*.[158]

The same happened with the zamindars of Mahisadal in the East Midnapur district. They claim to have migrated from a place near Allahabad in the sixteenth or seventeenth centuries, and are now connected with the Lalgola family by marriage.[159] Their palace museum abounds in war weapons and hunting trophies, indicative of their family tradition as warriors.[160] Their sympathy and support for a rebel like Fateh Sahi and the uprisings in Bihar and Awadh could have been a natural response.[161] Likewise, the zamindars of Chanchal and the babus of Nainjore, protagonists of the famed eponymous story by Rabindranath Tagore,[162] who had migrated from Bihar and Awadh, are likely to have similar empathies for uprisings in the western provinces.

No wonder that, in view of such widespread connections and concealed empathy for Fateh Sahi, the provincial council in Patna was now desperate to capture him.

The heavy reward on the head of Fateh Sahi had failed to bring him to book. From time to time, the Company forces combed the countryside for him, but he remained at large. His incursions upset the British thoroughly and compelled them to counter his menace with all the resources at their disposal. Hectic correspondence among the Company officials in this connection speaks volumes about their frustrations. Eventually, the Company began stooping to nasty tricks. When they got wind of Fateh Sahi's daughter's impending marriage, they seized the chance to trap him. Since Sahi was supposed to be present at his fort on the day of the marriage, it was surrounded by Company forces and intelligence, waiting for the kill. But Fateh Sahi slipped past their guard, it is said, disguised as a pandit in traditional wooden sandals, who walked past the waiting battery of soldiers. He had escaped the Company—yet again.[163]

5

The Parting of the Siblings

As time passed, the British seemed to come to terms with the situation on the ground. Fateh Sahi also reduced his incursions. There seems to have been little provocation from the Company officials under Cornwallis's regime. The Governor-General had been directed by the home government to avoid confrontation with neighbouring native rulers and concentrate instead on the consolidation of possessions already acquired. Under the circumstances, Fateh Sahi now had the time to consolidate his own position and property. He had, under his control, a portion of the Huseypur Raj, to which he was adding more from the territory of Awadh. By 1808, he had 100 villages under his control.[1] This phase of comparative peace offered the East India Company immense opportunity to strengthen their control over the cadet line of Basant Sahi and the remainder of their estate. After the death of Basant Sahi, the estate remained under the direct management of the East India Company for some time. Dhujju Singh acted as the guardian of the minor son and heir of the deceased Basant Sahi, who lived with Dhujju's family at Bhurtawlee, a village close to Huseypur. This was the perfect time for the Company to sneak into the internal management of the estate and control its affairs at different levels.

Politically, this was a period of hectic transition, marked by rivalry among political stakeholders and partners of the declining Mughal Empire. Entering the fray was as much an opportunity as a hazard for the British. Awadh was a powerful deterrent, but so was the fear of attacks of invaders from the north-west like Ahmad Shah Abdali, the Rohillas and the Satnamis. The sanyasis and Banjaras were another menace. Above all, there was the terror of the Marathas, who had ruthlessly invaded eastern India in the early 1760s. They posed a constant danger to the Company's burgeoning authority. The last vestiges of Mughal rule over local society were fading fast and various types of administrative controls came into operation. Besides the indigenous rajas like those of Huseypur, the provincial Mughal officers, who had gradually become hereditary, acted as independent rulers; some Afghan chiefs behaved similarly in their territorial pockets, and there were other freebooters who tried to exploit the situation.

In south India, the strong opposition by Hyder Ali, Tipu Sultan, the Nizam of Hyderabad and the Marathas was a nagging problem. Their individual or joint opposition apart, their alliance with the French and the use of European mercenaries in their wars were a real threat for the Company. In the northern plains, mercenaries like Walter Reinhardt Sombre and his wife Begum Samru, and George Thomas were regular operators. Sombre had fought against the British on behalf of Mir Kasim and Thomas was Sombre's collaborator. Both of them had lent their services to the Marathas, whose Chitpawan connection (through the Peshwas) linked many indigenous rulers of Awadh and Bihar, like Benares, Huseypur and Tikari, in the diplomatic loop of central and north India.[2]

British Stake in Hathwa

The Company had gradually gained supremacy over other non-British Europeans, but it is difficult to assume that the latter's influence had diminished in eastern India, which they had entered very early. Even if they were no longer politically assertive in the region, their presence at the commercial and social levels cannot be overlooked. Many of them had also entered the East India Company services during the course of time. George François Grand and Catherine Grand were both of non-British origins. Grand was an employee of the East India Company, and Catherine, his wife, who shifted to Europe after their break-up and joined the anti-British group there. Others operated as traders or engaged in plantation in the region, and yet others worked as Christian missionaries.[3] Many served native rulers as doctors, engineers, technical advisers, military aides, suppliers of machines, gadgets and the like.[4]

Fateh Sahi's successors leased out a sizeable farmland for plantation to a Dutchman, which is now a state farm at Sipah in the Gopalganj District of Bihar.[5] Can the genesis of this deal and similar interactions be traced to their friendly relations since earlier times? The history of these non-British Europeans in the region is little explored. Generally speaking, they operated neutrally and did not exhibit any apparent animosity towards the English; many of them settled in the region and assimilated themselves with local society. Some of the currently existing Christian families claim their descent from them. In fact, the intra-national hostility among the Europeans was confined mostly to diplomatic levels, rather than at levels of social interaction; but quite often, European mercenaries joined the ranks of the adversaries of the Company.

The British administrators were aware of this. Therefore, to counter a persistent danger from both Indian rulers as well as the Europeans, they required resources in terms of money, men and war supplies. Additionally, they needed to strategically ally with local rulers. This could be done only by diplomacy and acquisition of more areas under their control and access to the resources of other powers, together with an increase in their own military might. They had already gained control over a greater part of eastern India in and around Bengal; now, in the Gangetic heartland, their operations in Benares, Awadh and Saran were destined to be their top priority. But beyond Benares and Awadh, Fateh Sahi was a vexing hurdle. This region was one of the most fertile tracts of the Indian subcontinent, full of the natural resources in demand at the time (such as saltpetre, opium and indigo) and situated far away from southern enemies. South of the Ganga, prospects of some basic minerals could have been attracting many. Coal, for instance, was first mined in 1774 when John Sumner and Suetonius Grant Heatly of the East India Company commenced its commercial exploitation in the Raniganj coalfield along the western bank of the Damodar River. Soon coal became one of the most sought-after resources for the Company.[6]

The Company was increasingly becoming aware of the great prospects of natural resources in India and was curious about everything it came across. Not long after, Francis Buchanan (1762–1829) came to India and joined the East India Company as a doctor in 1794. From 1803 to 1804, he was physician to Governor-General Wellesley in Calcutta, before he developed an interest in India's geography and society. He travelled to many parts of south and eastern India and presented a comprehensive account of his surveys in his journal. The East India Company showed considerable interest in his expeditions and supported them officially. After the defeat of Tipu Sultan and the fall of Mysore in 1799, Buchanan was asked to survey south India, resulting in his *Journey from Madras through the Countries of Mysore, Canara and Malabar* (1807).[7] Between 1807 and 1814, he made a comprehensive survey of the areas falling within the jurisdiction of post-Buxar Bengal, including Bhagalpur, Patna, Shahabad, Palamu and Gorakhpur. As mandated, he reported on topography, history, antiquity, society, religion, natural products, occupation, landed property, fine arts, crafts and trade and commerce.[8] His findings were reported in a series of volumes, which have been recently reissued in new editions. He also studied the flora and fauna of the region up to Nepal, and collected their watercolours, painted probably by Indian artists, which are now in the library of the Linnean Society of London.[9] He visited Gorakhpur briefly.[10]

This brief profile and the mandate for his survey amply demonstrate the Company's keen interest in the resources of the region and, understandably, the appreciation of their value for trade and industry at home and abroad. Almost a contemporary of Fateh Sahi, Buchanan visited areas surrounding his territory towards the end of his operations. Even if there is no evidence of Buchanan's interaction with the Huseypur estate until now, his presence in the neighbouring districts (Patna, Shahabad, Gorakhpur, Champaran and Nepal) is significant. His exploratory expeditions so close to Huseypur and Tamkuhi suggest the Company's active interest in the area in view of tax returns, its strategic location and natural resources, forest products in particular, especially given its increasing hold on its cadet line. The control over the area was crucial, as despite his exit to the jungle, Fateh Sahi was a constant menace along with the raids of the Marathas and others from the west.

Claims for Legitimacy

The Company was thus fast learning that war alone was not the most effective weapon against an enemy like Fateh Sahi, with long grounding in the local soil. An opportunity to utilize other methods soon appeared on their horizon. As soon as the minor son of Basant Sahi, Mahesh Dutt, achieved his majority, he applied for a sanad for the zamindari of Huseypur, which the committee of revenue forwarded to the higher authorities. In reply, the government wrote to them on 2 November 1784, saying that if it was thought advisable to invest the petitioner with the zamindari of Huseypur, it should be done on the express conditions of his effectively suppressing the depredations of Fateh Sahi, and if possible, delivering him in person to the government within a year. The fulfilment of these conditions would be evaluated by an official committee at the end of the ongoing Bihar year; and in case the petitioner failed to fulfil these conditions and his response was unsatisfactory, he would immediately lose every claim on the estate in question.[11] It was a clever move by the Company, but equally partisan and excessive—intended to keep Hathwa on their side, but only on its own terms.

But just as the Company was about to formally declare Mahesh Dutt as the Raja of Huseypur, he passed away in 1785. Astrologers had predicted he would live only for twenty-two years, hence his guardian Dhujju Singh had hastened to marry him off at an early age to the daughter of the Chainpur Babu, so that he might have a child to continue the lineage. But the marriage was not consummated, as the bride's family refused to immediately send her to her in-laws on account of some family tradition. Worried, Dhujju Singh terminated the marriage, only to have Mahesh Dutt married off for a second time to a country girl, who gave birth to a child about two months after Mahesh Dutt's demise.

This child was the future Maharaja Chhattaradhary Sahi (1785–1858). The government of Lord Cornwallis conferred on him the rajaship of the confiscated estate of Huseypur on 21 January 1791. But as he was then only five years of age, the estate came under the protection of the Court of Wards, and Dhujju Singh continued to be his guardian. In 1802, the minor attained majority and formally took actual charge of his zamindari. Now he shifted from Bhurthawlee, where he and his late father had lived for a long time under Dhujju Singh's protection, and founded his new capital at Hathwa, where he built his palace and a fort surrounded by moats.[12] As a gesture of gratitude, he granted to Dhujju Singh a village as jagir, which was named Hathwa Buzurg (meaning guardian of Hathwa), named after his own capital Hathwa. However, the title of Maharaja Bahadur to the Raja was not conferred until 1837. It was thought that there could not be two Maharajas of Huseypur as long as Fateh Sahi was alive. So, when Fateh Sahi vanished from the scene and was not heard of for several years, the government of Lord Auckland (viceroy between 1836 and 1842), on 27 February 1837, conferred the title of Maharaja Bahadur on the Hathwa Raja, with the usual khillat.[13] On the occasion, the Raja paid a *peshkash* of Rs 50,000, which was placed at the disposal of the General Committee of Public Instruction to promote education.[14]

The Rise of Hathwa

This was an effort to push the last vestiges of the Huseypur Raj into oblivion, and sneak into the royal household of the cadet line. The ground was under preparation for long but now it was readied to force the two siblings apart and create their separate identities—Hathwa and Tamkuhi. Thus, the seat of power now shifted from Huseypur to these two new capitals. Yet, historically, Huseypur still commanded a position of awe in popular memory. It had traditionally been at odds with some of its neighbours, but its rajas had succeeded in subduing them. They suppressed Majhauli when it asserted its power, and checked the persistent inroads of the Afghan chief Kabul Muhammad of Burharia. But Huseypur was in perpetual conflict with the Betia Raj on the issue of the demarcation of boundaries between the two estates. Countless were killed on both sides. This happened principally because of frequent changes in the course of River Gandak and its minor channels, which upset the territorial boundaries of the two estates.[15]

Since Fateh Sahi had been dislodged from Huseypur and was now operating from his far-flung jungle refuge, the clout of the Huseypur Raj was significantly compromised for adversaries—actual or potential. The new sibling estates were yet to regain the same status once enjoyed by their parent state of Huseypur. With a minor heir put under the Court of Wards, Hathwa was all the more vulnerable to adversaries and new challenges. The first spark of an impending explosion came in 1842, when Maharaja Chhattaradhary Sahi petitioned against the government's plans to institute survey operations in Saran, saying that it was against the principle of the Permanent Settlement. His real concern was the disputes it would foment between the estate and the vested interests who had secured privileges from the Huseypur line. The petition was, however, dismissed. [16]

The Raja's apprehensions proved true. In early 1844, petitions were submitted to the government by persons claiming themselves to be *britdars* (rent-free grantees) of villages that included one-third of pargana Kalyanpur Kuari. They claimed they had acquired these rights before and during the tenure of Raja Fateh Sahi. In fact, some of these privileges were created by the rebel Raja to maintain his supporters in the protracted struggle against the Company. But the petitions were rejected, provoking anger among their authors. On 2 April 1844, when they assembled before the Deputy Collector to plead their case, they were assaulted by the local police and arrested. More protests followed. Curiously, the official inquiry revealed subsequently 'that this attack was instituted by the police in collusion with the Hathwa retainers to intimidate the petitioners'.[17]

On 21 June, Bujhawan Misir of Bhore appeared with a band of 500 people, while another britdar, Ishri Prasad, claimed fifty-two villages in Bhore. They ignited a 'flame' that soon spread over the whole pargana; and at its height, the protest involved as many as twenty 'ring leaders', supported by about 6000 men armed with swords, matchlocks and clubs. The britdars seem to have been supported by the family and supporters of the disinherited Huseypur line, now organized around Fateh Sahi's grandson, the britdars of Gorakhpur and many tenants of villages held by the Betia Raja.[18] Bujhawan

Mishir became very powerful with the help of turbulent local Rajputs and other vested interests. He claimed the whole territory on the other side of the Jharahi River as his brit, donated by the Huseypur Raja, which comprised even the fort of Huseypur. Each time the Hathwa troops were sent to dispossess him, they were beaten back. Bujhawan held the area in such terror for some time that no one from the Hathwa side dared cross the river. At last, the Maharaja had to seek the help of the Company government, which marched its forces into the area. Bujhawan was confronted, captured, tried and imprisoned for ten years. In this way, the country controlled by him was reclaimed and order restored.[19]

Around this time, all those who had suffered because of the wars and incursions of Fateh Sahi and who were loyal to the junior line rushed to the Company government for help. The sons of Dhujju Singh (Lall Singh, Shah Singh and Gauree Singh) were the most important of them. Dhujju Singh had already been granted a pension of Rs 200 per month after the decisive battle against Fateh Sahi. When Dhujju Singh passed away, his sons were apprehensive that the pension and other facilities given to the family might be seized. Therefore, they petitioned the government to not only continue and extend its existing support, but also to increase its volume and expand it to help more of the loyalists who had fought against Fateh Sahi. The sons narrated their present abysmal economic condition and the inability of the cadet line to maintain them, hence the urgency for the Company's help. This, they emphasized, was necessary in view of their increasing liabilities, arising out of their responsibilities. The need to look after their own families apart, now they had the liabilities of looking after the war widows and orphans whose guardians had lost their lives or had been maimed in battles against Fateh Sahi. They reiterated their loyalty to the cadet line and the Company, and reminded them of the sacrifices and contributions of their father, the family and their private militia and followers.[20] For the Company government, this gave them an opportunity to oblige the Raja and many others who would remain loyal in return for the generosity and benevolence of the Company government.

This and other contingencies helped the Company gain the trust of the cadet line of Hathwa, participate in its internal matters and influence their policy. Hathwa needed help against adversaries in order to stabilize their administration. But, for the Company, it was a great opportunity to use Hathwa's resources in order to operate unhindered in the area. Sadly, the Hathwa family was also periodically disturbed by the glitches in succession—premature death of the Raja and the succession of a minor heir, leading to imposition of the Court of Wards. This allowed the British to control the administration of the estate almost directly. Under this arrangement, its important functionaries, such as the diwan and the manager were nominated by Company authorities to whom they, naturally, owed allegiance. An English Resident was also deputed at the capital (Hathwa), to liaise between the Raja and the British-Indian government.[21]

Thus, the Court of Wards was used as an effective instrument of the Company's control over the estate in the garb of help. Until then, the Huseypur Raj had worked with an indigenous administrative set-up evolved over centuries.[22] It was manned by locals who wielded power in the areas of their operations, served as pillars of strength for the Raja and acted as deterrents for intruders and enemies. Apart from personal experience and efficiency, and a deep understanding of their territory, they derived power from their kin and clan connections. Moreover, they communicated in the local language and understood the various nuances of the ryots' responses.

Now, the British gradually increased their own presence in the estate—directly as well indirectly. The English army was stationed at Baragaon ever since the first clash with Fateh Sahi at Huseypur; and despite his opposition, revenue farmers were appointed by the Company in the estate. In view of its larger plans, the Company posted its agents and troops in the neighbouring Awadh territory, as at Gorakhpur and Benares, and at several places along rivers Saryug-Ghaghra and Gandak, and bordering Bagaha and Betia in the east. With the introduction of the Permanent Settlement of land revenue under Cornwallis, the Company found a new group of supporters in the new zamindars. This increased the presence of the English and their agents in the region. The English traders fast gained supremacy in the district, and an increasing number of British planters began to engage in the cultivation of opium and indigo in north Bihar and eastern UP. All of them acted as British loyalists and helped consolidate the position of the new regime. Recently, Amitav Ghosh tried to portray the life of that time in the region in his *Sea of Poppies* (2008).[23]

With their strengthened position in the region, the British were now free to focus on Hathwa. During the Court of Wards tenure of 1871-1874, they started replacing the indigenous lineage of internal functionaries of the estate with outsiders who could speak English and would be loyal to the Company as their patron. One of the first casualties was Chaudhur Lal, the grand uncle of Rajendra Prasad, the first President of independent India, and a local. He was removed from the post of diwan, where he had served for over a quarter of a century.[24]

In ensuing years, they appointed Europeans and Bengalis to manage the Hathwa Raj. The trend began with the Dutt family. Originally, the Dutts belonged to Shaoli village in the Chinsura District of Bengal, now in Bangladesh. The earliest of them, Bhubaneshwar Dutt, was appointed superintendent of the Court of Wards (1872) and diwan and manager in 1874. His nephew, Devendra Nath Dutt, was first appointed private secretary to the Maharaja (1885), and diwan and joint manager in 1891; he was succeeded by his son Brajendra Nath Dutt as diwan in 1915.[25] Although these outsiders lacked local anchorage, they enjoyed a close working relationship with the Hathwa family. By the 1890s, Bengalis occupied all major positions below that of the estate manager, A.M. Markham. Under the Dutt family, the 'estate's management often appeared to be largely a Bengali enterprise'.[26] Many of the Hathwa maharajas spoke Bengali. The Dutts forged such a close bond with them that Maharaja Krishna Pratap Sahi regarded Bhubaneshwar Dutt as his 'father'.[27] This augured well for the English, because these appointees owed allegiance to the British; they could speak English, and they did not have any local social roots to be strong enough to ever defy their British patrons. Some of the descendants of the Dutt family still live in Patna and fondly remember the happy Hathwa days and royal patronage.[28]

With the ever-growing regional threats, Hathwa constantly needed additional help, which was provided by the Company. This facilitated a closer relationship between the two that proved to be both long and cordial. Under the circumstances, each side took advantage of the other. Once stabilized and safeguarded by the Company, the Hathwa rajas flourished; and some of them made significant contributions to internal administration as well as public welfare, especially in the field of education, healthcare and public works.

Chhattaradhary Sahi was a patron of Sanskrit and learning. He hosted in his durbar learned scholars from Mithila, Benares and elsewhere in the country, including Ram Niranjan Svami, a great savant of the time. The Raja also opened a Sanskrit school under the Svami, wherein about 1000 students from all parts of India were maintained at royal expense. Chhattaradhary Sahi was an able administrator. On his death on 16 March 1858, he left behind about Rs 40 lakh in his treasury.[29]

The Company, in the meanwhile, had a field day with a resourceful ally that also acted as a buffer against potential adversaries. With the Company's patronage, Hathwa was now upscaled on the imperial protocols and lavished with decorations and honorifics of the Empire (like Sir and the Kaiser-i-Hind Gold Medal).

Rajendra Pratap Sahi died in 1871, leaving behind a minor son of fifteen, the late Krishna Pratap Sahi; and the Court of Wards took over the administration of Hathwa yet again. Such eventualities often compelled the minor heirs of the Hathwa Raj to go under the Court of Wards and guardianship of others, even those from outside their blood relations, like Dhujju Singh. This seems to have forced the Hathwa line to depend increasingly on the British government, a predicament which the latter took full advantage of. In the following years, they used the resources of Hathwa lavishly, including its army, for suppressing revolts and consolidating their own authority. Moreover, Hathwa acted as a buffer state against several adversaries. In return, they showered successive rajas with pompous honorifics and regularly invited them to colonial celebrations like imperial durbars and other public events.[30] Thus, Fateh Bahadur and his successors were left to gradually fade from popular memory.

On their part, the Hathwa rajas took advantage of the situation: their growing prominence in official protocols added to their status, and military security, privileges and immunities provided by the British allowed them to act freely in their territory, which had salutary outcomes—the story of their running a free Sanskrit School on state expenses and their huge donations in times of famines, epidemics and the like have already been discussed. In fact, many later Hathwa kings did more for the welfare of the people than the British ever did in Bihar. They also tried to protect and promote cultural heritage. With the decline of the Mughals, artistes under their patronage moved eastward from Delhi and Agra to provincial towns like Lucknow and Patna; the Hathwa rajas welcomed some of them. It is said that a troupe of courtesans travelled from Delhi to Lucknow and finally arrived at the Hathwa court. They pioneered the Bhojpuri folk theatre—*Nautanki*. Two of them, Sundari Bai and Duniya Bai, later earned great fame as Nautanki artists, and inspired others to write plays in Bhojpuri.[31] The Hathwa rulers promoted education, launched projects of public utility such as hospitals, wells and tanks, embankments along water bodies and public orchards. They also undertook various measures, including financial donations to deal with difficult times, such as famines.[32]

The regimes of Rajendra Pratap Sahi and Krishna Pratap Sahi were marked by two major famines in Bihar, when the Hathwa Raj spent more than Rs 10 lakh to relieve the distress of its tenants. Later, the Maharani of Hathwa contributed

Rs 1 lakh to the Famine Fund raised by Lord Curzon, for the relief of the distressed people in the Central Provinces and Rajputana. Another Rs 1 lakh was donated to the Victoria Memorial Fund, Rs 50,000 to the Lady Dufferin Zenana Hospital, Rs 30,000 to the Soldiers' and Sailors' Families Association Fund and Rs 25,000 to the Chapra Charitable Hospital, besides numerous minor contributions. In recognition of her generous charity and kindly feelings towards her tenants, the Queen Empress of Great Britain conferred on the Hathwa Maharani the Kaiser-i-Hind Gold Medal. It was invested by Sir John Woodburn, the Lieutenant-Governor of Bengal, at a grand durbar at Hathwa in January 1902.[33]

This could have been a consolation for the Hathwa family and the people of Bihar to an extent; but as it happened in most other cases of charities and munificence by other notables, the British channelled them in a way as to project their own image. Many such contributions from the notables of Bihar, the United Provinces and other provinces went into the projects of public welfare launched by the Central or Provincial British-Indian governments in bad times or wars, depriving the original donors of any credit or recognition. This happened in the case of education and health, to which the Hathwa Raj, along with Benares, Darbhanga, Tamkuhi, Tikari and many others from the region made significant contributions, as to the Banaras Hindu University (BHU) and the universities of Calcutta, Patna and others.

Public welfare was not a priority for the British; whatever they did was done under compulsion or by outside agencies. For example, the contribution by an American millionaire led to the establishment of the famous Imperial Institute of Agricultural Research at Pusa in 1905, and two decades later, the Rockefeller Foundation initiated landmark measures to help India gain self-reliance in health management.[34]

Thus, taking advantage of the situation articulated with astute diplomacy, the British finally succeeded in breaking apart the centuries-old Huseypur Raj, forcing its siblings—the lines of cousin brothers—to part forever.

6

The Royal Retreat

Sporadic incursions continued after 1790, though Fateh Sahi did not launch any major attack on his erstwhile territory. This may be largely attributed to decreased British interference consequent upon Lord Cornwallis's conciliatory policy. After 1786, Cornwallis launched projects aimed at consolidating the Company's rule by creating local support and endeavouring to present it as a benevolent regime. The introduction of the Permanent Land Revenue Settlement and the Cornwallis Code focused on administrative reform and the establishment of the Asiatic Society of Bengal were efforts in this direction.[1] Since his regime avoided confrontation with neighbours, it preferred to nurture its partner Hathwa, which was now owner of the huge Huseypur property, instead of fighting with the fugitive Fateh Sahi, who was in no mood to surrender.

Farewell to Arms

Fateh Sahi's last raid was in Champaran in 1795, when he herded hundreds of cattle to his hideout, from their grazing grounds along the Gandak River. He is also believed to have held periodic *panchayats* (a traditional social platform of negotiators) in the riverine area of Champaran in order to resolve local disputes. This shows his influence in the area. Some believe he was killed by British agents during one such panchayat. However, there is no credible evidence of the episode; had it been so, then it would have had repeated reference in the British sources. The British would have trumpeted the killing of their most daring enemy. There does not seem to be any reason why the Company would not have done so.[2] This may suggest at most an encounter with Company forces, resulting in his disappearance that was rumoured to be his assassination. Maybe it was just a hoax, as the occurrence of encounters and skirmishes with Fateh Sahi was an almost daily affair. One may also note that Betia Raj was situated in Champaran and touched Huseypur territory as well as Nepal. Thus, this tri-junction often triggered border clashes between the three parties; as such, the reference to the clash with Fateh Bahadur might have been with either of them, and not with the British. In all eventualities, however, it suggests that Sahi operated in the area and commanded some influence over it.

Fateh Sahi's first revolt against the British in 1767 and his subsequent departure for the jungles was driven by his political urge and for the sake of his autonomy. Now his motives were very different—much more personal and spiritual than political and public. So far, he had lived through bloody wars and violence. He had retreated into the jungle of his own volition in order to fight the British. But meanwhile, his minor nephew Mahesh Dutt, the posthumous child of Basant Sahi, had fallen prey to the predators of the East India Company, and its officers were doing everything, in the guise of protectors, to keep the minor under their control and influence.

This could have been a touching situation for his uncle Fateh Sahi. Unfortunately, we do not have any written account of his mental and emotional state. However, in view of the close interpersonal relations within the traditionally joint families of the region, it is unthinkable that he could have been indifferent to the plight of the nephew and his extended family, despite his past differences and spats with them. This was all the more possible because here the protectors of the cousin line were the British, his enemies. His last-minute hesitation while attacking Basant Sahi on the fateful night of the latter's killing, Fateh's deep religiosity in personal life and concern for his own children later, strongly negate the possibility of his being unmoved at the plight of his nephew. Couldn't it have been one of the reasons behind the dramatic change in the later life of the rebel?

What, then, led to this dramatic change? What about the life of his family members, the royals who were forced to live like nomads? Their life in the forest would have been terribly difficult, with dangers lurking all around. We have already discussed about Sahi's maternal grandfather (Chapter 4), but we know very little about the early life of Fateh's wife. She is said to have been born to Pahalwan Singh, a zamindar of Benares.[3] However, she was in the limelight after the revolt of her husband. He had left Huseypur in a great hurry, leaving his family behind, and his wife was constantly worried about her safety being breached by Englishmen. To ward off such an eventuality, she had got a device prepared that would blow up the aggressor and herself before the English attempted molestation. For this, she had hidden a box of gunpowder in the litter with a taper in her hand so that she could explode it before any harm was done.[4] Fortunately, this never happened.

Yet, she was always on the alert, carrying a dagger on her person to defend herself, and poison to commit suicide, if she were ever captured by the enemy.[5]

Indeed, it was extremely difficult for Sahi to maintain his army and war supplies so cut off from human settlements. To maintain a regular flow of supplies would also have been extremely difficult; constant Company vigil aside, he was stationed in the interiors of a dense tropical forest infested with deadly animals, reptiles and poisonous insects. With every monsoon shower, the rivulets in the vicinity would have gone into spate, flooding the area around and jeopardizing communication.[6] Moreover, he would have to be on constant alert against the enemy. A situation such as this needed indomitable courage, grit and a burning desire for freedom. Fateh Sahi possessed this in abundance. But a stable life could have been a better option for the king in his old age.

The Emergence of Tamkuhi

Thus, the royal household of Huseypur was now clearly divided and the ground was prepared for the two siblings to live as two separate estates—Hathwa and Tamkuhi. The British sided with the Hathwa family; and effectively helped it get rid of the initial irritants and obstacles, such as the revolt of the britdars like Bujhawan Mishir. In return, the British enhanced their intervention in its internal management. Over and above the Court of Wards, they brought in a successive line of diwans and managers, and finally their Resident. Somehow, Hathwa continued to be in need of a guardian, which the British readily fulfilled with the Court of Wards arrangement. This provided Hathwa with both a period of peace and an opportunity to prosper; but it perpetuated, at the same time, its dependence on the British in the future.

For Fateh Sahi, this was the time to consolidate his possessions, and restore and reassert his identity as Raja. He had grown old by now. So, in 1790, he relinquished his gaddi in favour of his son and gradually inclined towards *sanyas* (renunciation). After the parting of Hathwa and Tamkuhi as separate estates, the Company's animosity to Fateh Sahi slowly eased as well, since they had a foothold of power in his cousin's branch of the family. Fateh Sahi, on the other hand, maintained his sway over the north-western part of the Huseypur state adjoining the Bhagjogni jungle, and consolidated it gradually. He also entered secretly into some kind of land settlement with the Awadh Nawab regarding the territory under his possession in the forest, which we have already discussed. He continued to assert his authority as the legitimate ruler of the entire Huseypur Raj, but the British authorities did not approve; instead, they recognized the successors of Basant Sahi as the rulers of the original estate. However, this did not deter Fateh Sahi or his successors from maintaining their claim.

In 1790, Fateh Sahi crowned his son Dalmardan Sahi as his successor. He had four sons—Amardhan Sahi, Dalmardan Sahi, Samsher Sahi and Ran Bahadur Sahi. The eldest, Amardhan Sahi died issueless and was succeeded by his brother, Dalmardan Sahi. His successors continued to try to recover their lost patrimony in the meanwhile. When Fateh Sahi wished to settle down permanently with a new capital, the vizier of Awadh allowed him to clear as much forest land as he would require. Initially, about a hundred acres were acquired and a palace with the infrastructure required for a royal establishment was constructed. First came a mud fort, which was gradually replaced with elaborate structures—residential quarters, a darbar hall, a court for public hearing, a garrison with stables for horses and elephants, a hospital and a temple. The main capital was surrounded by a moat. Today, only a few of these structures survive, the Sheesh Mahal being the most impressive of them. It is in a dilapidated condition now, but its bold design reflects its past grandeur and the personality of its creator.[7] Going by the minor variations in its design and the bricks used in it, it seems to have undergone certain changes in the original structure over the successive generations.

In 1790, the youngest son of Fateh Sahi petitioned Montgomery, the settlement officer of Saran, to be allowed to settle for the revenue of the Huseypur Raj on behalf of Fateh Sahi, but the claim was treated as inadmissible. Similar applications were also made in 1816 and 1821, but with the same results. Fateh Sahi's wife also petitioned the Company government to restore her rights to the lost estate but to no avail, once again.[8] In June 1829, the great-grandson of Fateh Sahi brought a regular suit for the recovery of the Raj but it was dismissed as barred by limitation. A similar claim was made again in 1848 with the same result.[9]

The third son, Shamsher Bahadur Sahi, later managed to acquire some of the lost villages by purchase between 1830 and 1840, and settled at Salempur, laying the foundation of another eponymous estate. Raja Dalip Sahi, son of Dalmardan Sahi, had no issue, and his widow transferred her rights to Kharag Bahadur Sahi, the grandson of Ran Bahadur Sahi, the fourth son of Fateh Sahi. Kharag Bahadur Sahi was recognized by the British as the 'Raja' of Tamkuhi, although they had actually never prohibited them from using the title, and it continued to be in use even in the court proceedings.[10]

Thus, Fateh Sahi consolidated the territories of the Huseypur Raj under his control, with additions from Awadh territories, into a new estate with its capital at Tamkuhi, in the Sidhua Jobana pargana of Gorakhpur, known as Tamkuhi Raj. Subsequently, his descendants acquired many zamindaris and came to have influence in certain pockets of Uttar Pradesh and Bihar. The Tamkuhi rulers responded to public concerns and welfare, and gradually sympathized with the nationalist cause. They came close to nationalist leaders and freedom fighters like Motilal and Jawaharlal Nehru, participated in the functioning of local municipal bodies and entered the provincial assembly.

Thus, the Tamkuhi rajas, like some others in India, forged an easy passage for old indigenous rulers to join the mainstream life of the nation, and set the tone of national integration soon after Independence in 1947. The genesis of this trend may be clearly traced to Fateh Sahi in the case of eastern India, in view of his association with the common masses right from the beginning in his long-drawn opposition to British rule.

With the passage of time, Fateh Sahi gradually inclined towards spirituality and adapted to the life of a sanyasi.[11] Legends and family sources testify that he was a disciplinarian and a man of determination from his early days. He believed in Sanatan Hindu Dharma and was especially disposed towards the Shakti cult. Before leaving for any military campaign, he would worship Satvahini Durga at the family temple located on the bank of the adjoining Jharahi river. He is also believed to have annually offered sacrifices (*bali*) of a male buffalo calf and goat to the goddess at the family temple during the Dussehra pooja.[12] This seems to suggest his faith in power and the use of force for a cause—freedom from newly imposed colonial rule, in his case. But these traits might have also aroused fear in the hearts of his adversaries, and loyalty among his associates and supporters. His descendants claim that the Durga idol, which he always carried with him, was part of the family collection until it disappeared some years ago; though his sword used in the sacrificial ritual is still a prized possession of the family (see photo insert).[13]

In some sources, Fateh Sahi is referred to as 'Fakir'. However, this appellation may not be taken to distinguish between sanyasi for a Hindu and fakir for Muslim ascetics, as they have often been used interchangeably without distinguishing one from the other. This region has had a long history of religious and spiritual diversity and intermixture. Apart from Hinduism and Buddhism, it experienced the influence of Kabirpanth, Nathpanth and Sufism, leading to a deep and widespread cultural assimilation; as such, these sects seem to have admirers both among the Hindus and the Muslims, and many of their rituals, idioms and maxims have been traditionally shared by the local communities across religious orientation.[14] The region is full of the tombs of their saints who are still revered and worshipped by all.

Fateh Sahi is believed to have had in his army Naga sanyasis, fakirs and even bandits, which reminds one of the old traditions of the Sanyasi Revolts against the foreign invaders and their oppression in India. This re-emerged, particularly in eastern India, in the early days of the British rule. The Nagas, Satnamis and the Nathpanthis were prominent among them. The Satnamis had revolted against Aurangzeb not long ago; the sanyasi revolts took place in Bengal soon after the introduction of Company rule. The Nathpanthis, who had an older history, did have a major centre in Gorakhpur, close to Huseypur.

We have already discussed this aspect of Sahi's revolt; further research should be able to unravel its deeper roots and expanse.

The question of whether the sanyasis joined Fateh Sahi out of any grudge against foreign rule or whether it was just a coincidence arising out of other reasons needs to be probed. Besides the other reasons discussed earlier, there is an additional probability: many sanyasis lived in the forests, foothills and the higher reaches of the Himalayas. They did not have any personal earnings and often depended on offerings from visitors or local devotees. With the coming of British rule, the approaches to their abodes were increasingly policed and sealed, making it difficult for the common people to reach them. As their traditional patrons—the rajas and nobility—declined and grew impoverished under colonial rule, they stopped visiting these ascetics, depriving them of their sustenance. This could have prompted them to join Fateh Sahi in the revolt against the English.

The Voyage to Ultimate Freedom

Eventually, Fateh Sahi renounced his Raj and the family to become an ascetic in 1808. His family sources say he went to Nasik, a pilgrimage of great importance for Hindus. His departure must have been a touching affair. We do not have any eyewitness account; but in view of the location and circumstances, one may visualize the scene: Fateh Sahi leaving his Tamkuhi palace along with a retinue caravan of guards, advisers and loyal aides, with provisions for their day-to-day needs. A contingent of cavalry headed the convoy to provide advance security; the Raja sat on his favourite elephant in the middle, with more elephants, camels and a long line of followers trailing the convoy.

Popular memory visualizes the Raja pausing at the bank of the Jharahi to have a last glimpse of his kingdom, of the capital and the surrounding forest. He visited his favourite Durga temple and paid his respects to the deity. Soon, he bowed towards Huseypur, then stared stoically towards Hathwa for a while pensively, before he looked one last time upon his Tamkuhi palace and the wooded landscape around. He bowed in all directions to bid his final farewell. Lastly, he took leave of his followers. Nobody would be accompanying him on this final journey, except for a handful of security men, aides and trusted loyalists. The cavalcade moved towards the west. Dust clouded the atmosphere, against the golden glow of the setting sun. As dusk fell, so did an eerie silence, with nothing but the bells of the elephants tinkling faintly in the air. Slowly, the silhouette of the convoy grew smaller, fading into the night. All of a sudden, there was commotion in the jungle. Birds screeched, animals howled, before a couple of thunderous roars from deep inside the jungle overwhelmed the ambience.

The gloom deepened, and the darkness of the night set in over the Ganga valley.

Since Gwalior was not on a direct route from Tamkuhi, the journey of over 400 miles was extremely hazardous, as the royal entourage had to cross countless ravines and an unending stretch of wilderness infested with thugs and pindaries.[15] The Raja halted several times on the way before reaching Gwalior, where he stayed for some days. Mahadaji was no more by then, but Chait Singh was alive. Did they discuss another assault on the British? We are not sure.

From Gwalior, Sahi is said to have gone to Nasik, over 600 miles further into Maharashtra, on the River Godavari. This part of the journey was more arduous and dangerous due to its rough and craggy terrain and Bhil raiders, unless the Raja had local contacts and support. Nasik is one of the holiest cities for Hindus in India, and it made sense for a man as deeply religious as Fateh Sahi to go there. Apart from its temples, it is the site of the Kumbh, the greatest congregation of devout Hindus held every twelve years. Mythically, Lord Rama is said to have lived there during his exile. Nasik gets its name from the tale of Ram's brother, Lakshman, cutting off the nose of Ravana's sister demoness, Surpanakha, who tried to seduce Ram. Valmiki, Kalidas and Bhavabhuti have paid rich tributes to the place, and it is discussed at length in the *Ain-e-Akbari*. In the time of Shivaji, it was known as the 'land of the brave'. This background is likely to have attracted the rebel Raja; more so because it was still free from British control.

No one knows what actually became of Fateh Sahi after reaching Nasik.[16] We may presume he formally accepted sanyas there in the quest for *mukti*—the ultimate freedom.

What a unique journey of life—from Raja to rebel to monk!

Epilogue

The Rebel in Retrospect

It's been over two centuries since Fateh Bahadur Sahi was last seen in 1808. He was active in the latter half of the eighteenth century and exited the scene at the start of the nineteenth century. That was the period of transition from medieval to modern times and, politically, of consolidation of the British rule in India. Sahi was part of that turbulent process, and its victim, too. Old ideas, values and institutions were giving way to new ones that were yet to take clear shape. As a rebel in exile, Fateh Sahi was fated to be in the saddle all the time. He was never caught, nor did he ever surrender. His farewell to arms and his sudden retreat from war was neither forced nor accidental. This reminds one of two greats of Indian history—Maharana Pratap of Chittor, and, farther back in time, Emperor Asoka of Magadha.

Two centuries before Fateh Sahi, Maharana Pratap (1540–97) fought for his independence for about the same duration and in almost similar conditions as Sahi—in the extremely difficult terrain of Rajasthan. Pratap's own brother, like Sahi's cousin, was friendly with the enemy.[1] The Mughal Emperor Akbar was on a mission of territorial expansion at the time; so, as soon as Pratap was crowned, the Emperor wanted him to become his vassal. But the Maharana refused to submit and war became inevitable. Eventually, the two confronted each other at Haldighati in 1576. Pratap's troops were outnumbered by the huge Mughal army. A short but fierce battle lasting over six hours left the Maharana wounded; however, he managed to retreat into the hills and lived to fight another day. He had many encounters with Mughal forces thereafter, but he did not surrender.[2] Finally, taking advantage of Akbar's preoccupation with rebellions in other parts of the Empire, Pratap captured the Mughal post at Dewar (1582) and recovered his lost territories. Like Fateh Sahi, he also built a new capital at Chavand near modern Dungarpur. He died in a hunting accident in 1597; but, while breathing his last, he asked his successor to never submit to the enemy.[3]

Still further back in time, over two millennia ago, Emperor Asoka (c.304–232 BCE), too, fought ruthless battles, killing thousands in the Kalinga War. However, in his crowning moments of victory, he gave up arms, renounced his worldly ambitions and accepted Buddhism. He preached compassion and worked for the welfare of all lives on earth. He was inspired by the Buddha, propagated his ideas and memorialized the important events of his life with public works and the installation of rock edicts and memorial pillars.

Incidentally, the most important events in the life of the Buddha took place around the kingdom of Fateh Sahi: the Buddha was born at Lumbini not very far off, across the northern border in Nepal. He gained enlightenment at Bodh

Gaya on the southern side of the Ganga, delivered his first sermon at Sarnath in the south-west near Varanasi and died at Kushinagar, just a couple of hours' walk from Sahi's capital at Tamkuhi. And, finally, may we remember Sahi's remote connection with the Buddha via the Mallas (see Chapter 2).

These comparisons may sound utterly incongruous, but some similarities among the three are striking. History has strange ways of remembering its actors! We honour a few but forget many. Fateh Sahi is one of the forgotten ones.

We know very little about Sahi's personal life, as he spent most of his time in the jungle, cut off from local society. As a rebel, he operated stealthily, leaving no trace of his movements and activities. To tell his story, we must substantially depend on unconventional and popular sources—folklore, historical remnants and artefacts from the households of his descendants and relations. His maternal grandfather, the chief of Lilkar in Balia district, seems to have supported Fateh Sahi in hard times, especially during his rebellion against the British. We do not have any clear information about the background of Sahi's in-laws, except that his father-in-law, Pahalwan Singh, was a zamindar in the district of Balia near Benares.[4] We do, however, know about his wife: of her fearlessness and dynamism, and about her hectic efforts to regain the estate of Huseypur when Fateh was in exile.

Vaidurya Pratap Sahi, an eighth-generation scion of Fateh Sahi, recounts: 'Raja Fateh Bahadur Sahi was a man of honour and principles. I grew up hearing tales of his valour and honour. Drawing from the literary sources and oral tradition, I visualize him as a tall man with an athletic build and good martial skills. He was a disciplinarian.' Vaidurya Sahi further recalls Sahi's ability to disguise himself in any situation. We have already seen how he bluffed Company forces in order to enter his fort, dressed as a pundit on the occasion of his daughter's marriage, and escaped to his jungle hideout safely. He 'was married to one woman in an era when polygamy was common among the rajas,' adds Vaidurya Sahi. 'Surprisingly, he didn't strictly follow the rule of male primogeniture and divided his kingdom into four—one for each son, rather than passing on the whole raj to the eldest. After handing over his property to his sons, he became a fakir and left for Nasik.'[5]

Unfortunately, we do not know much about his life afterwards, although popular memory recounts his arduous journey to Nasik through an extremely unfriendly terrain. His two contemporaries, Mahadaji Shinde and Ahilya Bai Holkar, might have provided some clues, but both of them had passed away by then. Yet, a closer look at their life histories is likely to shed some light on the activities of Fateh Sahi. Mahadaji Shinde, for instance, was a crucial link between the English and Chait Singh, although he was ambivalent towards the latter. It is believed that Shinde did not help Chait Singh during his war with the English despite an earlier commitment, but when Chait Singh arrived in Gwalior as an exile, Shinde granted him a jagir, on the advice of the Peshwa.[6] Chait Singh lived in Gwalior until his death. Unfortunately, we don't know whether Fateh Sahi, who had fought along with Chait Singh in the Benares rebellion, met the exiled Raja and some old supporters. In all probability, it was an occasion for the two old friends fallen in a similar situation, to share feelings and express gratitude to each other for the last time. Chait Singh died three years later on 29 March 1811.

Ahilya Bai Holkar could be another connecting link. Her visit to Kashi and restoration of the Kashi Vishvanath Temple and several others in north India, tempt one to presume that she was aware of political developments in the region. She encouraged Mahadji to play a decisive role in north Indian politics.[7] Under the circumstances, even though we don't have concrete answers, could she have been uninformed about the revolts of Chait Singh and Fateh Sahi?[8] In a letter to Mahadji in 1772, she warned him against association with the British and likened their embrace to a deadly bear hug that was sure to kill its prey, unless assaulted straight in its face.[9]

Fateh Sahi is said to have gone from Gwalior to Nasik, over 600 miles further in Maharashtra. This was a still more hostile terrain, with rough and craggy topography ridden with Bhil raiders. Yet, going by the religious temperament of Fateh Sahi, his visit to Nasik is a strong possibility. Its mythological and religious sanctity apart, Nasik was also the site of the Kumbh, which Sahi had earlier attended at Prayag to recruit the Naga warriors for his militia. A petition filed in the court for recovery of Huseypur estate, by the granddaughter-in-law of Fateh Sahi, states that he died in 1817. Yet, no one really knows what became of him.[10] It is possible that he took sanyas, seeking *mukti*—the ultimate freedom.

Despite his adherence to orthodox religious customs, Fateh Sahi was not orthodox in many aspects of life. He seems to have given considerable freedom to his wife, as she took up the case of his estate with the British government and pursued it, though without success, up to the Privy Council in London.

Fateh Bahadur's love for his subjects earned him their support in his fight against the Company. His followers came from all sections of society and were not only Hindus. Some sources suggest that he became a fakir in the end. This appellation may not be taken literally to mean a Sufi or Muslim ascetic; yet, it suggests some association with them. Many Muslims, most notably the Nawab of Awadh and, nearer home, the Afghan chief of Siwan and others from his region, supported Sahi secretly. The fact that several *mazars* exist around Huseypur and Tamkuhi, gives an impression that either he encouraged their construction, or else, at least allowed them to be built there.[11] The influence of Sufi saints is still visible in the region, as it could have been then. His army was a unique amalgam of diverse social classes from all sects and segments of society—virtually everyone deprived of a livelihood, pushed to the margin and dissatisfied with the newly imposed political order. Yet, its diversity itself was an innovation, something that French revolutionaries replicated years later.

The management of such a disparate body of people hailing from different communities, faiths and professions demanded superior acumen and leadership qualities. Fateh Bahadur was unique and unparalleled in many ways, blessed with varied personality traits—he was emotional and impulsive, yet resolute, daring, gritty and ruthless at the same time. No wonder he bid farewell to arms voluntarily in the end and became a sanyasi.

In the longer historical sweep, however, the line of Fateh Bahadur appears to be eclectic and liberal in religious faith. Shubhrendru Kumar of the Chainpur-Salemgarh estate informs us about a later Rani of the family—Maiji, and how she became famous for generously distributing alms to the poor and the needy of all creeds and communities at the family temple. After her death, the locals installed her idol in the temple, now named Maiji Mandir after her, where both Hindus and the Muslims worship her.

Beyond India, this was a period of incubation and outburst of two revolutions against imperialism and oppression: first, the American War of Independence (1776) against British imperialism, and the second, the French Revolution (1789) against an oppressive monarchy and the church in France. Apparently, neither of them had any connection with what happened in Huseypur—a small principality in an obscure corner of the Indian subcontinent. Yet, the revolt of Fateh Sahi foreshadowed some of the traits of these world events. For example, Sahi's first and foremost concern was to oppose British imperialism right at its start in his territory. When dislodged from his seat of power, he operated from his jungle hideout, with the support of the masses, acting, as in France, at the grassroots from 'below'. When his engagement with the English turned violent, he was joined by supporters who were dissatisfied with the colonial dispensation. This is reminiscent of the agrarian unrest in the French countryside on the eve of the historic upheavals of 1789, the participation of the crowd and vagrants in them, and of the unprecedented violence and killings during the Reign of Terror.[12]

These were times when human societies were not so tightly insulated from each other. Trade, war, diplomacy, missionary activities and colonialism created circumstances for societies to interact beyond their borders, as far as the nature and environmental factors allowed them.[13] This explains the resemblance between the happenings in a small principality like Huseypur and in the larger expanses of America and France.

In this overarching process, traders, adventurers, explorers, religious missionaries, scholars and royal emissaries acted as channels of communication and exchange, influencing the societies concerned.[14] They introduced new artefacts, techniques and ideas in the lands they visited or, back home, in their own countries. We must not forget that many such travellers and traders had entered the Indian subcontinent, too. After all, the East India Company and its French and Dutch counterparts had come to India through this process, and with them entered many other players. In medieval times, many such people had come with Muslim invaders, serving them when the latter established their rule in India. Eastern India did have a good share of them.[15] The Christian missionaries were another important group that entered the region. They made Betia one of their earliest centres, along with Patna and other places in the region.[16]

Earlier, we have referred to Begum Samru's association with many Europeans. Her husband Walter Reinhardt Sombre had fought several wars in north India and was the perpetrator of the Patna Massacre, in which hundreds of soldiers of the East India Company were butchered by him in 1763.[17] The presence of formidable mercenaries like Sombre, his wife Begum Samru and their collaborator George Thomas in the region was important because, in the course of time, they carved out principalities of their own, acquiring real personal diplomatic and material stakes in north India.[18] Notably, most of them had non-British roots and they belonged to an anti-British clique. Sombre also fought in the Battle of Buxar against the English, in which Fateh Sahi, too, fought along with other supporters from Saran, Champaran and Muzaffarpur, from the side of the Indian allies. There is all likelihood that he helped Sahi in his rebellion.[19]

We may briefly revisit the Madam Grand–Francis affair (see Chapter 4) to assess its fallout on the career of the people involved, its impact on the Company administration and the implications for local opposition to it, as by Fateh Sahi. Madam Grand's scandal spoke a lot about the state of affairs, as it involved the two highest functionaries of the Company government—a member of the supreme council of the Governor-General and the Governor-General himself.[20] The duel between Francis and Warren Hastings only a few days after the episode was not only a show of chivalry by the two suitors, but it also revealed the rowdyism and criminality of the top bureaucratic circles of the Company. The fact that on his return to England, Francis did not lose his public standing and was repeatedly elected as a member of Parliament was a reflection on contemporary British society as well.

Francis was plotting Hastings's impeachment in London, and so Hastings probably thought it would be a good move to win George Grand over to his side. Appointing a clerk who looked after petty commercial activities, such as loading goods at a commercial establishment, to the newly created post of Collector to administer revenue and justice in Tirhut and Hajipur, two important commercial hubs of the Company in Bihar, could not have been without ulterior motives.

Grand was given a free hand in the administration in Tirhut. He encouraged indigo plantation and its processing on European lines in north Bihar, and founded three factories as a personal investment. He was one of the earliest to do so in India. This enhanced his popularity and clout in the area but also alarmed the top management in Calcutta. They imposed various checks on his powers, and finally, he was replaced by Robert Bathurst in 1787.[21]

Before these events, the Grands' marriage had broken down in 1778 and Catherine left to eventually settle in Paris. She befriended many notables and then married Talleyrand, allegedly under some pressure from Napoleon Bonaparte. Talleyrand ensured she had a life of luxury, and when

Grand's business in north Bihar collapsed and he fell out of the Company's favour, Catherine came to his rescue with financial help.[22]

In view of the huge commercial value of the region, Grand was keen to continue his business operations there. Aggrieved with his top management and sensing the rebellious situation in the region heightened by Chait Singh's revolt, Grand leaned towards the local zamindars around Muzaffarpur. Most of them were clansmen of both Chait Singh and Fateh Sahi, or, in some cases, their relations, such as Betia, Sheohar, Madhuban and Narhan.[23] They were likely to empathize with Grand as a partner in the anti-establishment faction. Since Fateh Sahi had personally commanded forces with Chait Singh during the Benares rebellion, it is difficult to believe Grand was unconcerned with its undercurrents in Bihar.[24]

The fact that the British had stooped to the worst levels of wickedness and malice, bereft of any legal or moral conscience, to subjugate India and extract its resources, was amply vindicated by the British Parliament's impeachment of their three highest officials in India—Robert Clive, Warren Hastings and Chief Justice of the Supreme Court of Judicature Elijah Impey. Haunted by the guilt of his misdeeds done in India, Clive committed suicide on 22 November 1774. Then, Warren Hastings was impeached. Leading its proceedings, Edmund Burke charged him of heinous crimes, corruption, manipulation and mischief.[25] We may recall that the prime facilitator of the impeachment now was Philip Francis, the main accused of the Madam Grand scandal, who was bent upon avenging his humiliation at the hands of Hastings in Calcutta. Spread over nine years, it was the longest proceedings of its type but failed in the end. Was it really an impartial and just trial? A closer reading of it would not absolve the East India Company of the crimes its officers committed in India. All these developments showed the extremely low level of human material and ethical values running the colonial enterprise in India.[26]

Against this murky background, Fateh Sahi's indomitable resolve kept his family members inspired and unyielding, even after his exit from the scene. Under the circumstances, they preferred to create and consolidate a separate domain of their own. Fateh Sahi had left behind sizeable assets. He had created a parallel government with a new capital at Tamkuhi, no doubt; but what about its legitimacy vis-à-vis the original Raj of Huseypur? His family took it squarely. His wife petitioned the government to restore her rights on the lost estate, as did his sons, but to no avail. Their efforts continued for a long time without success until the scions gained their recognition as rajas, after a century. Even after the legal battle arising out of the exit of Fateh Sahi from Huseypur and its transfer to the cadet line as its natural heir, with a new capital at Hathwa, the English patronage continued. But, until the end, the colonial government saw to it that Tamkuhi did not gain the legitimacy and status it claimed. On their own, however, the Tamkuhi branch continued to assert itself. They acquired revenue rights over hundreds of additional villages; many more territories were gained as patrimonial gifts of succession from maternal sides, such as the Maksudpur estate in Gaya and Anapur near Allahabad. This enhanced their status greatly. Already, one of Fateh's sons had shifted to another village and established what emerged as the Salemgarh Raj.

The British, on the other hand, devised a way to block their aspirations to return to the Huseypur gaddi. Instead of entertaining this demand for restoration, they recognized

Tamkuhi as a separate estate, and designated Kharag Bahadur Sahi, then successor in line, as its Raja. He was succeeded in 1856 by his son, Raja Kishan Pratap Sahi, who died in 1892. Of his two sons, the elder, Satrujit Pratap Bahadur Sahi, was crowned the next Raja. He died in 1898, and was succeeded by Indrajit Pratap Bahadur Sahi who was just five years old at the time. As a result, the estate went under the Court of Wards. When Indrajit Sahi reached majority in 1914, he assumed actual charge of the estate. It comprised 362 villages—232 in the district of Gorakhpur (UP) and 130 in Bihar.[27] The villages in Gaya were obtained partly as a legacy to Raja Kharag Bahadur from his maternal grandfather, the Raja of Tikari, and partly by purchase. Besides, the Sursand zamindari in Muzaffarpur had been bequeathed to Satrujit Pratap Bahadur Sahi.[28]

Thus, British diplomacy worked once again. With one stroke, the British almost obliterated Huseypur from popular memory. As the official heir of Huseypur, they reinforced the status of Hathwa, but appeased, at the same time, the elder-line claimants of Tamkuhi by bestowing rajaship on them as a separate estate. Everyone felt happy in their positions—a great relief for the British. No wonder, as they had done in Hathwa, the British now started placating the Tamkuhi rajas with official decorations, protocol privileges and the like. In response, the Tamkuhi rulers were drawn under the colonial ambit. Raja Indrajit Sahi was awarded a silver medal at the Delhi Coronation Durbar in 1911 for initiating public welfare measures within his territory. For his war services, he was presented a sanad by the War Board and a sword of honour by the Lieutenant-Governor of UP.[29]

However, in spite of this mutual bonhomie, there was a streak of independence of thought and approach among the

Tamkuhi rajas. From the beginning, they remained inclined towards their subject people, through various welfare measures and socio-cultural activities. In his own fraternity, Indrajit Sahi was a member of the All-India Zamindars' Association and president and vice president of its affiliates at district levels in the United Provinces and Bihar. He was an elected chairman of the Gorakhpur District Board and also to the Legislative Council of the United Provinces for three consecutive terms, and served on several civic bodies in different capacities in UP.[30]

During his stewardship, he launched measures to educate his people, and planned some home industries for their economic betterment. At an agricultural farm, improved farming methods, seeds and implements were publicized, and an annual cattle show was organized to promote well-bred livestock. These welfare measures endeared him to his people,[31] which shows the family's bond with the masses. Most of all, during the last quarter of the freedom movement, they leaned towards the national leaders. Though not vocal on the political front, they discreetly sided with them. In the course of their protracted property suits, they engaged Motilal Nehru as their lawyer and maintained a good reciprocal relation with him. Although Nehru spoke against big zamindars during the Kishan Sabha movement in Uttar Pradesh, personally, he had cordial relations with the Tamkuhi family, the descendants claim.[32]

Thus, Fateh Sahi's greatest legacy remains his pro-people stance, his ethos of protest against injustice and oppression, and an unshakeable yearning for freedom. He demonstrated that it was not the material wherewithal, but the will to stand, endure and fight for one's cause. We do not know if he had read the *Bhagavad Gita*, but he seemed to have followed its ideals. His accomplishments exuded *Purusharth*,[33] and in his actions, he was an inspiration to others not to ever yield before injustice. He was resolute in his goals and ruthless to his adversaries. These qualities ensured his camaraderie with and support of other chiefs across the Gangetic plain.

In later times, his region remained a hotbed of anti-British activities that imploded during the Revolt of 1857. Beginning with his own rebellion and that of Chait Singh and Jagat Singh, the revolts of the nawabs of Awadh, of Mangal Pandey of Balia, Kunwar Singh of Shahabad and others during 1857, to the Chauri Chaura massacre and the extraordinary feat of defiance by Chitu Pandey in the Quit India Movement of 1942, there are countless examples that reflect the spirit of Fateh Sahi.[34]

The heritage of his Huseypur Raj has survived in the Tamkuhi Raj, with a difference in comparison to its Hathwa counterpart. Deprived of colonial generosity, Tamkuhi rajas found satisfaction in promoting the welfare of their people and development within their jurisdiction. They promoted education and cultural activities, initiated public works of social welfare and materially helped educational institutions in Uttar Pradesh and Bihar.[35] They patronized scholars, artists and writers. Noted polymath and writer Rahul Sankrityayan sought their help for the promotion of Hindi, and he has written about their history. The family also played host to singers and musicians, and exponents of indigenous arts like wrestling.[36] Interestingly, the Tamkuhi scions took an interest in innovative farming; and they leased out some land to a non-British European planter for farming, which later developed into an agricultural farm at Sipaya, now a government farm near Gopalganj.[37]

Such contributions to socio-cultural amelioration were also made by their cousin line of Hathwa and, in many cases, on a much larger scale, as towards the promotion of education and public health, and relief in natural calamities. But since that was routed mostly through colonial channels, it was often projected as a colonial initiative; hence, in public perception, the credit went to the British-Indian Government. As a reward, the British kept Hathwa higher in their roll of honour, but away from public life and the freedom movement. A few instances of efforts to break away from the colonial net are glossed over in public memory. For example, the Hathwa family claims that before Mahatma Gandhi left Patna for his first visit to Champaran in 1917, he had a confidential meeting with the Hathwa Raja in Patna. Similarly, their contributions to educational institutions in Bihar, Bengal and Uttar Pradesh, are generally overlooked in the sweeping nationalist stance against the native states in the later phase of the freedom struggle.[38]

There are also instances of occasional irritants cropping up in the Tamkuhi family's relations with British authorities. Family sources recount how Raja Indrajit Pratap Sahi expressed his displeasure about colonial protocol at a public gathering. During that meet, the guests were expected to sit in two designated enclosures demarcated by signboards—one for Europeans and the other for Indians. The European section was meant for the whites, but it also accommodated Indian notables like local chiefs, though it was not indicated anywhere. Irritated at this discrimination, the Tamkuhi Raja sat in the Indians' enclosure. However, the moment the colonial authorities noted it, they rushed and requested him to move to the enclosure meant for the Europeans. The Raja refused, explaining the simple meaning of the official announcement. It was a great embarrassment for the officials; but the Raja did not budge until they apologized and respectfully persuaded him to move to the other section.[39]

On their part, the British tried their best to wipe out the memory of Fateh Sahi. So much so that today there does not exist any authenticated portrait; and the only available picture seemingly of him is one with Raja Chait Singh of Benares, in which Chait Singh is captioned by name, but Fateh Sahi is believed to have been depicted just as a rais—a nobleman.

Finally, can we consider his rebellion to be India's First War of Independence? The opinion may be divided, essentially because the documentary sources on Fateh Sahi are fewer. Those that exist originate mostly from the British—his enemies; and the real side of his story was little recorded in black and white, as he was a rebel who had to work secretly. Above all, even if he did not surrender, he chose to go into exile. Finally, he lost his ancestral principality. As such, he lost all chances of being in the news and remembered by posterity. Any association with him was a crime under colonial rule; the remoteness of time and his geographical location have further obscured his existence.

Fateh Sahi rose against the British about a century before the Revolt of 1857—generally considered as India's First War of Independence. Of course, the revolt of 1857 was spread over a larger part of India; yet, Sahi's rebellion was far wider in expanse than is generally believed. Since his rebellion was against the Company with huge resources at their command, his operations were bound to be secretly planned and executed, and kept unrecorded, as in the case of the Revolt of 1857, too. His collaborators and sympathizers maintained secrecy to escape the ire of the Company government, and destroyed all evidence likely to reveal their connections with him. To add to the problem, most of the estate's records and other sources of information about him and his family were destroyed right in the beginning, when his fort at Huseypur was demolished by the Company forces in 1767. Later, a great volume of the family's possessions (records, artefacts, etc.) was wantonly taken away by the office bearers during the Court of Wards tenures.[40]

However, he is fondly enshrined in the minds and hearts of the local people. Aided by colonial records and contemporary memoirs, we have been able to recreate a tangible profile, good enough to recount his deeds. After the nawabs of Bengal and Awadh and the Mughal emperor of Delhi lost the Battle at Buxar and accepted the Company's control over eastern India, Fateh Sahi was probably the first and only hereditary ruler of an ancient origin to revolt against the East India Company. Hyder Ali, who rose against the English in the south, was not from a ruling dynasty; and his son Tipu Sultan rose against them over thirty years later than Fateh Sahi; but he was defeated, killed and his territory taken away. Fateh Sahi, on the other hand, was never arrested or submitted to the British. Tactically, he chose to go into exile and pursued a guerrilla war for nearly three decades. This was a rare instance of its kind, not only in India but anywhere. Even in exile, he did not relinquish his position: he considered himself the Raja of Huseypur; collected revenue in the areas under his control, and recreated a capital at his jungle hideout at Tamkuhi. When he became old, he handed over his gaddi to his son to continue his lineage.

Notably, the ancestors of some of the native states who participated in or supported the 1857 Revolt also backed Fateh Sahi. The nawabs of Awadh are a glaring example. It may be recalled that they allowed him to run his government-in-exile from their territory, and eventually let him establish his new capital there. Further research on such estates in UP, Bihar and

Bengal, with new sources released after Independence, is likely to support our view further.

The preliminary research in this direction hints at Sahi's operations extending far beyond his territory around Huseypur, or his jungle hideout. They seem to have reached Awadh, if not Delhi, in the west, Bihar in the east, into Nepal in the north, and to a very large area of Chhota Nagpur plateau, reaching into Bengal. The region situated between Camur Hills in the west and Rajmahal Hills in the east, was also the active zone of the uprising of Chait Singh, in which Fateh Sahi, too, fought with his forces. Both of them closely collaborated against the English.[41]

In line with the Benares rebellion, the conspiracy against the British by Jagat Singh of Benares deserves attention. After the fall of Chait Singh and his exit from Benares, Jagat Singh conspired with Vazir Ali, now detained in Benares, to remove the British from Benares, but the plan leaked. How he was tried and convicted, but committed suicide before transportation, are already discussed. Here, we may return to his collaborators for a while to understand the enormity of the episode: of the close collaborators, Bahadur Singh, Gudge Rauj Singh (a subadhar in the 2nd Battalion of the 9th Native Regiment) and Jagarnauth Singh were apprehended. They were tried and found guilty. Bahadur Singh was sentenced to death for being privy to Jagat Singh's interaction with Jagarnauth Singh for the purpose of raising troops against the Company. He was sentenced to be executed in Benares and his body to be suspended on a gibbet in or around the city to inspire fear in the local population.[42]

The episode is little known in history; but it speaks volumes about the smouldering embers of protest against the Company government in Benares and Awadh, after the exit of Chait Singh.

The British worry is well reflected in their choice of remote Saint Helena. Curiously, while the British authorities wanted to keep Jagat Singh fully cut off from his native land, they did not dare hang him, fearing a violent retaliation by his followers. Therefore, they wanted to keep him most comfortably, with two personal servants, necessary provisions and all arrangements made for the 'indulgences' befitting his status as a raja and desirable in his situation.[43] The repeated emphasis on 'indulgences' in many documents smacks of a conspiracy to push him into a life of addiction and similar aberrations.

Around Huseypur, Chainpur, Manjha and Khaira wielded considerable power and influence in their areas, and were undergoing similar humiliation under the Company rule, and they were tacitly supporting Fateh Sahi. The Tikari state in Gaya district had a large zamindari and a sizeable army, and there are indications of their opposition to the British Raj. They supported Chait Singh during his rebellion. Regrettably, things changed later. Problems of succession arose there, too; and in the absence of natural heirs, the estate was taken over by the British. It slipped into oblivion, thereafter.[44]

Likewise, the possibilities of Fateh's contacts with the same caste of the Betia Raj in Champaran, its offshoots at Sheohar and Madhuban in Muzaffarpur district,[45] the zamindars of Lalgola, Singhabad and Mahisadal in West Bengal and the zamindars of Maheshpur in Pakur and others, need to be probed.[46] The Betia Raja had revolted against the Company just before clashes with Fateh Bahadur, and the Rani of Maheshpur, Sarveshwari Devi, was arrested by the British for her anti-government activities and left to languish and die in Bhagalpur jail at about the same time. On allegation of forgery by Warren Hastings, Maharaja Nandkumar (1705–1775) was tried in 1775 by the first Chief Justice of India, Elijah Impey, and sentenced to death, which must have stirred most Indian rulers. This official excess later formed a major charge for the impeachment of both Hastings and Impey.[47]

As to the Maharashtra connection, we may note that around this time, groups of Chitpawan Brahmins from there and their affiliates from Gujarat were migrating towards the eastern Gangetic plain north of the Vindhya range, in order to evade oppression by their local rulers, lawlessness and lack of livelihood. The process accelerated especially after the Third Battle of Panipat (1761), when the Marathas were defeated. A large chunk of their army consisted of Chitpawans, who now moved eastward in search of employment and fortune. A branch of Chitpawans had migrated long ago from Bijapur and settled, as at Bharatpura, near Patna; others followed. Gradually they established major zamindaris and entered into matrimonial relations with the Bhumihar Brahmins of Bihar, and, later, also married into the Sahi families. Some of them trace their origins to Bhatt Brahmins, to which belonged Mayyur Bhutt, the earliest known ancestor of Fateh Sahi.[48]

At present, relatives connected with Huseypur vouch for Fateh Sahi's close contact with the Marathas.[49] How could a veteran military strategist and organizer like Fateh Bahadur forgo using their military skill? Occupational affinity and a deep faith in Hinduism were uniting factors among them, and all of them had a common enemy in the British.

That this inference could have some substance may also be derived from Sahi's visit to Gwalior, and to Nasik from there (1808). The fact that the British formally installed the successor of the Huseypur Raja at Hathwa only in 1837 gives some hint in this regard, particularly when one remembers that

Fateh Sahi was presumed dead by this time. This intervening period between these two dates is noteworthy, as it poses many questions: Did Fateh Sahi go to Gwalior and Nasik on the way to taking sanyas, or did he try to forge an alliance with the Marathas against the British? Was his visit to Nasik aimed at attaching some religious groups like the sanyasis in his forces, as he had done earlier during the Kumbh at Prayag? Did he survive beyond 1808, because the British fear of his re-emergence seems to have persisted at least up to 1837? A few later sources indicate Fateh Sahi died in 1836. A positive answer to any of these questions may credibly extend the area, scope and duration of his rebellion.

Since Fateh Sahi resorted to guerrilla warfare and used speed and vengeance to surprise and outwit his enemy, and acted brutally with his adversaries, he was projected by the British as a ruthless outlaw—an image that persisted for long, even among nationalist historians. This perception, however, started changing since India's Independence, after revelations of similar ruthlessness were reported during the Revolt of 1857. Between the Swadeshi Movement and Independence, countless English men, women and their associates were butchered, even as Indian revolutionaries indulged in disruptive activities and serious crimes like looting the government treasury and dacoity in the houses of British supporters.[50] Fateh Sahi had preceded them by well over a century. It is time now to evaluate him from this perspective.

From the viewpoint of leadership, determination, intensity and duration of struggle, Fateh Sahi's rebellion appears to have surpassed almost all revolts before or after him. We know of the debacles at Plassey and Buxar. Indeed, Tipu Sultan offered a formidable challenge to the British; but he lost both his life and kingdom, ultimately. No doubt, his iconic tiger toy attacking a white soldier menacingly depicts his deep hatred and wrath against the British.[51] The possibility of some interaction between Tipu and Fateh Sahi, the two arch-enemies of the British at the time, is not ruled out. If so, then how can we overlook the possibility of Sahi trying to gain French support against the British, through Tipu?[52] Already, Sahi was in close proximity with Madam Grand, Walter Reinhardt Sombre and his wife Begum Samru, and many other non-British generals fighting from the side of the anti-British clique.

Fateh Sahi's rebellion may be considered among the earliest instances of the people's participation in a common cause against an alien oppressive political authority. No wonder, he continues to live in their hearts in his homeland. In sombre moments, they still remember him, and admire his courage and sacrifice, and his love for motherland and freedom.

Indeed, he was the hero of India's First War of Independence.

Bibliography

In order to make this bibliography user-friendly, its subdivisions have been kept to the minimum. On account of the remote antiquity of events and lack of any pioneering work on the subject, at times, the sources used are very indirect and are likely to puzzle the readers. In fact, many of them do not refer to Fateh Sahi at all, but they closely talk of events and their handlers as well as the contemporary situation and circumstances that influenced and prompted Sahi's plans and moves. For the sake of ease, again, various types of sources have been kept together, as in several cases it is difficult to categorize them. Likewise, under Secondary Sources, books and articles have been clustered together to simplify the search. Besides the conventional repositories, many sources were consulted on the Internet, whose details are not given beyond footnotes. Since many entries of this bibliography were accessed in digitized format at various serving portals, variation and distortion in their pagination and format from the hard-print editions are not ruled out.

PRIMARY SOURCES

Archival Sources

Bengal State Archives, Kolkata: Proceedings of the Department of Revenue, Fort William Correspondence and Bengal Revenue Consultations.

Bihar State Archives, Patna: Proceedings of the Departments of Revenue, Home and Military, Foreign Affairs, Proceedings of the Chief and Council of Revenue.

National Archives of India, New Delhi: A few associated digitized files from the groups mentioned above.

India Office Library & Records, and British Library, London: East India Company Papers.

Published Primary Sources

Allahabad High Court, "In the High Court of Allahabad: First Appeal No. 214 of 1901, decided on: 24.05.1904: Appellants: Sarabjit Partap Bahadur Sahi and ors. Vs. Respondent: Indarjit Partap Bahadur Sahi and ors. (Hon'ble Judges/Coram: Sir John Stanley, Knight, C.J. and William Robert Burkitt, J. Counsels: For Appellant/Petitioner/Plaintiff: Sir Walter Colvin, Babu Jogindro Nath Chaudhri and Munshi Jang Bahadur Lal; For Respondents/Defendant: Mr. Conlan, Mr. G.A. Wood, Pandit Sundar Lal and Pandit Moti Lal Nehru)," MANU/UP/0014/1904; Equivalent Citation: (1905) ILR 27All203.

Babur, Zahiruddin Mohammad, *Baburnama*, trans. A.S. Beveridge, London: OUP, 1921.

Bhargava, K.D., ed., *Browne Correspondences* (Indian Record Series, 1919); New Delhi: Govt. of India, 1960.

British Parliament, *Parliamentary Papers (Commons)*, 1812-13, running vols. 285 until now, London: British Parliament.

Browne, James, *India Tracts*, Eng. trans., in the Asiatic Researches (1788); Paperback Handbooks, 2020.

Buchanan, Francis, *An Account of the Districts of Bihar and Patna in 1811-1812*, Patna: Bihar & Orissa Research Society, 1928;

—& Montgomery Martin, *Eastern India*, Vol. 2, *Bhagalpur, Gorakhpur*, Reprint, Delhi: Cosmo Publications, 1976;

—, *An Account of the District of Shahabad in 1812-1813*, Patna: Bihar & Orissa Research Society, 1934;

—, *Journal of Francis Buchanan Kept during the Survey of the District of Bhagalpur in 1810-1811*, ed. by C.E.A.W. Oldham, Patna: Govt. Printing, 1930.

Burke, Edmund, *Articles of Charge of High Crimes and Misdemeanours, Against Warren Hastings, Esq., Late Governor General of Bengal: Presented to the House of Commons, in the Months of April and May 1786*, London: J. Debrett, 1786.

Calendar of Persian Correspondence, being Letters, referring mainly to Affairs in Bengal, which passed between some of the Company's Servants and Indian Rulers and Notables, 10 vols., Calcutta: Imperial Record Dept., 1911.

Calendar of Persian Correspondence, with Introduction by Muzaffar Alam and Sanjay Subrahmanyam, 5 vols, 1759-1780, New Delhi: reprint, Primus Books, 2013.

Champaran District Gazetteer, Patna: Govt. Printing, 1930. [*Bengal District Gazetteer Series* is prefixed with all district *Gazetteers*, but removed here for easy accessibility]

Chatterjee, R.P. & K.R. Khosla, *His Imperial Majesty King George V and The Princes of India and The Indian Empire (Historical-Biographical)*, Lahore: Imperial Publishing Co., 1937.

Chaudhury, P.C., *Sarkar Saran (based on old correspondence regarding Saran District in Bengal during 1785 to 1866)*, Patna: Gazetteer Revision Office, 1956.

Chief of Factory at Patna, *Copy-Book of Letters, Apr. 1771 to Mar. 1773*, Corrected Paperback, Gale Ecco, 2010.

Cook, Andrew S., 'Alexander Dalrymple's "A Collection of Plans of Ports in the East Indies (1774-1775): A Preliminary Examination"', *Imago Mundi*, 33 (1981): 46–64;

—, 'Rennell, James (1742-1830), *Oxford Dictionary of National Biography*, Oxford University Press, 2004, (online)'.

Crosthwait, H. L., 'The survey of India', *Journal of the Royal Society of Arts*, 72 (3716), (1924): 194–206.

Darbhanga District Gazetteer, Patna: Govt. Printing, 1930.

Datta, K.K., comp., *Old Zamindari Records of Bihar*, Patna: Bihar State Archives, 2014;

—, *The Dutch in Bengal and Bihar* (1946), Delhi: Motilal Banarsidas, 1968;

— *Selections from Unpublished Correspondence of the Judge-Magistrate and the Judge of Patna, 1790-1857*, ed. with an Introduction by K.K. Datta, Patna: Superintendent, Government Printing, Bihar, 1954.

—, *A Contemporary Account of the Indian Mutiny*, Patna, 1950.

Daulah, Asafud, *History of Asafud Daulah: Nawab Vizir of Oudh*, Eng. trans. from Persian by W. Honey, Allahabad: NWP & Oudh Govt. Press, 1885.

Dutt, Devendra Nath, *A Brief History of the Hatwa Raj*, Calcutta: K.P. Mukherjee, 1909.

Dutt, Girindra Nath, 'History of the Hutwa Raj, with some unrecorded events of the administration of Warren Hastings and of the Indian Mutiny', *Asiatic Society of Bengal*, Vol. LXXIII, Part I., Nos. I-IV and Extra No.—1904;

—, *History of the Hutwa Raj*, Bankipur: Lahiri & Co., 1905;

—, 'History of the Hathwa Raj', *Journal of the Asiatic Society of Bengal*, Calcutta,1904;

—, 'Chronicles of the Hatwa Raj', *Calcutta Review*, Vol. 12, No. CC IX, Jul. 1897:35-36.

Fazl, Abul, *Ain-i-Akbari*, vol. I, trans. H. Blochmann & Colonel H.S. Jarnet, vols. II & III, Calcutta: The Asiatic Society of Bengal, 1891; rep. 2010.

Firminger, W.K., ed., *Report from the Select Committee on the Affairs of the East India Company* (1812), 3 vols., Calcutta, 1917.

Fort William--India House Correspondence, ed., N K Sinha, Vol. V: 1767-1769 (Indian Records Series), New Delhi: Govt. of India, 1949.

G.P.S., 'The Aristocracy of Bihar', *Calcutta Review*, Vol. LXXVI, Calcutta, 1883.

Gentil, Jean Baptiste Joseph, *Memoires Sur L'Indoustan* (1822), rept. Kessinger Publishing, 2010.

Ghoshe, Jamini Mohan, *Sanyasi and Fakir Raiders in Bengal*, Calcutta: Bengal Secretariat, 1930.

Gleig, G.R., *Memoirs of the Life of the Right Honourable Warren Hastings: First Governor General of Bengal*, Vol. I, London: Richard Bentley, 1841.

Grand, George François, *Narrative of the Life of A Gentleman long Resident in India: Comprehending A Period the most eventful in the history of that country, with regard to the revolutions occasioned by European interference, and interspersed with interesting anecdotes, and traits characteristical of those eminent persons who distinguished themselves at that juncture*, Cape of Good Hope: Author, 1814.

Grierson, George A., *Bihar Peasant Life* (1885); Reprint Delhi: Cosmo Publication, 1975.

Hand, J. Reginald, *Early English Administration of Bihar, 1781-85*, Calcutta: Bengal Secretariat Press, 1894.

Harvey, Robert, *Clive: The Life and Death of a British Emperor* (1998); Thomas Dunne Books, St. Martin's Press, 2000.

Hastings, Warren, *The History of the Trial of Warren Hastings, Esq. Late Governor-General of Bengal, Before the High Court of Parliament in Westminster-Hall: On an Impeachment by the Commons of Great-Britain, for High Crimes and Misdemeanours: Containing the Whole of the Proceedings and Debates in Both Houses of Parliament, Relating to that Celebrated Prosecution, from Feb. 7, 1786, Until His Acquittal, April 23, 1795*, London: J. Debrett. John Logan, 1788; London: J. Debrett & Vernor and Hood, 1796.

—, *The Answer of Warren Hastings to the Articles: Delivered at the Bar of the House of Peers, on Nov. 28, 1787*, London: John Murray, 1788.

Hodges, William, *Travels in India During the Years 1780, 1781, 1782, 1783* (1794); Digitized OUP, 2007.

Holwell, John Zephaniah, *India Tracts by Mr. Holwell and Friends*, Paperback: Nabu Press, Primary Source ed. 2013.

Hunter, W.W., *Annals of Rural Bengal* (1868), Smith, Elder and Company, (1871); rept. 1965.

Imperial Gazetteer of India: United Provinces of Agra and Oudh, Vol. II, Calcutta: Govt. Printing, 1908.

Indian Year Book 1944-45, The, Vol. XXXI, Bombay: Bennett, Coleman & Co., Ltd, 1945.

James, J.F.W, *Selections from the Correspondence of the Revenue Chief of Bihar, 1781-1786*, Patna: Government Printing, 1919.

Johnson, Alison M., 'The Renell Collection', *The Geographical Journal*,148 (1) (1982):38-42.

Khadilkar, Ramchandra Raghunath, *Bhojpur Kshetra ke Pahle Vidroh ki Kahani*, in Vishwanath Mukherjee, *Yah Banaras Hai*, Varanasi: Thalua Club, 1978.

Lee, Sidney, ed., 'Renell, James', *Dictionary of National Biography*, 48, London: Smith, Elder & Co., 1896.

Logan, John, *A Review of the Principal Charges Against Warren Hastings Esquire, Late Governor General of Bengal*, London: John Stockdale, 1788.

Malcolm, Sir John, *The Life of Robert Clive,* India: Life Span Publishers, 2012.

Malleson, Col G.B., *History of the French in India*, London: Allen, 1893.

Marx, Karl, *The Eighteenth Brumaire of Louis Bonaparte* (1852); Paperback: Independent Pub, 2016.

Motilal Nehru Collected Works, multi-vols. (1926-1928), eds., Ravinder Kumar & Hari Deov Sharma, New Delhi: NMML-Vikas Publishing, 1982.

Mukherjee, Vishwanath, *Yah Banaras Hai*, Varanasi: Thalua Club, 1978.

Mundy, Peter, *The Travels of Peter Mundy*, Vol. 2: *Travels in Asia, 1628-1634*, [Travel to India, 1655-56], ed., Lt-Col Sir Richard Carnac Temple, London: Hakluyt Society, 1914.

Muzaffarpur District Gazetteer, Patna: Govt. Printing, 1930.

Nevill, H.R., *District Gazetteers of the United Provinces of Agra and Oudh*, vol. 31: Gorakhpur, Allahabad: Govt. Press, 1909.

O'Malley, L.S.S. (Author), A.P. Middleton, ed., *Bihar and Orissa District Gazetteers: Saran*, Patna: Govt. Printing, Bihar & Orissa, 1930.

O'Malley, L.S.S., *History of Bengal, Bihar and Orissa under British Rule*, Calcutta: Govt. printing, 1925. Also refer under district-wise *Gazetteers.*

—, *Bengal District Gazetteers: Saran*, Calcutta: Bengal Secretariat, 1908;

—, *Bengal District Gazetteers: Shahabad*, Calcutta: Bengal Secretariat, 1906.

Oldham, Wilton, *Historical and Statistical Memoir of the Ghazeepoor District*, Allahabad: 1870.

Orme, Robert, *A History of the Military Transactions of the British Nation in Indostan: from the year MDCCXLV*; to which is prefixed A dissertation on the establishments made by Mahomedan conquerors in Indostan, (1803); Madras: reprinted Pharaoh Collection, 1861.

Renell, James (1742-1813), *India- A Bengal Atlas: containing Maps of the Theatre of war and Commerce on that side of Hindoostan compiled from the original surveys...*, London, s.n., 1780;

—, *The Journals of Major James Renell*, Calcutta: Baptist Mission Press & Asiatic Society, 1910;

—, 'James Renell: The Father of the Indian Survey,' Online Exhibits;

—, (https://apps.lib.umich.edu/online-exhibits)❖Maps and Map-making in India (/online-exhibits/exhibits/show/India-maps).

Ross, *Correspondence of Charles, First Marquis Cornwallis*, Vols. I-II, London: John Murray, 1859.

Royal Society of Edinburgh, *Biographical Index of Former Fellows of the Royal Society of Edinburgh 1783–2002 (PDF)*, Royal Society of Edinburgh. 2006.

S.R. Kerr, J.H., *Final Report on the Survey and Settlement Operations in the Saran District, 1893 to 1901*, Calcutta: Bengal Secretariat Press, 1903.

Salim, Ghulam Husain, *Riyaz-us-Salatin* (Persian, 1786-87); Eng. trans. *A History of Bengal*, by Maulvi Abdus' Salam, (Calcutta, 1788); rept. Nabu Press, 2010.

Salatore, G.N., U.P. State Records, *Selections from English Records: Banaras Affairs (1811-1858)*, Vol. II, Allahabad: Central Record Office, 1959.

Saran District Gazetteer, 1960, comp. P.C. Roy Chaudhury, Patna: Bihar Secretariat Press, 1960.

Saran District Gazetteer, B Vol.: *Statistics, 1901-02 to 1910-11*, Allahabad: Govt. Press, 1914.

Saran District Gazetteer, by L.S.S. O'Malley, Rev. ed. by A.P. Middleton, Calcutta: Bengal Secretariat Book Depot, 1908.

Saran District Gazetteer, by L.S.S. O'Malley, Rev. ed. by A.P. Middleton, Calcutta: Govt. Print, 1930.

Saran District Gazetteer, Statistics, 1901-02, Calcutta: Bengal Secretariat, 1905.

Scranton, Luke, *Reflections on the Government of Indostan* (1763); London: reprinted by W. Strahan Jun. for G. Kearsley. Internet Archive.

Singh, Bhagwati Saran, *An Appeal to Zamindars*, [Private appeal by the author], 1931.

Stevenson-Moore, J., *Champaran Survey and Settlement Report*, Survey 1803.

Tabatabai, Ghulam Husain Khan (b. 1727), *Siyar-ul-Mutakherin* (an eighteenth century history in Persian completed in 1782), Eng. trans. Haji Mustafa, 4 vols., Calcutta, 1902.

The Hathwa Raj Family, (an account of services rendered to government by the Hutwa Raj), 1914.

Twain, Mark, 'Mark Twain's itinerary', retrieved from website.

Tull, Walsh J.H., *A History of Murshidabad District (Bengal)*, (1902); Paperback, Franklin Classics, 2018.

Valentia, George Viscount, *Voyages and Travels to India etc.*, 3 vols., 1809, Facsimile Publisher, 2020.

Vansittart, Henry, *Narrative of the Transactions in Bengal, From the Year 1760, to the Year 1764, During the Government of Mr. Henry Vansittart*, 3 vols. (1760); rpt. Forgotten Books, 2018.

Wickwire, Franklin B. and Mary Wickwire, *Cornwallis, the Imperial Years*, North Carolina: University of North Carolina Press, 1980.

Wilson, Minden, *Histories of the Bihar Indigo Factories; Reminiscences of Behar;*

—, *Tirhoot and its Inhabitants of the Past;*

—, *History of the Light Horse Volunteers*, Calcutta: General Printing, 1908.

PRIVATE SOURCES

Documents & Heirloom Collections

Hathwa Raj Collections: Papers, artifacts and pictures

Tamkuhi Raj Collections: Papers, artefacts and pictures:

—, Tamkuhi Raj Court Case Documents, as cited in the text, and the major ones entered in the Bibliography;

— Miscellaneous unpublished typed or handwritten papers, photographs of Fateh Sahi's belongings—sword (khukri), dagger (khukri), shield, matchlock, axe, and other possessions of the family, such as, a tiger-head-mounted Nalki (reminiscent of Tipu Sultan's iconic Tiger-Soldier machine), which the Tamkuhi family possessed till 1948, etc.

Interactions

Hathwa Raj Family (Bihar): Mrigendra Pratap Bahadur Sahi, head of the family; his son and next in line, Kastubmani Pratap Sahi, Hathwa, Bihar, Camp: Patna.

Tamkuhi Raj Family (UP): Vaidurya Pratap Sahi, A.P. Sahi, R.P. Sahi, Maheshwar Pratap Sahi, Veena Sahi, Tamkuhi, UP. Camp: Allahabad, Delhi.

Salemgarh- Chainpur Family (UP-Bihar): Shubhrendu Singh, Salemgarh, UP.

Sheohar Family (Bihar): Krishna Nandan Singh, Sheohar, Bihar. Camp: Patna.

Banaras Raj Family (UP): Chait Singh's descendants: Dileep Singh and Anurag Singh Kashiwale, Gwalior.

Parsa Garh Family: Kashinath Singh and Aditya Narayan Singh, Parsa Garh, Bihar, Camp: Benares.

Ghataro Chaturbhuj-Dharahara Family (Bihar): Priyadarshini Sharma, a history and heritage enthusiast, with *The Hindu*, Kochi.

Singhabad (Tilasan) Family (West Bengal): Rakesh Rai (Tilasan), and Shefali Roy (Patna University).

Lalgola Family (West Bengal): Yatindra Narayan Rai, Lalgola.

Mahisadal Family (West Bengal): Hara Prasad Garg, Kolkata.

Jagat Singh Family (Varanasi): Pradeep Narayan Singh, Varanasi.

Manjha Family (Bihar): Amiteswarendra Shahi, Manjha Gopalganj, Bihar.

SECONDARY SOURCES

Ahmad, Qeyamuddin, 'Aspects of Historical Geography of Medieval Bihar', *Indian Historical Review* 5 (1975): 119-35.

Amin, Shahid, *Conquest and Community: The Afterlife of Warrior Saint Ghazi Miyan*, Paperback: University of Chicago Press, 2016.

Ansari, Tahir Hussain, *Administration and the Zamindars of Bihar*, New Delhi: Manohar, 2019.

Askari, S.H. & Qeyamuddin Ahmad, eds., *Comprehensive History of Bihar*, Vol. ii, Part i-ii (1983); Patna: K.P. Jayaswal Research Institute, 1987.

Barnett, Richard B., *North India between Empires: Awadh, the Mughals, and the British, 1720-1801,* (1980), Delhi: Manohar, 1987.

Basra, Amrit Kaur, '*1757 se 1857 ke beech British Bharat men jan-vidroh*', in Ramlakhan Shukla, ed., *Adhunik Bharat ka Itihas,* (in Hindi, 1987), Delhi: Delhi University, 27th edn. 2016.

Bayly, C.A., *Rulers, Townsmen and Bazaars: North Indian Society in the Age of British Expansion 1770-1870* (1983); New Delhi: Oxford, 2002.

Bhattacharyya, Ananda, ed., *Sannyasi and Fakir Rebellion in Bengal: Jamini Mohan Ghosh Revisited,* Delhi: Manohar, 2014.

Bhura, Sneha, 'How Satyajit Ray immortalised "a little-known place called Nimtita,"' *The Week,* New Delhi: 22 June 2018

Bihar District Gazetteer: Saran, ed., P.C. Chaudhury, Patna: Secretariat Press, 1960.

Bloch, Marc, *The Historian's Craft: Reflections on the Nature and Uses of History and the Techniques and Methods of Those Who Write It,* Vintage, Paperback: Mass Market, 1964.

Borpujari, Priyanka, 'India's forgotten power broker—what was her secret?' *National Geographic,* 5 July 2019.

Chandra, A.N., *The Sanyasi Rebellion,* Calcutta: Ratna Prakashan, 1977.

Chatterjee, Kumkum, *Merchants, Politics and Society in Early Modern India: Bihar: 1733–1820,* Brill, 1996.

Chatterjee, Parth, et al, *Subaltern Studies,* 12 vols., Delhi: OUP, Permanent Black and Ravi Dayal Publisher, 1982-2005.

Chatterjee, Suranjan, 'New Reflections on the Sannyasi, Fakir and Peasants War,' *Economic and Political Weekly,* Jan. 28, 1984, Vol. 19, No. 4 (28 January 1984): PE2-PE13.

Chattopadhyay, Bankim Chandra, *Anandamath,* Eng. trans., Lipner Julius, UK: Oxford University Press, 2006;

—, ed., *Anandamath, or The Sacred Brotherhood,* India: OUP Online edn.

Chaudhuri, S.B., *Civil Disturbances during the British Rule in India, 1765-1857,* Calcutta: World Press, 1955.

Chaudhury, Sushil, *From Prosperity to Decline: Eighteenth Century Bengal,* New Delhi: Manohar, 1999.

Cohn, Bernard. S., 'Political Systems in Eighteenth Century India: The Banaras Region', *Journal of American Oriental Society* 82, 1962:312-20.

—, 'Structural change in Indian rural society 1596-1885' in R.E. Frykenberg, ed., *Land Control and Social Structure in Indian History*, Madison, Wisconsin, 1969.

Cotton, C.W.E., *Handbook of Commercial Information for India*, Calcutta: Govt. Press, 1919.

Dalrymple, William, *The Anarchy: The Relentless Rise of the East India Company*, London-New Delhi: Bloomsbury, 2019.

Datta, K.K., ed., *The Comprehensive History of Bihar*, 3 vols., Part i-ii, Patna: K.P. Jayaswal Research Institute, 1976;

—, *Anti- British Plots and Movements before 1857*, Meerut: Meenakshi, 1970;

—, *History of the Freedom Movement in Bihar*, 3 vols, Patna: Govt of Bihar, 1957;

—, *History of the Bengal Subha*, Vol. i, Calcutta, 1935.

Dixit, Akshaywar, *Bharatiya Swatantrya Sangram ka Pratham Veer Nayak* (in Hindi), Muzaffarpur: Abhida Prakashan, 2007;

—, 'Bharatiya Swatantrya Sangram ka Pratham Veer Nayak Maharaj Fateh Bahadur Shahi—Ek Singhavlokan', in Akshaywar Dixit, *Vimarsh*, New Delhi: Ayan Prakashan, 2010.

Durant, Will, *The Case for India* (1930), reissued: Mumbai: Standard Book Stall, 2015.

Dutt, Devendra Nath, *A Brief History of the Hathwa Raj*, K.P. Mookherjee, Calcutta, 1909.

Dutt, Girindra Nath, *History of the Hutwa Raj*, Bankipur: Lahiri & Co., 1905;

—, 'History of the Hathwa Raj', *Journal of the Asiatic Society of Bengal*, Vol. 73 (Calcutta), 1904;

—, 'Chronicles of the Hathwa Raj', *Calcutta Review*, Vol. C.V. (Calcutta), July 1897.

Dutt, Ramesh Chander, *The Economic History of India under Early British Rule: From the Rise of the British Power in 1757 to the Accession of Queen Victoria in 1837* (1950); rept. New Delhi: Govt. of India, 1963.

Fraser, Hugh, 'Folklore from Eastern Gorakhpur', *Journal of Asiatic Society of Bengal* 52 (Calcutta): 7-8.

Frykenberg, R.E., ed., *Land Control and Social Structure in Indian History*, Madison: University of Wisconsin Press, 1969.

Frykenberg, Robert, *Christianity in India: From Beginnings to the Present*, Oxford History of the Christian Church, 2008.

Ghosal, H.R., *Economic Transition in the Bengal Presidency 1793-1833* (PU PhD Dissertation 1950), Calcutta: 2nd edn. Firman K.L. Mukhopadhyay, 1966.

Hagen, James R., and Anand. A Yang, 'Local Sources for the Study of Rural India: The "Village Notes" of Bihar', *IESHR* 13 (1976):75-84.

Hasan, S. Nurul, 'The Position of the zamindars in the Mughal Empire,' *IESHR*, Vol. I, No. 4, April-June 1964: 107-19.

Heaney, G.F. 'Rennell and the Surveyors of India', *The Geographical Journal*, 134 (3), 1968: 318–325.

Holmes, T.R., *History of the Indian Mutiny and of the Disturbances which Accompanied it Among the Civil Population* (1898); 5th. edn., Macmillan, 1904.

Hussain, Taiyab, *Ek Gumshuda Itihas* (Hindi drama), Patna: Shabd Sansar, 2009.

Jha, Murari Kumar, *The Political Economy of the Ganga River: highway of state formation in Mughal India, c. 1600-1800*, Leiden: Leiden University, 2013.

Jharap, Kuldeepnarayan, 'Meer Jamal Buddh' (a *khand kavya* in Hindi) in Akshaywar Dixit, ed., *Aur Kampani Kanpti Rahi* (in Hindi), 2010.

Kalapura, Jose, *The Case of the Bettiah Christians in India*, 2015;

—, *Christian Missions in Bihar and Jharkhand till 1947: A Study by P.C. Horo*, Delhi: Christian World Imprints, 2014.?

Kantak, Suresh, *Pahila Nayak* (Bhojpuri drama), Baksar: Navshakti Prakashan, 2010.

Keay, Julia, *Farzana: The Woman who Saved an Empire*, I.B. Tauris, 2014.

Khosla, K.R., comp., R.P. Chatterjee, ed., *His Imperial Majesty King George V and the Princes of India and the Indian Empire (Historical Biographical)*, Lahore: Imperial Publishing Co., 1937.

Kochuchira, John, *Political History of Santal Parganas from 1765 to 1872*, Inter-India Publications, 2000.

Lefebre, Georges, *The Great Fear of 1789: Rural Panic in Revolutionary France (1932)*, Eng. trans., Pantheon, 1973;

—, *The French Revolution*, vol. I: *From Its Origins to 1793*, trans. (1951); Vol. II: *The French Revolution: From 1793 to 1799*, (1957); Columbia University Press, 1962–64.

Lipner, Julius. J., ed., *Anandamath, or The Sacred Brotherhood*, Oxford Univ. Press Online edition;

—, "'Icon and Mother': An Inquiry into India's National Song," *The Journal of Hindu Studies*, 2008: 26-48.

Maharatna, Paramita, 'Explaining Chait Singh's Revolt in Bihar (1781): The Role of the Refractory Bihar Zamindars,' *Proceedings of the Indian History Congress*, 2007, Vol. 68, Part I 2007: 565-72;

—, 'The British in Bihar: 1757-1781', unpublished M. Phil. Dissertation, University of London, 1992, esp. Chap. 6 [also for repercussions of Chait Singh's revolt in Bihar in 1781].

Marshall, P.J., *The impeachment of Warren Hastings* (1965);

—, P.J. Marshall, 'Hastings, Warren (1732–1818)', *Oxford Dictionary of National Biography* (Oxford University Press, 2004); online edn, October 2008.

McLane, John R., *Land and Local Kingship in 18th century Bengal*, Cambridge University Press, online 2009.

Mishra, G.S., *British Foreign Policy and Indian Affairs 1783-1815*, Bombay: Asia Publishing, 1963.

Misra, B.B., *The Central Administration of the East India Company, 1733-1833*, Manchester: Manchester Univ. Press, 1950.

Misra, Shree Govind, *History of Bihar*, New Delhi: Manohar, 1970.

Moon, Penderel, *Warren Hastings and British India*, Macmillan, 1949: esp. chap. XVII for Impeachment: online.

Moreland, W.H., *The Agrarian System of Moslem India*, Cambridge: Heffer, 1929.

Mukherjee, Mithi. 'Justice, War, and the Imperium: India and Britain in Edmund Burke's Prosecutorial Speeches in the Impeachment Trial of Warren Hastings,' *Law and History Review* 23.3 (2005): 589-630 online.

O'Malley, L.S.S., author, A.P. Middleton, ed., *Bihar and Orissa District Gazetteers: Saran*, Patna: Govt. Printing, 1930.

Oldham, Wilton, *Historical and Statistical Memoir of the Ghazeepoor District*, Allahabad: Govt. Printing, 1870.

Pandey Kapil, *Phoolsunghi* (1977), Eng. trans. (New Delhi: Penguin, 2020).

Pandey, Manager and Anjala Upadhyay, 'Truth Fears No Test', *Indian Literature*, Vol. 44, No. 1 (195), January–February 2000:12-23.

Pathak, Shreya, *The Ruling Dynasty of Benares State*, New Delhi: Anamika, 2014.

Pradhan, Awadhesh, '*Samrajya-Virodhi Sangharsh ka ek aur bhula-bisra naiyak Fateh Shahi*,' in Akshaywar Dixit, ed., *Aur Kampani Kanpti Rahi* (in Hindi), 2010: 106-15.

Prasad, Leela, *Opposition to British Supremacy in Bihar, 1757-1803*, New Delhi: Janaki Prakashan, 1981.

Qureshi, H.A. and Shreya Pathak, *The Lost Hero of Banaras: Babu Jagat Singh*, Delhi: Primus Books, 2024.

Rai, Kuldeep Narayan, '*Maharaj Bahadur Fatehshahi aur Swatantra ka 1857 tak ka Itihasey*,' *Brahmarshi-Sandesh* (Hindi), Kanpur 29-40.

Ramusack, *The New Cambridge History of India: The Indian Princes and Their States*, Paperback 2005.

Ray, Aniruddha, 'Revolt of Vizir Ali of Oudh at Benares in 1799,' *Procs. of the Indian History Congress, 49th Session*, Karnatak Univ., Dharwad, 1988: 331–38.

Ray, Ratnalekha, 'The Bengal Zamindars: Local magnates and the state before the Permanent Settlement,' *IESHR* 12:3 (1975): 263–92.

Raye, N.N., *The Annals of the Early English Settlement in Bihar*, Calcutta: Kamla Book Depot, 1927.

Rizvi, S.A.A., *Freedom Struggle in Uttar Pradesh*, 6 vols., New Delhi: OUP, 2010.

Rodd, Rennell, 'Major James Rennell. Born 3 December 1742. Died 20 March 1830', *The Geographical Journal*, 75 (4): 289–99.

Rudé, George, *The Crowd in the French Revolution*, US: Paperback: OUP, 1968.

Sahi, Vaidurya Pratap, 'Fateh Sahi's Religious Belief,' *Writers Pouch*, 21.2.2020;

—, *Sahi's Anecdotes: Tales from Tamkuhi*, Writers Pouch, 2024.

Sankrityayan, Rahul, *Puratatwa-Nibandhavli*, Prayag: Indian Press, n.d.

Sanyal, Suprakash, *Benares and the English East India Company, 1764-1795*, Calcutta: World Press, 1979.

Shukla, R.L., ed., *Adhunik Bharat ka Itihas* (in Hindi), Delhi: Dilli Visvavidyalaya (1987); 18th edn., 2020.

Shukla, Ramdev, *Kavita aur Kudal* (Hindi novel), New Delhi, n.d.

Singh, Bholanath, 'Saranya Janpad ka Uttaranchal: Aitihasik Vivechan', in Akshayvar Dikshit, *Bharatiya Swatantrya Sangram ka Pratham Veer Nayak* (in Hindi), 2007.

Singh, Rana P.B., *Clan Settlements in the Saran Plain (Middle Ganga Valley): A Study in Cultural Geography*, Varanasi: BHU, 1977.

Sinha, J.C., *Economic Annals of Bengal*, (1927); Digitized: University of Michigan, 2007.

Sinha, J.N., 'Vignettes from the Age of War', *The Hindu*, Chennai, 22 May 2011.

Smith, Brian. 'Edmund Burke, the Warren Hastings trial, and the moral dimension of corruption.' *Polity* 40.1 (2008): 70-94 online.

Tharoor, Shashi, *An Era of Darkness: The British Empire in India*, New Delhi: Aleph, 2016.

Tripathi, Pt. S.N.M, *Autobiography*, [refers to Tamkuhi's donations to BHU], VP Sahi's post: 8 June 2021.

Tull, Walsh J.H., *A History of Murshidabad District (Bengal)*, (1902); Paperback, Franklin Classics, 2018.

Tyagi, Sanjiv, *Aur Hathi Bik Gaye evam anya Kahaniyan* (in Hindi), Sarv Bhasha Trust.

Yang, Anand A., *The Limited Raj: Agrarian Relations in Colonial India, Saran District, 1793-1920*, New Delhi: OUP, 1989;

—, *Bazaar India: Market, Society, and the Colonial State in Gangetic Bihar* (1999), paperback: New Delhi: Munshiram, 2000;

—, 'Social History and Local Records: Sources for the Study of Modern Bihar,' *Indian Archives* 28, 1979: 1-23.

ONLINE RESOURCES

Tamkuhi Samachar: www.tamkuhisamachar.com.

Royal Archives: **oroyalarchives.com**. https://oroyalarchives.com/h, *Wikipedia Commons* and other web platforms, including some personal, family and ethnic portals.

Hathwa Raj - Alchetron, The Free Social Encyclopedia, alchetron.com.

Online resources of several internet platforms: Including National Archives of India, National Library (Kolkata), Jai Gyan, Indian

Culture, Internet Archive, digitallibraryindia; Project Gutenberg online library of free eBooks; and portals of the Universities of Chicago, California, Toronto, Amsterdam, etc.

Notes

Introduction

1. Bankim Chandra Chattopadhyay, *Anandamath*, Hindi trans. Dilipkumar Banerjee (New Delhi: Rajkamal, 2011). English trans. Julius Lipner, *Anandamath* (UK: Oxford University Press, 2006).
2. Ibid. Also see J.J. Lipner, '"Icon and Mother": An Inquiry into India's National Song', *The Journal of Hindu Studies*, 2008, 1:26–48.
3. J.J. Lipner, 2008, 45.
4. Vaidurya Pratap Sahi of the Tamkuhi Raj family informs me that his grandmother was connected from her mother's side with the Lalgola zamindars. For Lalgola, see Walsh J.H. Tull, *A History of Murshidabad District, Bengal* (1902); Paperback (Franklin Classics Trade Press, new edn. 2018: Chapter V).
5. Sneha Bhura, 'How Satyajit Ray immortalised a little-known place called Nimtita', *Week*, New Delhi, 22 June 2018.
6. Girindra Nath Dutt, *History of the Hutwa Raj* (Bankipur: Lahiri & Co., 1905).
7. Devendra Nath Dutt, *A Brief History of the Hutwa Raj* (Calcutta: Hutwa Raj, K.P. Mukherjee, 1909).
8. L.S.S. O'Malley and A.P. Middleton, eds., *Bihar and Orissa District Gazetteers: Saran* (Patna: Govt. Printing, 1930).

9. *Bihar District Gazetteer: Saran* [hereafter *DGS*], ed. P.C. Roy Chaudhury (Patna: Secretariat Press, 1960): 51–55.
10. *The Comprehensive History of Bihar*, ed., K.K. Datta, Vol. III, Part I, (Patna: K.P. Jayaswal Research Institute, 1976).
11. Leela Prasad, *Opposition to British Supremacy in Bihar, 1757-1803* (New Delhi: Janaki Prakashan, 1981): 52–61; Paramita Maharatna, 'Explaining Chait Singh's Revolt in Bihar (1781)', *Procs. Indian History Congress, 2007*, Vol. 68, Part I, 2007: 565–72.
12. Anand A. Yang, *The Limited Raj: Agrarian Relations in Colonial India, Saran District, 1793-1920* (New Delhi: Oxford University Press [hereafter OUP]), 1989.
13. Anand A. Yang, *Bazaar India: Market, Society, and the Colonial State in Gangetic Bihar* (1999); (New Delhi: Manohar, 2000).
14. B.S. Cohn, 'Structural Change in Indian Rural Society 1596–1885', in R.E. Frykenberg, ed., *Land Control and Social Structure in Indian History* (Wisconsin: Madison, 1969), 89–114; S. Nurul Hasan, 'The Position of the Zamindars in the Mughal Empire,' *IESHR*, Vol. I, No. 4, April–June 1964, 107–19; Richard B. Barnett, *North India between Empires: Awadh, the Mughals, and the British, 1720-1801,* (1980); (Delhi: Manohar, 1987).
15. Leela Prasad, 1981: 52-61; Paramita Maharatna, 'Explaining Chait Singh's Revolt in Bihar (1781)', 2007: 565–72.
16. George Rudé, *The Crowd in the French Revolution*, Paperback (US: OUP, 1968). The 'Eighteenth Brumaire' refers to 9 November 1799 in the French Revolutionary Calendar, the day Napoleon Bonaparte had become dictator by a coup d'état. In his works, Marx traced how the conflict of different social interests manifests itself in the complex web of political struggles.
17. C.A. Bayly, *Rulers, Townsmen and Bazaars: North Indian Society in the Age of British Expansion 1770-1870* (1983); (New Delhi: OUP, 2002).
18. Shashi Tharoor, *An Era of Darkness: The British Empire in India* (New Delhi: Aleph, 2016); William Dalrymple, *The Anarchy* (London: Bloomsbury, 2019). Most recently, Tahir Hussain Ansari, *Mughal Administration and the Zamindars of Bihar* (New Delhi: Manohar, 2019),

236–50, has discussed Fateh Sahi in greater detail; but, once again, primarily as a revenue defaulter.

19. Rahul Sankrityayan, *Puratatwa-Nibandhavli* (Prayag: Indian Press, n.d.).
20. Amrit Kaur Basra, '*1757 se 1857 ke beech British Bharat men jan-vidroh*', in Ramlakhan Shukla, ed., *Adhunik Bharat ka Itihas* (in Hindi) (1987); (Delhi: Delhi University; 27th edn, 2016).
21. Rahul Sankrityayan, *Puratatwa-Nibandhavli*; and Awadhesh Pradhan, '*Samrajya-Virodhi Sangharsh ka ek aur bhula-bisra naiyak Fateh Shahi*,' in Akshaywar Dixit, ed., *Aur Kampani Kanpti Rahi* (in Hindi), 2010: 106-15.
22. Akshaywar Dixit, *Bharatiya Swatantrya Sangram ka Pratham Veer Nayak* (in Hindi), (Muzaffarpur: 2007), and his other writings; Kuldeepnarayan Jharap, *Meer Jamal Buddh* (Hindi *khand kavya*), (publication details not available); Ramdev Shukla, *Kavita aur Kudal* (Hindi novel), (New Delhi: n.d.); Taiyab Hussain, *Ek Gumshuda Itihas* (Hindi drama), (Patna: 2009); Suresh Kantak, *Pahila Nayak* (Bhojpuri drama), (Baksar: 2010).
23. J.N. Sinha, 'Vignettes from the age of war', *The Hindu*, Chennai, 22 May 2011, for an introductory profile of Fateh Sahi.

Chapter 1: A Hero Forgotten

1. The earliest account of Fateh Bahadur Sahi appeared over a century ago in Girindra Nath Dutt, *History of the Hutwa Raj* (Bankipur: Lahiri & Co., 1905), which was followed by Devendra Nath Dutt, *A Brief History of the Hutwa Raj* (Calcutta: K.P. Mookerjee, 1909).
2. K.K. Datta, *The Comprehensive History of Bihar*, Vol. III, Part I (Patna: K.P. Jayaswal Research Institute, 1976): 138–39.
3. Ibid. Also see William Dalrymple, *The Anarchy: The Relentless Rise of the East India Company* (London-New Delhi: Bloomsbury, 2019).
4. James Rennell, *A Bengal Atlas: containing Maps of the War and Commerce on that side of Hindoostan*, (1779), 1781; and his *Memoir of a Map of Hindoostan* (London: Court of Directors for the East India Company, 1781).

5. The European penetration for saltpetre and plantation in the region, for example, was a part of the process, but these aspects are yet to be studied in the context of the local geography and environment, independent of Gandhi's Champaran Satyagraha and the freedom movement.
6. Ferrell's Lawexplains the changes in the course of rivers universally, and can predict the direction of their flow in the northern and southern hemispheres, subject to local topography and the nature of the soil.
7. *DGS*, ed., P.C. Roy Chaudhury (Patna: Secretariat Press, 1960): 43–44.
8. *Darh* is a mock hunt by villagers of an animal, especially of boar. The villagers assemble their domestic animals in an open ground and incite them to attack the pig, which is eventually killed by the participants and its meat distributed among them.
9. C.A. Bayly, *Rulers, Townsmen and Bazaars: North Indian Society in the Age of British Expansion 1770-1870* (2002), 17–18.
10. These 'populous clans of warrior-cultivators deepened and extended their local sway' in various ways. They suppressed pockets of resistance among aboriginals, tribals and nomads living in the wild terrain, and pushed cultivation into the forest zones, north and south of the great plains between the Himalayas and the Ganga. This was first explored by Wilton Oldham in his *Historical and Statistical Memoir of the Ghazeepoor District* (Allahabad, 1870); and more recently by Bernard Cohn, 'Structural Change', in *Land Control*, 53–69. In the hilly borders of central India, the Baghel, Bundela and Gaharwar Rajputs conspicuously gained most from the decline of Mughal control and expansion of the arable land (See C.A. Bayly, 2002, 17–18).

Chapter 2: Prelude to Power

1. The town was associated with Jainism as well. Legends apart, the archaeological remains and the living traditions practised in Shravasti reflect these associations even now. It was one of the

six largest cities in India in the time of the Buddha (ref: https://en.wikipedia.org/wiki/Shravasti, retrieved 1.9.2021). In order to trace Fateh Sahi's lineage, we may occasionally return to the Shravasti connection, not only to prove his royal ancestry but also in relation to his war operations, using sanyasis from around this region.

2. Anand A. Yang, *The Limited Raj* (New Delhi: OUP, 1989): 58–59. Also see Kuldeep Narayan Rai, *'Maharaj Bahadur Fatehshahi aur swatantra ka 1857 tak ka itihasey'*, *Brahmarshi-Sandesh* (Hindi), (Kanpur, n.d.): 29–40.
3. G.P.S., 'The Aristocracy of Bihar', *Calcutta Review*, Vol. LXXVI, Calcutta, 1883, 80ff, appears to be the earliest discussion on their origins.
4. The Mallas were one of the sixteen Mahajanpadas (republics) in ancient India: Kasi, Kosala, Anga, Magadha, Vajji, Malla, Chedi, Vats, Kuru, Panchala, Machcha, Surasena, Assaka, Avanti, Gandhara and Kamboja.
5. Rahul Sankrityayan, *Puratatva-Nibaandhawli* (Hindi), (Prayag: Indian Press Ltd, n.d.).
6. Ibid.
7. Ref: Wikipedia, under the Creative Commons, retrieved on 1.9.2021.
8. Girindra Nath Dutt, *History of the Hutwa Raj* (Bankipur: Lahiri & Co., 1905), 179–80. Also see his 'History of the Hathwa Raj', *Journal of the Asiatic Society of Bengal*, 1904; and 'Chronicles of the Hathwa Raj', *Calcutta Review*, Vol. C.V. 12. No. CC IX, July 1897: 35–36.
9. G.P.S., 'The Aristocracy of Bihar', *Calcutta Review*, 1883, Vol. LXXVI, 83.
10. Girindra Nath Dutt, 1905, 180.
11. Banabhatta, *The Harsa-carita of Bana*, Eng. trans. E.B. Cowell and F.W. Thomas (London: Royal Asiatic Society, 1897).
12. Others claim he lived in the Gaya district of Bihar. Ref. Wikipedia, retrieved on 1.9.2021.
13. G.P.S., 'The Aristocracy of Bihar', *Calcutta Review*, 1883: 84–85. Also see the elaborate genealogical table provided with D.N. Dutt, 1909.

14. Anand A. Yang 1989, 58.
15. Ibid. Also see Kuldeep Narayan Rai, '*Maharaj Bahadur Fatehshahi aur swatantrey ka 1857 tak ka itihasey*', *Brahmarshi-Sandesh* (Hindi): 29–40.
16. Ref: http://ledoestate.blogspot.com/2017/11/rai-title-india-html?=1.
17. Many of the tribal chiefs who gained power over time claimed higher caste status and married among the Kshatriyas and assumed their titles, such as Singh, because Kshatriyas symbolized the ruling class. Others donned new titles as honorifics. But there are extreme examples, such as the sudden emergence of an entirely alien caste or social group in a distant land. The matrimonial alliances in ancient and medieval times aside, the establishment of a Punjabi Khatri as the Raja of Burdwan in Bengal in the time of Jahangir is still closer. This Raja is said to have originally been a commander of Jahangir who defeated the ruler of Burdwan, Sher Afghan, and captured his wife, Meherunnessa, for Jahangir, who married her with a new name, Noorjahan. Jahangir is said to have rewarded the commander with the jagir of Burdwan; and, thus, suddenly a new dynasty with the surname of Chand came into existence.
18. K.K. Datta, *The Comprehensive History of Bihar*, Vol. III, Part I, 1976, 284.
19. Anand A. Yang, 1989: 56–61.
20. K.S. Singh, Gen. ed., *People of India: Bihar, including Jharkhand*, authors: Surendra Gopal and Hetukar Jha (Calcutta: Anthropological Survey of India, Seagull Books, 2008).
21. Not far off in the Baharaich area to the west of Huseypur, Ghazi Miyan was a cult figure admired both for his fighting skill and spiritual powers. (See Shahid Amin, *Conquest and Community: The Afterlife of Warrior Saint Ghazi Miyan*, Chicago-London: University of Chicago Press, 2016).
22. Anand A. Yang, 1989: 58.
23. Abul Fazl, *Akbarnama*, ed. Maulawi Abdur Rahim, Calcutta: Asiatic Society of Bengal, 1877.
24. Babur, *Baburnama*, trans. A.S. Beveridge (London: OUP, 1921): 520–21.

25. Abul Fazl, *Ain-i-Akbari*, ed. Saiyad Ahmad Khan (Delhi: Private Press, 1856), Vol. I, 120, quoted in Tahir Hussain Ansari, (2019), 13.
26. W.H. Moreland, *The Agrarian System of Moslem India* (Cambridge: Heffer, 1929): 122, 191–94, 279. Parmatma Saran has defined them as vassal chiefs found in some parts of the Empire, and has also highlighted their position and role in it (ref. *Provincial Governments of the Mughals 1526-1658* (Allahabad: Allahabad Law Press Kabistan, 1941): 111.
27. Irfan Habib, *Agrarian System of Mughal India 1556-1707* (New Delhi: OUP, 1999): 169–75.
28. S. Nurul Hasan, *Thoughts on Agrarian Relations in Mughal India* (Delhi: PPH, 1990).
29. Tahir Hussain Ansari, 2019: 14–15.
30. Anand A. Yang, 1989: 59–60.
31. D.N. Dutt, 1909.
32. J.H. Tull Walsh, *A History of Murshidabad District (Bengal)*, 1902; Digital Library of India: Item 2015.211145. Also, my interaction with Vaidurya P. Sahi on his family's relationship with the Lalgola zamindars.
33. Refer also to authors who have written on Betia, Maheshpur and others, such as T.H. Ansari 2019.
34. Anand A. Yang, 1989: 55.
35. Ibid.
36. Ibid.: 55–56.
37. Shaad Azimabadi, *Tarikh-i-Suba Bihar*, Vol. I, Patna: Fine Art Printing Works, 1924: 121–22, quoted in Tahir H. Ansari, 2019: 254, 257.
38. G.N. Dutt, 1905: 181.
39. Anand A. Yang, 1989: 59.
40. S.H. Askari and Q. Ahmad, *The Comprehensive History of Bihar*, Vol. II, Part II, Patna: K.P. Jayaswal Research Institute, 1987: 302.
41. Raja Inderjeet Pratap Sahi of Tamkuhi, Court document, p. 149. Courtesy: V.P. Sahi.
42. L.S.S. O'Malley, *Bengal District Gazetteers: Saran* (Calcutta: Bengal Secretariat Book Depot. 1908): 21; also see Anand A. Yang, 1989: 59.

43. G.N. Dutt, 1905: 182 (vide Note on p. 227).
44. Legend says that a statue of the goddess was later found in the jungle, with one leg sunk in the ground and the other placed on a lion at the site where the Thawe temple exists today. This temple was built by the Hathwa Raj family, along with a resort house for their visits for worship. The food *bali* (sacrifice) is still offered to the legendary jackal in the adjoining jungle. The place is highly venerated by the local people and is the site of an annual fair.
45. D.N. Dutt, 1909; Anand A. Yang, 1989: 59.
46. Anand A. Yang, 1989: 59.
47. The Oiniwar dynasty ruled in the Mithila region during 1325–1526, after the Karnat dynasty. Following the end of the Oiniwars, there was a period of lawlessness in the region until the dynasty of the Raj Darbhanga emerged.
48. Abul Fazl, *Ain-i-Akbari*, Vol. I, trans. H. Blochmann and Colonel H.S. Jarnet, Vols. II & III, The Asiatic Society, 2010.
49. Anand A. Yang, 1989: 57.
50. Tahir H. Ansari, 2019: 237–39.
51. G.N. Dutt, 1905: 182. Also see Tahir H. Ansari, 2019: 38–39.
52. *DGS, 1960*, comp. P.C. Roy Chaudhury (Patna: Secretariat Press, 1960): 47.
53. Peter Mundy, *The Travels of Peter Mundy, 1608-1667*, Vol. II: *Travels in Asia, 1628-1634*, ed., Lt-Col Sir Richard Carnac Temple (London: Hakluyt Society, 1914).
54. G.N. Dutt, 1905: 185.
55. C.A. Bayly, *Rulers, Townsmen and Bazaars: North Indian Society in the Age of British Expansion 1770-1870* (1983); (New Delhi: OUP, 2002): 17–18. This was discovered by Wilton Oldham over a century later, which has more recently been analysed by Bernard Cohn.
56. See Wilton Oldham, *Historical and Statistical Memoirs of the Ghazipur District*, 2 vols, Allahabad, 1870; and Bernard S. Cohn, 'Structural Change in Indian Rural Society 1596-1885', in Frykenberg, ed., *Land Control and Social Structure in Indian History* (Madison, Wisconsin, 1969): 53–69.

57. C.A. Bayly, 2002: 17–18.
58. Ibid.

Chapter 3: At War for Freedom—1767–1772

1. Kuldeep Narayan Rai, '*Swatantray Sangram men Maharshi Vansh ka Yogdan*,' *Brahmarshi-Sandesh*, Vol. 1, 1687 BS (in Hindi), (Brahmarshi Samaj, Kanpur, 2022).
2. See K.K. Datta, ed., *Comprehensive History of Bihar* (hereafter *CHB*), Vol. III, Part I, (Patna: K.P. Jayaswal Research Institute, 1976): 1–71.
3. Ibid.: 19.
4. For details, see K.K. Datta, *CHB*, 1976.
5. See James Renell, *A Bengal Atlas: containing maps of the theatre of war and commerce on that side of Hindoostan compiled from the original surveys...* (London, s.n., 1780).
6. For a significant discussion on this aspect, see Murari Kumar Jha, 'Ganga-polity: Mughal Decline, the Zamindars and the Diwani Raj' in *The political economy of the Ganga River: highway of state formation in Mughal India, c. 1600-1800*, Leiden University Repository, 2013: 233–69.
7. William Dalrymple, *The Anarchy* (London-New Delhi: Bloomsbury Publishing, 2019): 167–68.
8. Warren Hastings was fast rising in the colonial bureaucratic hierarchy; after a successful stint at Murshidabad, he became the deputy of Henry Vansittart, and was looked upon as a future Governor. Anxious to make the dual government of the Mughals and the Company a success, he took up a positive posture, in view of the long-term prospects for the Company in India. He disliked the Company officials and agents indulging in rampant extortion and corruption, and their soldiers engaging in rapacious behaviour. Conflicts and clashes between the men of the Bengal Nawab and the Company became a common feature. Mir Kasim constantly complained of this to the Governor in utter desperation and helplessness, but to no avail.
9. William Dalrymple, *The Anarchy*, 2019: 171.

10. Ibid.
11. Ibid.: 172.
12. Ibid.: 174.
13. *Tarikh-i-Muzaffari* of Muhammad Ali Khan Ansari of Panipat, 703, quoted in William Dalrymple, *The Anarchy*, 2019: 174–75.
14. William Dalrymple, *The Anarchy*, 2019: 176.
15. R.R. Diwakar, Gen. ed., *Bihar Through the Ages* (Calcutta: Orient Longman, 1959), chapters I-II.
16. Pandey Kapil, *Phoolsunghi* (Bhojpuri novel; Eng. tr: India: Penguin Books, 2021) has portrayed his life close to reality.
17. For more details on the Dutch in Saran and the inland trading-ports like Revelganj, and other market centres such as Maharajganj, in and around Saran, see DGS: 484-85ff; also see P.C. Roy Choudhury, *Sarkar Saran*, Patna: Free Press, 1956.
18. Anand A. Yang, *The Limited Raj*, 1989; and his *Bazaar India: Market, Society, and the Colonial State in Gangetic Bihar*, (New Delhi: paperback Munshiram Manoharlal, 1999).
19. Renell's maps, op. cit.
20. For the settlers' recollections, see Sylvia Dyer, *The Spell of the Flying Foxes* (New Delhi: Penguin India, Paperback, 2011).
21. *District Gazetteers* of Champaran, Muzaffarpur and Darbhanga. For Mark Twain, refer to 'Itinerary of Mark Twain's Lecture Tour in India January 18–April 5, 1896', at website. Also see Keshav Mutalik, *Mark Twain in India* (Bombay: Noble House Publishing, 1987).
22. *DGS*, ed., P.C. Roy Chaudhury (Patna: Secretariat Press, 1960), 54.
23. Curiously, these boats were procured from Tripura (*DGS*, 1960): 55.
24. K.K. Datta, *CHB*, Vol. III, Part I, 1976: chaps. II and III.
25. Shashi Tharoor, *An Era of Darkness*, 2016: 12.
26. K.K. Datta, *CHB*, Vol. III, Part I, 1976, chap. II. For more details, see R.C. Dutt, *Economic History of India*, 2 vols. (Kegan Paul, 1902).
27. Sushil Chaudhury, *From Prosperity to Decline: Eighteenth Century Bengal* (Delhi: Manohar, 1999); Kumkum Chatterjee, *Merchants, Politics and Society in Early Modern India: Bihar: 1733–1820* (Leiden: Brill, 1996); John R. McLane, *Land and Local Kingship in 18th Century Bengal*

(Cambridge: Cambridge University Press, revised edn. 2002); Sir William Wilson Hunter, *The Annals of Rural Bengal* (New York: Leypoldt & Holt, 1868), seen at Internet Archive.

28. K.K. Datta, *CHB*, Vol. III, Part I, 1976: 138–39. May also see H.V. Bowen, *Revenue and Reform: The Indian Problem in British Politics 1757–1773* (Cambridge University Press, 2002).
29. K.K. Datta, *CHB*, Vol. III, Part I, 1976, 138.
30. Ibid.: 139.
31. See page 71, footnote 118; for details, William Dalrymple, *The Anarchy*, 2010: 139–40.
32. Ibid.: 117–18. Details of Clive's wealth and investment on return to London vary in sources, William Dalrymple gives a comprehensive break-up in his *Anarchy*, 2019: 139–40.
33. K.K. Datta, *CHB*, Vol. III, Part I, 1976: 129–30.
34. Ibid.; also, *DGS*, 1960: 51.
35. K.K. Datta, *CHB*, Vol. III, Part I, 1976: 131.
36. Ibid.
37. *Journal of the Bihar and Orissa Research Society*, 1940: 15. (6)
38. K.K. Datta, *CHB*, Vol. III, Part I, 1976: 132.
39. Ibid.
40. Ibid.: 133. For more details, see *Calendar of Persian Correspondence,* Vol. IV: 228, 236.
41. Suranjan Chatterjee, 'New Reflections on the Sanyasi, Fakir and Peasants War,' in *Economic and Political Weekly*, (Vol. 19, No. 4, 28 January 1984: PE2-PE13) presents an incisive synoptic view of these uprisings, including Sahi's rebellion. Also, see J.M. Ghosh, *Sanyasi and Fakir Raiders in Bengal* (Calcutta, 1930).
42. In the sixteenth century, Madhusudana Saraswati of Bengal organized an armed group of sanyasis to protect Hindus from the tyranny of the Mughal and oppressive local rulers. These sanyasis lived naked, and were called Nagas. They were also called Goswami or by its phonetic variances. Their main centres were called Akhara, prefixed with specific names such as Juna, Niranjani, Anand, Atal, Awahan, Agni and Nirmal Akhara.

43. These sanyasis belonged to the Hindu monastic order called Dashanami (connoting ten names), generally associated with the Vedanta tradition, organized in its present form by eighth-century-theologian Adi Shankara. They sought to achieve spiritual union with the *swa* (self). After renunciation, they generally wore robes of ochre, saffron or orange colour, as a symbol of non-attachment to worldly desires, and chose to roam independently, in a group, or join an ashram (spiritual centre). Its Swami order has ten subdivisions: Giri, Puri, Bhāratī, Vana, Āraṇya, Sagara, Āśrama, Sarasvatī, Tīrtha and Parvata. The Dashanamis are associated mainly with the four *maṭhas*, established by Shankara, in the four corners of India. They still assemble periodically at Kumbh melas at Prayag and elsewhere, posing an administrative challenge to control them.
44. Asit Nath Chandra, *The Sannyasi Rebellion* (1977); reprint (Ratna Prakashan, 2009).
45. Suranjan Chatterjee, 'New Reflections on the Sanyasi', 28 January 1984: PE2–PE13.
46. Ibid.
47. William Dalrymple, *The Anarchy: The East India Company, Corporate Violence, and the Pillage of an Empire* (Bloomsbury Publishing, London, 2019): 193–94.
48. Kuldeep Narayan Rai, '*Maharaj Bahadur Fatehshahi aur swatantra ka 1857 tak ka itihasey*', *Brahmarshi-Sandesh* (Hindi), (Kanpur): 29-40. Shubhrendu, a scion of the Chainpur-Salemgarh estate, is emphatic about Sahi's participation in the Battle of Buxar.
49. G.N. Dutt, 'History of the Hathwa Raj', *Journal of the Asiatic Society of Bengal*, 1904, 185–86; 'Chronicles of the Hatwa Raj', *Calcutta Review*, Vol. C.V., July 1897: 35–36.
50. K.K. Datta, *CHB*, Vol. III, Part I, 1976: 133–34.
51. Letter from Samuel Charters to Warren Hastings, Governor-General and the Council of Revenue at Fort William, with enclosures, dated 25 June 1782, Revenue Dept., G.G. in Council, 28 June 1782, L.R. No. 233–34, L.S. No. 86–89: 298-324, Bengal State Archives (College Street), Kolkata.

52. With the coup d'état of Eighteenth Brumaire, General Napoleon Bonaparte came to power as the first consul of France, which ended the French Revolution in the view of most historians. This bloodless coup overthrew the Directory, replacing it with the French Consulate. This occurred on 9 November 1799, which was Eighteenth Brumaire, Year VIII under the French Revolutionary Calendar. In his work on the Eighteenth Brumaire, Marx traced how the conflict of different social interests manifested themselves in the complex web of political struggles (Ref. Karl Marx, *The Eighteenth Brumaire of Louis Bonaparte* (1852); Paperback: Independent Pub, 2016).
53. K.K. Datta, *CHB*,Vol. III, Part I, 1976: 133–34.
54. K.K. Datta, *CHB*, Vol. III, Part I, 1976: 133–34.
55. *DGS*, 1960, Patna: Govt. Printing, 1960: 480.
56. *DGS*, 1908: 30. Also see Anand A. Yang, 1989: 63.
57. *DGS*, 1908: 30.
58. Shyam Narayan Singh, *History of Tirhut: From the Earliest Times to the End of the Nineteenth Century*, 1922 (Darbhanga: M.K. Singh Kalyani Foundation, 2012): 96.
59. With the passage of time, they lost their traditional sources of livelihood; so, while some shifted to other professions including farming, a section took to crime and became a social problem.
60. *DGS*, 1908: 30.
61. *Calendar of Persian Correspondence*, Vol. II (Calcutta: Govt. Printing, 1914): 202–03, quoted in A.N. Chandra, *The Sanyasi Rebellion*, 1977: 35–36.
62. Letter from Capt. Gabriel Harper to the President and Governor at Fort William, 25 June 1770.
63. Letter from the Controlling Council of Revenue at Patna to Capt. Carnac, December 1770, quoted in A.N. Chandra, 1977: 40.
64. *Calendar of Persian Correspondence*, Vol. II: 197.
65. A.N. Chandra, *The Sannyasi Rebellion*, (1977): 2009, 45.
66. Proc. of the Chief and Council of Revenue at Patna, 23 December 1771.
67. Anand Burdhan, 'The Sanyasi Revolt: A Critical Appraisal,' *History Today*, No. 19 (2018): 94–101.

68. Suranjan Chatterjee, 'New Reflections on the Sanyasi,' 28 January 1984, PE3, connects them to the peasant uprisings.
69. Ibid.
70. Ananda Bhattacharyya, *Sannyasi and Fakir Rebellion in Bengal: Jamini Mohan Ghosh Revisited* (New Delhi: Manohar, 2014). Also see A.N. Chandra, *The Sanyasi Rebellion* (1977); digitalized 2009.
71. Ibid.
72. See James Renell, *A Bengal Atlas: containing maps of the theatre of war and commerce on that side of Hindoostan compiled from the original surveys...*, London, s.n., 1780.
73. I personally travelled this remote and difficult terrain full of forests, varieties of water bodies, hills and tribal villages.
74. Golding to George Vansittart, Patna Council, 23 January 1771, Patna, Rev. Procs. 13 November 1770 to 28 May 1771: 45.
75. See Copy-book of letters issued by the Chief of Factory at Patna, April 1771 to March 1773.
76. For a broader perspective, see Murari Kumar Jha, *The Political Economy of the Ganga River: highway of state formation in Mughal India, c. 1600-1800*, Leiden: Leiden University, 2013; for finer details, *SDG* 1908: 138, 147-48, 150, 158-59; W.W. Hunter, *A Statistical Account of Bengal*, vol. 11, *Districts of Patna and Saran,* (London: Trubner & Co., 1877). *Account of Saran*: 328-31. Rankine, *Topography of Saran: 28.*
77. Anand A. Yang ,1997: 179.
78. Anand A. Yang, 1997: 178-79.
79. Robert Rankine, *Notes on the Medical Topography of District of Saran,* Calcutta: Military Orphan Press, 1839: 28; *SDG* 1908:138, 147-48, 150, 158-59; Hunter, *Account of Saran*: 328-31. Quoted in A.A. Yang 1997: FN 42: 179-80. Also see Alexander Wyatt, *Statistics of the District of Sarun and Chumparan, Calcutta: Military Orphan Press, 1847 [?]*; --, *Geographical and Statistical Report of the District of Tirhoot, Calcutta: Calcutta Gazette Office, 1854.*
80. For broader details, see *Gorakhpur: A Gazetteer*, Vol. XXXI: *District Gazetteers of the United Provinces of Agra and Oudh*, by H.R. Nevill, (Allahabad: Government Press, 1909); Montgomery Martin, *The History, Antiquities, Topography, and Statistics of Eastern India; Comprising*

the Districts of Behar, Shahabad, Bhagalpoor, Goruckpoor, Dinajpoor, Puraniya, Rungpoor, & Assam...., 3 vols.: Vol. II: *Bhagulpoor, Goruckpoor, and Dinajpoor* (London: W.H. Allen and Co., 1838). For later developments in the socio-economic spheres in Gorakhpur district, also refer to Ram Adhar Pandey, *Gorakhpur (c. 1813-1919 A.D.): A Study in Local History*, (Faizabad, RML Avadh University).

81. Yasmin Khan, *India at War: The Subcontinent and the Second World War*, (New York, Oxford, 2016).
82. See A.A. Yang, *Bazaar India*, 1997: 27–28.
83. Anand A. Yang, 1997: 30.
84. For more details on overland trade in the region, see Yang 1997: 180–87.
85. *DGS*, 1960: 55.
86. Ibid.: 53.

Chapter 4: Raids from the Jungle—1772–1795

1. The basic information on this aspect is available in K.K. Datta, ed., *The Comprehensive History of Bihar*, Vol. III, Part I, Patna: K.P. Jayaswal Research Institute, 1976 [shortened to *CHB*], chapters II-IV; also see *DGS*, by P.C. Roy Chaudhury (Patna: Secretariat Press, 1960): 55.
2. Letter to the Court, 8 Sep. 1766, para. 16, quoted in K.K. Datta, *CHB*, Vol. iii, part I, 1976: 135.
3. Ibid.: 135–36.
4. K.K. Datta, *CHB*, Vol. III, Part I, 1976: 136–37.
5. Ibid.: 137–38.
6. The Golghar is a huge beehive-shaped structure located to the west of the Gandhi Maidan at Patna in Bihar. As part of a long-term plan to prevent famine in the provinces, it was constructed as a granary on orders from Warren Hastings, during 1784–86. It was intended to be the first of a series of huge grain stores, though none others were ever built. It was designed by Captain John Garstin of the East India Company's Bengal Army (ref. the plaque at its base). Built in the Stupa architecture style, this 95-foot-high

structure has no pillars inside and a 145-step spiral stairway around it takes workers to the top to unload grain in it through a hole. The top presents a panoramic view of the city and the Ganga.

7. Anand Burdhan, 'The Sanyasi Revolt: A Critical Appraisal,' *History Today*, No. 19 (2018): 94–101.
8. Ibid.
9. James Pearson, Lt Commd., Barra Gawn, to Ewan Law, & c., Patna Council, 26 November 1777; A. Montgomerie, Colltr., to Wm. Cowper, BOR, 24 January 1792; Bengal Rev. Consltns., 2–27 January 1778, 13 January, no. 48, enc.; 4 May to 1 June. 1792, 24 January.
10. Ref. Patrick Turnbull (1975), *Warren Hastings* (New English Library); Moncton Jones, *Warren Hastings in Bengal* (Oxford, 1918).
11. Warren Hastings had an interest in the history and heritage of India. He encouraged the translation of the *Bhagavad Gita* into English by Charles Wilkins (Benares, 1784) and wrote its introduction. See William Dalrymple, *The Anarchy: The Relentless Rise of the East India Company* (London-New Delhi: Bloomsbury Publishing, 2019), XIII.
12. K.K. Datta, *CHB*, Vol. III, Part I, 1976, 142–43.
13. Ibid.
14. Ghulam Husain Khan Tabatabai, *Siyar-ul-Mutakharin* (Lucknow: Nawal Kishore Press, 1886).
15. K.K. Datta, *CHB*, Vol. III, Part I, 1976: 151–52.
16. Ibid.: 142, 145–46.
17. The origins of the kingdom of Kashi (also called Benares, Varanasi or Banaras) can be traced to ancient times. Since 1000 AD, its rajas belonged to the Gautam clan of Bhumihar Brahmins from Gangapur near Benares. In the late seventeenth century, Mansa Ram of this family entered the service of Rustam Ali Khan, the nazim of Benares. Soon, Mansa Ram rose to become the zamindar of Kaswar, recapturing the kingdom of his ancestors that had been lost to the Muslims. The Nawab of Awadh appointed him successor of Rustam Ali and, impressed by his administrative abilities, Mughal Emperor Mohammed Shah appointed him the Raja and nazim of the sarkars of Benares, Jaunpur, Ghazipur

and Chunar. His son and successor Balwant Singh (r. 1738–70) assumed this responsibility in 1738. He established his capital at Gangapur, but later shifted to Ramnagar, near Varanasi. In 1751, he expelled the representative of the Nawab in an attempt to carve out a principality in Benares, but had to flee after a fierce retaliation by the Nawab (1752). A settlement made between the two restored his titles. Emperor Alamgir II granted him a jagir in Bihar two years later. As the first of his house to fight with the East India Company, he joined Emperor Shah Alam and Nawab Shuja-ud-Daulah in their 1763 invasion of Bengal. After the Battle of Buxar in 1764, Shah Alam transferred Balwant's zamindari to the Company, but the Company refused to accept it. Instead, it reverted the zamindari once again to the Nawab of Awadh in 1765, five years before Balwant's death in 1770. His son Chait Singh (r. 1770–81) succeeded him as Raja of Benares, but he had to face a turbulent life thereafter. For further details, see Shreya Pathak, *The Ruling Dynasty of Benares State: Rise and Development 1740 to 1950 A.D.* (New Delhi: Anamika, 2014).

18. N.P. Verma, 'Repercussions in Bihar of the Rebellion of Chait Singh of Banaras,' *Procs. of the Indian History Congress*, vol. 66 (2005–06): 845–51.
19. Ibid. Also see Datta, *CHB*, Vol. III, Part I, 1976: 146–49
20. J.R. Hand, *Early English Administration of Bihar, 1781-1785*, 1–2.
21. So believed Lord Macaulay in his *Warren Hastings: Historical Essays*, quoted in N.P. Verma, 1976.
22. Chait Singh to Warren Hastings, 4 September 1781, in Foreign and Political Dept., Sec. Pr., 4 September – 22 October 1781, Vol. 68, No. 4, 2004–2008.
23. Hastings to Markham, 4 September 1781, in Foreign and Political Dept., Sec. Pr., 4 September – 22 October 1781, Vol. 68, No. 4, 2012–13.
24. Ibid.
25. Raja to Hastings, 4 September 1781, in Foreign and Political Dept., Sec. Pr., 4 September – 22 October 1781, Vol. 68, No. 4, 2012–13, quoted in Shreya Pathak, 2014: 131.

26. Shreya Pathak, 2014: 132.
27. In his letter to Major Scott, Hastings candidly mentioned the episode and referred to the 'repeated allusion to the insolent language' used by Cheitram, in the letter of the Raja. Cheitram, a dismissed mace-bearer, had often been found guilty of misbehaviour in the past; as such, he deserved the punishment, Hastings, too, felt. (Pathak 2014: 132–33).
28. Hastings to Wheeler, 4 September 1781, in Foreign and Political Dept., Sec. Pr., 4 September – 22 October 1781, Vol. 68, No. 4, 2022.
29. Hastings to Markham, 4 September 1781, in Foreign and Political Dept., Sec. Pr., 4 September – 22 October 1781, Vol. 68, No. 4, 2012–13.
30. However, Rani Golab Kunwar stayed in Benares along with her son-in-law Durgvijay Singh and his two sons. Was she unwilling to yield, or stayed for negotiating a settlement, as Durgvijay visited Hastings on the morning of 17 August?
31. Pathak, 2014: 135-36.
32. Charles Grome, Colltr., to Bengal Rev. Council, 15 September 1781, Bengal Rev. Consultns., 1 September to 23 October 1781, 28 September, No. 582.
33. Anand A. Yang, 1989: 68.
34. George Forest, ed., *Selections from the Letters, Dispatches and other State Papers Preserved in the Foreign Dept. of the Govt. of India,* Vol. I: 961–62 and 1004.
35. Pathak, 2014: 138.
36. The author is thankful to Kashinath Singh and his son Aditya Narayan Singh of Parsa Garh estate (Saran) for providing many related details.
37. Udit Narayan Singh (r. 1795–1835) was even more averse to British control. This embittered their relations further, and the Company projected him as a worse administrator than his father. In 1828, he petitioned the Company to annul the 1794 agreement and return the sarkars the family had lost under it. However, the Company retaliated with an inquiry into his personal affairs and governance that declared him guilty of gross mismanagement, and

they confiscated his last remaining landed property. He died in 1835. (Foreign and Political Dept., Secret Committee, 29 October 1781, no. 5).

38. Suprakash Sanyal, *Benares and the English East India Company, 1764-1795* (Calcutta: World Press, 1979): 155.
39. Pathak, 2014: 145.
40. Ibid., footnote 83.
41. G.N. Saletore, *Banaras Affairs*, Vol. II, Allahabad: Central Record Office, 1959: v.
42. Hastings to Major Scot, 21 February 1782, in G.R. Gleig, *Memoirs of Life of Warren Hastings*, vol. 3 (London: 1841): 428.
43. Hastings to Wheeler, 29 September 1781, in Foreign and Political Dept. 18 October 1781, No. 12.
44. Foreign and Political Dept., Secret Committee, 29 October 1781, No. 5: Proclamation made public at Benares on 29 September 1781.
45. Pathak, 2014: 147.
46. Sir Alured Clarke, commander-in-chief, etc, Juggut Singh / vide Benares Special Court and Resolution, in Judicial Dept. (Criminal), 24 October 1799; and acting registrar of the Nizamat Adawlat to G.B. Barlow, Secretary of the Govt., in Judicial Dept. (Criminal), 5 September 1799: 2–15, all at Bengal State Archives, College Street, Kolkata.
47. Ibid., which contains copies of various papers, from trial to the plan of transportation. Some people suspect he was poisoned by the Company authorities.
48. Foreign and Political Dept., Secret Committee, 16 June 1983, No. 11.
49. G.N. Saletore, *Banaras Affairs*, Vol. II: vii.
50. Interview with Anurag Chait Singh and his father, the descendants in Gwalior, July 2021.
51. N.P. Verma 2005–06; and Datta, *CHB*, Vol. III, Part I, 1976: 146–49.
52. Ibid.
53. Ibid. Also refer to Paramita Maharatna, 'Explaining Chait Singh's Revolt in Bihar (1781): The Role of the Refractory Bihar

Zamindars,' *Procs. of the Indian History Congress, 2007*, Vol. 68, Part I (2007): 565–72.

54. Ibid. Also see Tahir Hussain Ansari, *Mughal Administration and the Zamindars of Bihar* (New Delhi: Manohar, 2019), esp. chaps. 3–5.
55. K.K. Datta, *CHB*, Vol. III, Part, 1976: 146–49. Also, Shreya Pathak, *The Ruling Dynasty of Banares*, 2014, esp. chaps. 4–6.
56. For details, see correspondence between the board of revenue and revenue collectors, and the *5th Report from the Select Committee on the Affairs of the East India Company*, ed. by Firminger, Vol. II: 141–43.
57. J.L. Ross, revenue chief of Patna to Charles Grome, 31 August 1781.
58. J.L. Ross to Major Hardy, 6 October 1781: 16.
59. N.K. Singh, 'History of Territorial Aristocracy in Bihar, 1757-1793, unpublished PhD thesis, Patna University, Patna, 1967.
60. K.K. Datta, *CHB*, Vol. III, Part I, 1976: 146–49.
61. Samuel Charters to Warren Hastings, Governor-General and the Council of Revenue at Fort William, with enclosures, dated 25 June 1782, Revenue Dept., G.G. in Council, 28 June 1782, L.R. No. 233–34, L.S. No. 86–89, 298–324, Bengal State Archives, Kolkata (College Street).
62. Vazir Ali Khan (1780–1817) was the son of the daughter of a servant, who was adopted by Asaf-ud-Daulah. Aged thirteen, Vazir Ali was married in Lucknow at a staggering expenditure of £300,000. After the death of his surrogate father in September 1797, he ascended the throne with the support of the British.
63. Aniruddha Ray, 'Revolt of Vizir Ali of Oudh at Benares in 1799', *Procs. of the Indian History Congress, 49th Session*, Karnatak University, Dharwad, 1988: 331–38.
64. Finally, Awadh was annexed under the Doctrine of Lapse in 1856, and the following March, on the grounds of maladministration, it was placed under Henry Montgomery Lawrence as the chief commissioner. Under his predecessor, much of the local aristocracy had fallen from grace and widespread unrest had come to the fore. An added concern was the growing discontent among the sepoys of the Bengal Army, drawn largely from Awadh, who

were likely to command local support. Its Nawab, Wajid Ali Shah, was imprisoned and exiled to Calcutta. The Revolt of 1857 broke out soon after and the rebels took control of Awadh. The British could regain it only months later, after losing one of their ablest commanders—Lawrence. (https://en.wikipedia.org/wiki/Henry_Montgomery_Lawrence, retrieved on 7.9.2021).

65. The interference of the English and other Europeans in the socio-cultural life of the country was a persistent irritant for Indians. Sahi is said to have met with a poor mother begging with her small daughter who looked like a European in colour and features. On his query, the mother hinted that the child was the offspring of her rape by an Englishman. This enraged the Raja, his descendants claim.

66. K.K. Datta, *Comprehensive History of Bihar*, Vol. III, Part I, 1976: 114; also see William Dalrymple, *The Anarchy*, 2019: 161.

67. William Dalrymple, *The Anarchy*, 2019: 196–97, 279.

68. Ibid, 279. Also, see Julia Keay, *Farzana: The Woman Who Saved an Empire*, I.B. Tauris, 2014.

69. Catherine was born Catherine Noël Worlée (1761–1834) in the Danish possession of Tranquebar in south India, to a French colonial official stationed at Pondicherry. The family moved to Chandernagore near Calcutta in 1777, where she married George François Grand the next year.

70. Shyam Narayan Singh, *History of Tirhut during the English Period* (1922); Darbhanga: Kalyani Foundation, 2012: 105–06.

71. George François Grand, *Narrative of the Life of A Gentleman long Resident in India: Comprehending A Period the most eventful in the history of that country, with regard to the revolutions occasioned by European interference, and interspersed with interesting anecdotes, and traits characteristical of those eminent persons who distinguished themselves at that juncture* [hereafter *Narrative of the Life of A Gentleman*], (Cape of Good Hope: Author, 1814): 30–32.

72. George François Grand, *Narrative of the Life of A Gentleman*, 1814: 30–32.

73. Lesley Shapland, 'A Scandalous Annotation: the story of Madame Grand,' blog posted from India Office Records, London, 26 May 2021.

74. Lesley Shapland, 'A Scandalous Annotation', 26 May 2021.
75. George François Grand, 'Postscript to my Narrative', in *Narrative of the Life of A Gentleman,* 1814.
76. George François Grand, *Narrative of the Life of A Gentleman*, 1814: 30–32.
77. Ibid.
78. Lesley Shapland, 'A Scandalous Annotation', 26 May 2021; also see Abhijit Gupta, 'Scandals in old Calcutta,' *mint*, e-paper, 30 April 2016.
79. See the report by George François Grand in the *Final Report on the Survey and Settlement Operations in the Muzaffarpur district, 1892 to 1899*, Calcutta, 1901: 35–36. Also, my interaction with Krishna Nandan Singh of the Sheohar family, Patna, 2022.
80. Ref. my interview with Krishna Nandan Singh of Sheohar family (2022), and Kashinath Singh and Aditya Narayan Singh of Parsa Garh, Saran (2024).
81. Samuel Charters to Hon. Warren Hastings, G.G., No. 233, 25 June 25, 1782, Bengal Rev. Consltns., 16 April to 28 June 1782 (hereafter Charters Report 1782); and *DGS*, by P.C. Roy Chaudhury (Patna: Secretariat Press, 1960), 52.
82. *DGS*, 1960: 52.
83. Ibid.
84. Golding to Patna Council, n.d., Patna Rev. Procs., February–December 1773, 4 March and 24 July.
85. Golding to Patna Council, 8 and 26 January 1773, Patna Rev. Procs. 1772 to 1773, 1 February 1773.
86. *Arzees* (petitions) of Mahommed Ashruff Khan, Diwan of Saran to Patna Council, n.d., and encl. from amil of Gorakhpur, n.d., Patna Rev. Procs., 1774, 12 May 1926.
87. My interview with Shubhredu Singh of Salemgarh-Chainpur estate, 2.9.2023.
88. Another eyewitness account estimated the raiders to consist of twenty-five horsemen and 200–300 matchlock men.
89. Along with the sources quoted below, refer to the *DGS 1930*, quoted in its 1960 edition, 482–83.

90. Refer to Akshayabar Dixit and other authors of vernacular works.
91. Lt Jokh Erskin, 16th Battalion of Sepoys to Isaac Sage, chief of the provincial council of revenue, n.d., Appendix iii, Appendix V, in D.N. Dutt, *A Brief History*, 1909; also see *DGS*, 1960: 52–53.
92. Petition of Syed Golam to the Company authorities, n.d., Appendix V, in D.N. Dutt, *A Brief History*, 1909.
93. *DGS*, 1960: 52–53.
94. Derived from my interaction with the Hathwa and Tamkuhi families.
95. G.P.S., 'Aristocracy of Bihar,' *Calcutta Review*, Vol. LXXVI, 1883: 88–89.
96. D.N. Dutt, 1909: 14–15.
97. Ibid. Also Anand A Yang, 1989: 66.
98. Ibid.
99. Arzees from Mahommed Ashruff Khan, renter of Huseypur, Patna Rev. Procs., 4 August–31 December 1777, 17 November 24.
100. Patna Rev. Procs., 2 January to 28 December 1775, 21 September.
101. Nathaniel Middleton, Resident, Vizier's Court, Lucknow, to Ewan Law, chief of Patna, 15 March 1777, Patna Rev. Procs., 2 January–31 July 1777, 27 March. Majhauli paid Rs 32,000 revenues for the Saran portion of his holdings.
102. J. Harding, Lt Commanding at Barragong, to Simeon Droz, chief of rev. council, 8 and 15 January 1777, Patna Rev. Consultations., 2 January to 31 July 1777, 20 January.
103. Anand A. Yang, 1989: 66.
104. Lt T. Hardinge, 5th Battalion, Sepoys, to Simeon Droz, chief of Patna Council, 29 June 1777, Bengal Rev. Consultations., 21 May to July 1777, 1 July.
105. Alexander Hannay, Lt Col Nugger, 15 March 1781, Bengal Rev. Consultations., 1 September to 23 October 1781, 6 September.
106. Anand A. Yang, 1989: 66.
107. Ibid.: 66–67.
108. Ibid.: 68.
109. Samuel Charters to Hon. Warren Hastings, G.G., No. 233, 25 June, 1782, Bengal Rev. Consltns., 16 April to 28 June 1782, 300. Can

this Ramnagar be identified with present Salemgarh, where one of Fateh Sahi's sons later established a separate principality? I'm not sure. Once this entire area was covered with forest, for which the British appointed two revenue farmers—Bahadur Khan and Salim Khan, each of whom established their forts, known after them as Bahadurgarh and Salemgarh. Later, a son of Fateh Sahi, Shamsher Bahadur Sahi, is said to have vanquished them both, and established his citadel at what is now Salemgarh.

110. Samuel Charters Report, 1782: 300.
111. Ibid.: 300–01.
112. Ibid.
113. Major General Lucas from Husseypur to Commander-in-Chief Giles Stibbert, 19 October 1781.
114. Ibid.
115. G.P.S., 'Aristocracy of Bihar,' *Calcutta Review*, vol. LXXVI, 1883; 91.
116. *DGS*, 1960: 480. Also see Anand A. Yang, 1989: 72.
117. G.N. Dutta, *History of Hutwa Raj*, 1905: 192.
118. Patna Council to G.G. Warren Hastings and Council, 17 June 1776, Bengal Rev. Consultations, 25 October to 12 November 1776, 5 November, no. 776.
119. In case of serious ambiguities, I avoid identifying the names of persons and places spelt in the original sources, as here, with their real counterparts today, fearing committing errors. I hope the future researchers will work in this direction.
120. Yasmin Khan, *India at War: The Subcontinent and the Second World War* (New York: OUP, 2015), chap. 15: 200–19.
121. Samuel Charters to Hon. Warren Hastings, G.G., No. 233, 25 June 1782, Bengal Rev. Consltns., 16 April to 28 June 1782: 302–303.
122. Charters Report, 1782: 303.
123. Samuel Charters to Hon. Warren Hastings, G.G., No. 233, 25 June 1782, Bengal Rev. Consltns., 16 April to 28 June 1782.
124. See, for example, Isaac Sage and four others of the Patna Provincial Council to the Governor-General, 6 May 1775, Fort William, in Revenue Dept. G.G. in Council, 14 June 1775, O.C. No. 14,

2774–77, at Bengal State Archive. However, it is difficult to read many of them written in calligraphy.

125. Charters Report, 1782: 309–316A.
126. Ibid.:317–318.
127. Charters Report, 1782: 304.
128. W.R. Amherst, acting Collector, to Capt. John Archdeacon, commander at Baragaon, 4 September 1788. Bengal Rev. Consltns., 1 to 10, 1788, 10 October.
129. Coming from an aristocratic family, Charles Cornwallis (1738–1805) had joined the British army in 1757 and saw action in the Seven Years' War. Although defeated, he enjoyed the confidence of successive British regimes, and retained an active career. In 1786, he was appointed as Governor-General of India, with directive to avoid conflict with the Company's neighbours by keeping out of their internal affairs. Initially, he tried to extricate the Company from the Maratha-Nizam-Mysore politics of the South, and declined to intervene in the domestic affairs of Nepal. However, circumstances compelled him into the war with Mysore in 1790, when Tipu Sultan invaded Travancore, a Company ally. At that point, Cornwallis personally took over the command of his forces and compelled Tipu to surrender a major part of his territory, for which he was created Marquess Cornwallis (1792). During his tenure, he introduced many reforms, including the Permanent Settlement. He returned to England in 1794, where he acted as the chief British signatory to the 1802 Treaty of Amiens. He was reappointed the Governor-General of India in 1805, but he died soon after his arrival in India, on 5 October at Gauspur in Ghazipur. He was buried on the banks of the Ganga, and his mausoleum erected with public subscription.
130. Anand A. Yang, 1989: 68.
131. Ibid, 69.
132. Arzee of Baboo Maheiss Dut Sah, Zamindar of Pergunnah Hooseepur & c. and Nephew of Fatteh Sah, n.d., Bengal Rev. Consltns., 21 April to 20 July 1784, 26 May.
133. Grome to Sir John Shore, acting president, 6 July 1784, with Montgomerie to Hon. Chas. Stuart, president and member of

BOR, 16 June 1790, Bengal Rev. Consltns., 28 to 30 July, 1790, 28 July, no. 63.

134. Montgomerie to Stuart, BOR, 18 November 1790, Bengal Rev. Consltns., 7 January–25 February 1791, 21 February, Nos. 11,12.
135. Anand A. Yang, 1989: 69.
136. Ibid.
137. Translation of arzee of Ranee of Raja Futty Saw, n.d., Bengal Rev. Consltns., 23 June–9 July 1790, 23 June, No. 52.
138. Anand A. Yang, 1989: 69.
139. Charters Report, 1782.
140. Anand Yang, 1989: 67.
141. Ibid.
142. G.S. Mishra, 1970: 140.
143. Charles Grome, Collector, to Bengal Revenue Council, 15 September 1781, Bengal Rev. Consltns, 23 October 1781: 28 September, No. 582.
144. https://ledoestate.blogspot.com/, retrieved on 4/9/21.
145. Ibid.; also see Thursday, 19 October 2017. Ledo Estate: A Kharagdiha Gadi. Also see J.D. Shifton (1908–1915). *Final Report on the Survey and Settlement Operations in the District of Hazaribagh*: Appendix L, 36.
146. K.K. Datta 1976: 150. Also http://www.indianrajputs.com/view/maheshpur_raj.
147. *Amrita Bazar Patrika*, 8.1.1874.
148. *Amrita Bazar Patrika,* 15.1.1874.
149. Being of the same caste, it is not clear if Fateh Sahi was connected with the Lalgola zamindars, though in later times their descendants seem to have entered into matrimonial relations.
150. Including the river, tunnels, forest and embankment.
151. Kishan Chand Bhakat identifies Satyananda of the novel with Kali Brahma Bhattacharya, Dhirananda with the court poet and priest Trailokyanath Smritibhushan, and Bhabananda with Raja Jogindra Narain Roy. Bankim himself is reflected in Jibananda, who probably lived in the first-floor room that still exists in the Kali temple courtyard. In the ground-floor room, lived Dr

Parry of the Lalgola palace, who worshipped Kali and could be visualized in the physician loyal to the British in the novel. (Ref.: Author's telephonic interaction with Kishan Chand Bhakat, and many of his articles on this subject, which he has kindly shared with me).

152. Pradip Bhattacharya, blog, 2 August 2002.
153. The inspiration Bankim received from all this is reflected in his essay 'Aamaar Durgotsab' (1874).
154. Not far off from Lalgola, Rani Bhawani of Natore was popular as goddess Annapurna for devoutly feeding ascetics drawn from up to Benares. But this stopped after Warren Hastings confiscated a large portion of her estate in 1772–73.
155. Rakesh Roy of Singhabad (Tilasan) of Malda, claims that his forefathers, migrants from Ghazipur, were among the earliest to come across such sanyasis and tantrics in their neighbouring forest, as depicted in the *Anandamath,* and that idols of some of them are worshipped in his home as family deities.
156. They lived in the Deshwali area in the jungle on the banks of the Kalkali and Padma.
157. For a recap, see J.N. Sinha, 'The Facts about Fiction', *Telegraph* (Kolkata), 27 August 2023: 14.
158. My telephonic interaction with Rakesh Roy of Singhabad-Tilasan, West Bengal, 2023.
159. Interview on telephone with Hara Prasad Garg, Mahishadal, West Bengal, April 2023.
160. The author has visited the place. Also, ref. Mahishadal – Wikipedia: https://en.wikipedia.org › wiki› Mahishadal.
161. In a telephonic interaction, a descendant of Mahishadal Raj, Hara Prasad Garg recalled how the Raja of Hathwa (Fateh Sahi's cousin line) had once visited them in connection with some issue concerning property. Back in Bihar, there were several Hindu and Muslim zamindars and tribal chiefs, who maintained working relations with the English, but they nursed grievances against them, similar to those of Fateh Sahi, such as the Raja of Darbhanga. Even the Hathwa Raj family, generally viewed as the supporters of

the British, seem to have been later trying to wriggle out of their clutches.

162. Rabindranath Tagore, *Babus of Nayanjor and Other Stories* (Mindful Publisher: Paperback, 2016).
163. Some sources say he used a secret passage for his visit (Ref. Kuldeep Narayan Jharap).

Chapter 5: The Parting of the Siblings

1. Anand A. Yang, *The Limited Raj*, 1989.
2. Please see Chapter 4 for elaboration.
3. Refer to K.K. Datta, *Comprehensive History of Bihar*, vol. iii, part ii, 1976, chap. xvii, pp.109ff. Also, such works as Sylvia Dyer, *The Spell of the Flying Foxes* (India: Penguin Books, 2011), a memoir-cum-novel based on the life of the author on her family estate in the wilds of Champaran, near Huseypur.
4. Often, the professionals like engineers and doctors were hired by native rulers, and others supplied them exotic merchandise from Europe.
5. Interview with Vaidurya Pratap Sahi, Tamkuhi.
6. Nandini Gore and Khushboo Bari, 'India: A Brief History of Coal in India', https://www.mondaq.com/india/constitutional--administrative-law/986834/a-brief-history-of-coal-in-india, 21 September 2020.
7. *A Journey from Madras through the Countries of Mysore, Canara and Malabar*, 3 vols (London: T. Cadell and W. Davies / Black, Parry & Kingsbury, 1807).
8. In his account, he described over 100 species of fish of the Ganga and its tributaries unrecognized until then. See Francis Buchanan, *An account of the fishes found in the river Ganges and its branches* (1822).
9. Francis Buchanan, *An account of the fishes...*, 1822.
10. Francis Buchanan (1762–1829), later known as Francis Hamilton, was a Scottish physician who made significant contributions as a geographer, zoologist and botanist while living in India. An MD in medicine from the University of Edinburgh, he had also

studied botany. Initially, he served on merchant navy ships, plying between England and India and China. He reached Calcutta in September 1794 and joined the Medical Service of the Bengal Presidency, where he gradually evinced interest in the flora and fauna of India, and helped establish institutions promoting natural history. After the fall of Mysore under Tipu (1799), he surveyed South India, resulting in *A Journey from Madras through the Countries of Mysore, Canara and Malabar*, 3 vols, (1807). He also wrote *An Account of the Kingdom of Nepal* (1819). He surveyed the Bengal region in 1807–14. In 1804, he became in charge of the Institution for Promoting the Natural History of India founded by Wellesley at Barrackpore (1804), and superintendent of the Calcutta Botanical Garden in 1814; but had to return to Britain the next year due to ill health. (More details in Mark F. Watson and Henry J. Noltie (2016), 'Career, Collections, Reports and Publications of Dr Francis Buchanan, 1762–1829: Natural History Studies in Nepal, Burma (Myanmar), Bangladesh and India. Part 1', *Annals of Science*, 73 (4), 392–424; and Marika Vicziany, (1986), 'Imperialism, Botany and Statistics in Early Nineteenth-Century India: The Surveys of Francis Buchanan (1762-1829)', *Modern Asian Studies*. 20 (4): 625–60.

11. G.N. Dutt, *History of the Hutwa Raj* (Bankipur: Lahiri & Co., 1905), 194.
12. Ibid.
13. *DGS*, Patna: Govt. of Bihar, 1960: 480.
14. G.N. Dutt 1905, 195. Peshkash was a present given to the high British authorities by the Indian rulers and notables to gain some favour (ceremonial decorations, as Maharaja, Rai Bahadur, etc.).
15. G.N. Dutt, 1905: 196.
16. J.H. Young, deputy secretary to GOB, to Secretary Currie, No. 410, 13 April 1842, Bengal Rev. Consultns., 24 March to 13 April 1842, no. 85.
17. Revenshaw Report quoted in Anand A. Yang, 1989: 142.
18. Anand A. Yang, 1989: 143.
19. G.N. Dutt, 1905: 196; also see Anand A. Yang, 1989: 144.

20. 'Translation of a Petition from Lall Singh, Shah Singh, and Gauree Singh, sons of Dhujjoo Singh, deceased', in D.N. Dutt, 1909, Appendix XVIII.
21. Anand A. Yang, 1989.
22. Ibid.
23. Amitav Ghosh, *Sea of Poppies* (New Delhi: Penguin, 2008).
24. Anand A. Yang, 1989: 124.
25. Ibid.: 125.
26. Ibid.: 124.
27. Ibid.: 124–25.
28. Blog: 'The Noble Women of Hathwa Raj,' by Priyanjali Ray, with help from Ashok and Kaveri Dutt, at Indian Memory Project [contains details about Bengali Diwans and their families at Hathwa] https://www.indianmemoryproject.com/199-2/.
29. Anand A. Yang, 1989.
30. Ibid.
31. Jaikant Singh, *Bhojpuri Gadya Sahitya: Swaroop, Samagri, Samalochana* (Muzaffarpur: Rajshri Prakashan, 2013), 67, quoted in Pandey Kapil, *Phoolsunghi* (Eng. Trans. Delhi: Penguin, 2020): Introduction.
32. G.N. Dutt ,1905.
33. G.N. Dutt, 1905: 202.
34. Jagdish N. Sinha, *Science, War and Imperialism: India in the Second World War* (Brill: Leiden-Boston, 2008): 43–44.

Chapter 6: The Royal Retreat

1. In the USA and the UK, Charles Cornwallis is best remembered as a leading British general of the American War of Independence; but, in India, he was known for his administrative reforms aimed at consolidating the British rule in the country. Contrasted against his failure in America, his contributions in India were impressive. In South India, he succeeded in defeating a formidable enemy in Tipu Sultan. Tipu's rockets, firearms and military strategy, supported by the French, sent the Company forces helter-skelter, but, ultimately, he was overwhelmed, killed and his territory captured.

For Cornwallis, this restored his credibility in colonial circles, and seemingly served as a deterrent for the adversaries in North India. Internally, his measures to improve governance that would be known as the Cornwallis Code, proved a landmark, though at the cost of the rights and freedom of the indigenous population. Of them, the Permanent Settlement of land revenue (introduced in 1793) helped the British consolidate their possessions in India and create a powerful section of supporters in the new zamindars for the future. His interest in the Asiatic Society afforded the British a humanitarian façade of liberalism and generosity, enhancing their acceptability. For all this, he was hailed with honours and given important positions on his return to Britain in 1794. For more details about him, see the footnote under Chapter 4 (Raids from the Jungle).

2. The late Vijay Kumar, former director, Bihar State Archives, claimed to have seen some papers at the State Archive referring to such an encounter in the Gandak riverine.
3. See Suprakash Sanyal, *Benares and the English East India Company, 1764-1795* (Calcutta: World Press, 1979): 155.
4. Richard Joseph Sulivan, *Philosophical Rhapsodies: Fragments of Akbur of Betlis containing Reflections on the Laws, Manners, Customs and Religion of certain Asiatic, Afric, and European Nations*, Vol. II (London T. Becket, Pall-Mall Booksellers, 1776): 88.
5. Most sources, documentary and oral (a few cited in this book), speak of these safety measures adopted by the Rani.
6. James Rennel's maps, and the survey reports of the time, amply illustrate the point.
7. Information based on interviews with the Tamkuhi family members, and public memory of the locals.
8. See the court papers, op. cit.
9. G.N. Dutt, *History of the Hathwa Raj*, 1905: 194.
10. Allahabad High Court, 'In the High Court of Allahabad: First Appeal No. 214 of 1901, decided on: 24.05.1904: Appellants: Sarabjit Partap Bahadur Sahi and ors. vs. Respondent: Indarjit Partap Bahadur Sahi and ors.,' MANU/UP/0014/1904;

Equivalent Citation: (1905) ILR 27All203. Also see the synoptic account of the life of Indrajit Pratap Bahadur Sahi in a published article, anonymous, posted by Vaidurya P. Sahi on 3.10.23.

11. According to the Hathwa family chronicle, Fateh Sahi eventually became a fakir (ascetic) in 1808, perhaps finding his attempts to gain independence proved futile.
12. Vaidurya P. Sahi states that the huge sword is today a family heirloom. The practice of animal sacrifice was in vogue in the family until not long ago, when it was replaced by an ingenious practice of performing the ritual by cutting a bottle gourd, instead of a buffalo or goat.
13. This narrative reminds one of the future reformers, revolutionaries and the freedom fighters in India. Vivekananda and his guru Ramakrishna Pramahans were devotees of Kali, an avatar of Shakti. Bankim Chandra Chatterjee invoked the deity in his *Anandamath*, whose story is believed to be based on that of Fateh Sahi, we may recall. This was a natural response of Indians in difficult times when none appeared to help. Thus, they looked back into their cultural heritage, and invoked Kali, a female goddess from the Hindu pantheon as one who rose against the evil and destroyed its doer. In popular psyche, Kali was visualized as Mother Goddess (*Matrishakti*) and increasingly depicted as such in early nationalist literature. She appeared as a fiery persona, intolerant of any evil and unsparing to its perpetrators. Famous painter Abanindranath Tagore portrayed India as Bharat Mata (Mother India) in 1905; and around the same time, many posters depicted her as Durga seated on a tiger, with her usual weapons and accompaniments. The attraction for the Kali-Shakti cult continued among successive generations of revolutionaries throughout India's freedom struggle.
14. Author's personal observation.
15. Mike Dash, *Thug: The True Story of India's Murderous Cult* (Paperback India: Granta Books, 2018). For Pindaris, see William Raban, *Origin of the Pindaries* (Paperback RareBooksClub.com), 2013.
16. Even though the possibility of his falling prey to a British conspiracy cannot be ruled out, it is difficult to presume that he

was ever caught or killed by them. Had it been so, they would have trumpeted the capture of their most dreaded enemy.

Epilogue: The Rebel in Retrospect

1. Born Pratap Singh I (1540–1597), Maharana Pratap was the thirteenth king of Mewar, in the present Rajasthan in India. He ascended the throne in 1572 as the fifty-fourth ruler in the line of the Sisodia Rajputs, and ruled until his death in 1597. He was notable for his military resistance against the expansionism of the Mughals and known for his fierce battles of Haldighati and Dewar.
2. Sri Ram Sharma, *Maharana Pratap: A Biography* (Hope India Publication, 2002); Brishti Bandyopadhyay, *Maharana Pratap: Mewar's Rebel King* (New Delhi: Rupa Publications, 2007).
3. Ever since, Pratap has been celebrated as one of the greatest patriot warriors of India, and has been a favourite protagonist for successive movies. His method of sporadic warfare was later elaborated by Malik Ambar, the Deccani general, and Maratha ruler Chhatrapati Shivaji.
4. Kuldeep Narayan Rai, '*Swatantray Sangram men Maharshi Vansh ka Yogdan*', *Brahmarshi-Sandesh*, Vol. 1, 1687 BS (in Hindi), (Brahmarshi Samaj, Kanpur, 2022).
5. Vaidurya P. Sahi on e-paper on net, https://www.writerspouch.org/post/sahis-anecdotes; also refer to recently published Vaidurya Pratap Sahi, *Sahis' Anecdotes: Tales from Tamkuhi* (Writers Pouch, 2024).
6. Interview with Anurag Chait Singh and his father, who live in Gwalior (2022).
7. Mahadaji Shinde (1730–94), also called Mahadji Scindia, was a Maratha statesman and ruler of Ujjain in Central India. During his reign, Gwalior became the leading state in the Maratha Empire and one of the foremost military powers in India. He resurrected Maratha power in North India after the Third Battle of Panipat (1761). He subdued the Jats and Rohillas, countered Timur Shah Durrani's attack on Lahore, defeated Jodhpur and Jaipur, and

ruled over Punjab. After recurrent rebellions against the Mughals, he came to their rescue. When Rohilla chief Ghulam Kadir took over Delhi and deposed and blinded Mughal Emperor Shah Alam II, Mahadaji restored him to the throne (1788), and acted as his protector. Thus, Mahadaji earned a high position in the Mughal polity and played a vital role in establishing Maratha supremacy over North India. In the South, he defeated the Nizam and obliterated the prospects of his playing any role in north Indian politics. After peace was made with Tipu in 1792, Mahadaji prevented a British alliance against him. At the zenith of his power, Mahadaji died at his camp near Pune in February 1794. He had no heir, and was succeeded by Daulat Rao Scindia. His English biographer Keeney considers him the greatest man of South Asia in the eighteenth century. However, his relationship with the British was devious. He did not want to annoy Warren Hastings. So, he did not send his army to assist Chait Singh during his rebellion, disregarding his treaty cooperation with him. Scindia's sources claimed that Scindia had actually sent help, but it could not cross the river at Kalpi, as it was then in spate and a huge military detachment of the Company was deployed on the other side of the river. However, after Chait Singh's revolt failed and he had to leave Benares, Mahadaji granted Singh a jagir in Gwalior (Ref. Interview with Anurag Chait Singh and family, Gwalior, 2022).

8. Ahilya Bai Holkar (1725–95) was a hereditary noble sardar of the Maratha Empire. She took over the affairs of the Holkar fief in 1766, protected it from plunderers and personally led armies on the battlefield. She was a great pioneer, innovator and builder. During her reign, Indore developed from a small village to a prosperous and beautiful city; and she built forts and many public utilities in Malwa. Her capital at Maheshwar, south of Indore, emerged as a centre of literary, artistic and industrial activities. Outside Malwa, she built or renovated numerous temples, ghats, rest-houses and the like, all over the country. A woman of modern outlook, her rule is remembered as a golden age in Indore's history, and she is compared with the greatest of the Indian rulers. In North India,

she had restorations at Kashi, Gaya, Ayodhya, Mathura, Haridwar, among others. She is most remembered for the restoration of the Vishwanath Temple at Kashi (1780), one of the holiest Hindu pilgrimages.

9. John Keay, *India: A History* (New York City: Grove Press, 2000).
10. Source: Private Archive of Vaidurya P. Sahi, Allahabad.
11. Ref: Vaidurya Pratap Sahi, 'Religious Beliefs of Fateh Bahadur Sahi' (Writers Pouch, 21/2/2021); and his many discussions with the author.
12. Georges Lefebre, *The Great Fear of 1789: Rural Panic in Revolutionary France* (1932), (Eng. Trans., Pantheon, 1973); his *The Coming of the French Revolution* (1939); (Eng. Trans., Princeton University Press, 1947); and George Rudé, *The Crowd in the French Revolution* (Paperback: US: OUP, 1968).
13. Jaird Diamond, *Guns, Germs and Steel: A short history of everybody in the last 13,000 years* (1997), (London: Vintage Books, 2005); Lucian Fevre, with Lionel Bataillon, *A Geographical Introduction to History* (1922), 1925. For India, see K.M. Panikkar, *Geographical Factors in Indian History* (New Delhi, 1971).
14. Immanuel Wallerstein, *World-Systems Analysis: An Introduction* (US: John Hope Franklin Center, Paperback 2004). The world to Immanuel Wallerstein is a vast, integrated system that makes a strong case for vision that requires looking through a very different epistemological lens than habitually used.
15. For a general idea about this area, see *The Comprehensive History of Bihar*, eds., Syed Hasan Askari and Qeyamuddin Ahmad, vol. ii, part I, K.P. Jayaswal Research Institute, Patna, 1983.
16. P.C. Horo, 'Christian Missions and Communities in Bihar', in *The Comprehensive History of Bihar*, eds., K.K. Datta with Jatashankar Jha, Vol. III, Part II, 1976, chap. XVI: 109–292.
17. Infamous as Patna Massacre (1763). For his details, see Chapter 4.
18. See Chapter 4 for details.
19. Ref. my interview with Krishna Nandan Singh of the Sheohar family (2022), Kashinath Singh and Aditya Narayan Singh of Parsa Garh, Saran (2024).

20. H.E. Busteed, *Echoes from Old Calcutta* (Calcutta: Thomas Spink, 1888), ch. VIII.
21. For details, see the report by George François Grand in the *Final Report on the Survey and Settlement Operations in the Muzaffarpur district, 1892 to 1899*, Calcutta, 1901: cf. pages 35–36, quoted in Shyam Narayan Singh, *History of Tirhut* (1922), 2012, 105–06. Also, George François Grand, *Narrative of the Life of a Gentleman* (Cape of Good Hope, 1814).
22. Lesley Shapland, 'A Scandalous Annotation: the story of Madame Grand,' blog issued from India Office Records, London, 26 May 2021.
23. Shyam Narayan Singh, *History of Tirhut*, 2012, 105–06. Also, my interaction with Krishnanand Sinha of the Sheohar family, 2022.
24. Ibid.: 100–107.
25. Mithi Mukherjee, 'Justice, War, and the Imperium: India and Britain in Edmund Burke's Prosecutorial Speeches in the Impeachment Trial of Warren Hastings,' *Law and History Review* 23.3 (2005), 589–630, online.; Edmund Burke, *Articles of Charge of High Crimes and Misdemeanours, Against Warren Hastings, Esq., Late Governor General of Bengal...* (London: J. Debrett, 1786); and Warren Hastings, *The Answer of Warren Hastings to the Articles: Delivered at the bar of the house of Peers, on Nov. 28, 1787* (London: John Murray, 1788).
26. See Shashi Tharoor, *An Era of Darkness: The British Empire in India* (New Delhi: Aleph, 2016): 1–42.
27. K.R. Khosla (comp.), R.P. Chatterjee (ed.), *His Imperial Majesty King George V and the Princes of India and the Indian Empire (Historical Biographical)*, (Lahore: Imperial Publishing Co., 1937): 323.
28. Sarbjit Pratap Bahadur Sahi and Others vs Indrajit Pratap Bahadur Sahi and Others, First Appeal No. 214 of 1901, Decided on 24.05.1904, High Court of Allahabad, MANU/UP/OO14/1904.
29. K.R. Khosla and R.P. Chatterjee, *His Imperial Majesty King George V*.
30. Ibid.; also see Vaidurya Pratap Sahi, 'Raja Indrajit Pratap Bahadur Sahi,' *Tamkuhi Samachar*, March 2021: epaper in Hindi.
31. Ibid. for both references.
32. Motilal Nehru's letter to the Tamkuhi Raja, and interaction with Vaidurya P. Sahi.

33. In the Indian tradition, the four elements of *Purusharth* have been considered as righteousness, wealth, endeavour and liberation or salvation.
34. In the absence of deeper research, it is difficult to substantiate this statement and its mutual correlation with written sources at present, but local folk narratives eloquently recount Fateh Bahadur's inspirational legacy of courage and valour against foreign rule. A.A.A. Rizvi, *Freedom Struggle in Uttar Pradesh*, 6 vols. (New Delhi: OUP, 2010), especially Vol. 4.
35. As at the Langat Singh College of Muzaffarpur, BHU at Benares, AMU of Aligarh.
36. Later, they had good relations with the family of noted Indian painter Amrita Shergil, who were stationed at neighbouring Saraya near Gorakhpur. Tamkuhi had a large herd of elephants and Amrita was fond of one Ramprasad, the most majestic of them, recount the old-timers of the royal household. A present descendant speculates she painted a few of them.
37. Interaction with Vaidurya P. Sahi.
38. For Hathwa's contributions, refer to G.N. Dutt, 1905.
39. Vaidurya Pratap Sahi, *Sahis' Anecdotes: Tales from Tamkuhi* (Writers Pouch, 2024).
40. My telephonic interview with Maheshwar Pratap Sahi, Tamkuhi family, December 2024.
41. For a broader view, see Leela Prasad, *Opposition to British Supremacy in Bihar, 1757-1803* (New Delhi, 1981). Also, Paramita Maharatna, 'Explaining Chait Singh's Revolt in Bihar (1781): The Role of the Refractory Bihar Zamindars,' *Proceedings of the Indian History Congress, 2007*, Vol. 68, Part I (2007), 565–572; ibid, 'The British in Bihar: 1757-1781', unpublished M. Phil. dissertation, University of London, 1992, esp. Chap. 6 for repercussions of Chait Singh's revolt in Bihar.
42. Jagat Singh trial papers already quoted.
43. Ibid.
44. R.R. Diwakar, *Bihar Through the Ages*, K.P. Jayaswal Institute, Patna, 1959: 593–94.

45. Anand A. Yang, *Bazaar India: Markets, Society, and the Colonial State in Bihar* (Univ. of California Press, 1999): 69. Also see *District Gazetteers* of Champaran and Muzaffarpur. Interview with Krishna Nandan Singh of Sheohar, 2023.
46. For basic information, see R. Lethbridge, *The Golden Book of India: A Genealogical and Biographical Dictionary of the Ruling Princes, Chiefs, Nobles, and Other Personages, Titled or Decorated of the Indian Empire* (Delhi: Aakar Books, 2005): 67, retrieved 30 September 2020. Also, my interview with Kishanchand Bhakt of Lalgola and with Yatindra Narayan Rai, a scion of the Lalgola Raj family, June 2023.
47. Prachi Mangla, 'First judicial murder of India: Raja Nand Kumar case,' IJRASET43325, Open access article, 2022.
48. Consultations with Priyadarshini Sharma (a journalist), connected with the Hathwa-Tamkuhi families, traces her father's origins to Bijapur in Maharashtra from where an early ancestor came to Bihar in the time of Sher Shah Suri.
49. Interaction with Shubhrendru Kumar of Salemgarh-Chainpur family, 2022–23.
50. The deeds of Khudiram Bose, M.N. Roy, Bhagat Singh, Ramprasad Bismil and others illustrate the point.
51. Tipu's Tiger, c. 1793, Mysore, painted wood with metal fixtures (the Victoria and Albert Museum, © Victoria and Albert Museum, London), has long been one of the most popular items in the museum. A large automaton, the tiger is shown attacking a European man. When played, the man's left arm flails and the automaton emits the sounds of the roaring tiger and the cries of its victim. Originally made for Tipu Sultan to display his animosity against the British, it later became a tool for imperial propaganda in Britain.
52. In case of this possibility, we may again look back to the two ladies from the anti-British origins, Madame Grand and Begum Samru, in order to find any mutual cooperation.

Index

* Page numbers with *n* indicate number in Notes section.

Scan QR code to access the
Penguin Random House India website